THE MOUNTA~.

FROM THE FRENCH OF MICHELET.

BY THE TRANSLATOR OF "THE BIRD."

WITH FIFTY-FOUR ILLUSTRATIONS FROM DESIGNS
BY PERCIVAL SKELTON.

1872.

AUTHOR'S PREFACE.

" THE MOUNTAIN " continues the series of analogous books, whose publication commenced in 1856,—"The Bird," "The Insect," "The Sea."

That year was the starting-point of a movement which is still in progress, and shall not be arrested. The public from that epoch has felt an entirely new interest in Natural History. There were already in existence numerous scientific books which few people read. There were already in existence books of perhaps too subtle and speculative a character. It was the singular fortune of "The Bird" to find neither a critic nor an adversary. The least sympathetic minds were surprised, overcome, and defenceless before it. It bore upward on its wing both the public and the press.

Under their very modest guise—for they did not pretend to the honours of the octavo—the three books had the rare success of being the cause of many others. A flood of imitators followed. The booksellers published a number of special works, illustrated or not illustrated. Several firms even desired to possess their general treatises, their encyclopædias of natural history. There came an infinity of books

designed for the instruction of, or perusal by, the young. It
is sufficient to turn to the catalogue of books published since
1856 to see that a new branch of literature has sprung into
life since that epoch.

These little books, accepted as agreeable contributions to
literature, owe their success, nevertheless, mainly to their
truthfulness. They attempted, not to give a meaning of their
own to Nature, but to penetrate hers. They loved her and
they questioned her; from every creature they demanded the
secret of its little soul. The consequence was happy. For the
first time men learned the peculiar mystery of the Bird—the
peculiar mystery of the Insect. That sufficiently prolonged
education which certain species require is the secret of their
development. Hence we gather the following general law :—

"All species whose young live only through a prolonged
education attain prosperity. It is this which creates society."

See, now, what really impressed the public in these books,
far more than the picturesqueness or the magic of their style.
The best written works, replete with observations true,
curious, and approved, will leave their readers untouched, until
you might believe them to be materialists, and capable of
appreciating only the rude coarse fact. Yet the only books
which have powerfully affected them are those which appeal
to the soul.

The Bird is a personality. This fact is readily admitted.
But the Insect ! The difficulty here would seem to be much
greater; and among the Children of the Sea the transient
personality would appear still less capable of identification.

It was a daring attempt to fix and re-establish these obscure and confused souls, which had hitherto been denied and disdained—to restore them to their dignity as souls—to replace them in their fraternal rights and in the grand fellowship of life.

We pursue to-day the same labour in the Mountain and its forests. The greater portion of the present volume springs from our own travels, and relates what we ourselves have seen. It does not interfere with great scientific labours, with the all-instructive works of the Schachts or Schlagentweits. It derives its interest from our friendly relations with that lofty nature, so grand but so indulgent, which reveals itself willingly to those who sincerely love it. The reader will see with what a degree of intimacy we learned to admire the patriarchs of the Alps, the ancient and venerable trees, which men have so wrongly thought to be dumb. We cherish a grateful sentiment towards those august giants—those sublime mountains, in whose bosom we found ourselves so tenderly sheltered, which so generously (with their nourishing rivers, the life of Europe) poured out to us also their calm, profound, and serene soul.

Living spirit of regeneration! True heart-cordial in these days of too general decadence! May this book, while strengthening ourselves, steady others upon the slopes, where, through weakness or melancholy, so many fall! If it need an epigraph, it shall be this word—*Ascend!*

TRANSLATOR'S PREFACE.

THE present is a companion volume to "The Bird" and "The Sea," and, like those charming and popular expositions of zoological and physical science from a poetic point of view, is from the pen of M. Michelet. It is devoted to "The Mountain," to its external aspects and its inner life—its lava-streams and its canopies of snow—its torrents, ravines, and forests. It is not wholly scientific, and yet science is not entirely put aside; it is not wholly poetical or sentimental, and yet only by a man of mingled poetry and sentiment of disposition could it have been written.

It has been translated from the French by the Translator of "The Bird" and "The Sea," who, in this, as in the preceding volumes, has earnestly endeavoured to preserve in his version the force, and vigour, and graphic individuality of the original.

The reader will remember, with much pleasure, that its author, one of the most brilliant of modern French *littérateurs*, has recently recovered from a dangerous illness ; rendered doubly dangerous by his advanced age. For Jules Michelet,

"French historian and member of the Institute," having been born at Paris on the 21st of August 1798, is now in his 74th year. "The Mountain," written in 1868, shows no signs, however, of any decay of its writer's intellectual powers.

A list of his numerous works, corrected by himself, may prove acceptable to the reader, and will show how diversified is his range of subjects—how great his erudition—how comprehensive his genius. He frequently indulges in paradoxes, it is true, and is more frequently brilliant than profound; yet, as a writer, he is infinitely suggestive; his criticisms are always sparkling; his pictures are full of tone and vigour; and he possesses in perfection the happy art of concentrating a world of wit and wisdom into an epigrammatic phrase.

His greatest task, a "History of France," in nineteen volumes, and a "History of the Revolution" (down to 1795), in six volumes, has occupied, more or less, five-and-thirty years (1833–1868) of his laborious literary life. None but a man of genius could have written it; yet we doubt whether it will hand down his name to posterity so surely as some of his less elaborate compositions.

In 1831, he wrote, in one volume, an "Introduction to the Universal History"; in 1833, a "Memoir of Vico," two volumes (which had been preceded, in 1827, by a "Translation from Vico"). In 1827, also, appeared his "Précis of Modern History."

His well-known and judiciously written "Life of Luther" was given to the world in 1831 (two volumes), and was followed in 1832 by his "Histoire Romaine." His "Origines du Droit Français" appeared in 1837. His growing fame was largely increased in 1846 by his characteristic and highly original book on "The People," which, however, did not create so general a sensation as his severe satire, "The Priest and the Family," in 1849. In 1858 was published "L'Amour"; in 1859, "La Femme"; in 1862, "La Sorcière"; in 1862, his "Légende Nord"; in 1864, "La Bible de l'Humanité," another work which exercised a great influence on public opinion; in 1870, his tractate on modern education, "Nos Fils" (Our Sons); and in 1871, his statement of the political situation, "La France devant l'Europe."

In partnership with Madame Michelet, an amiable and accomplished woman, whose literary merits are just beginning to gain appreciation in England, he has written those agreeable semi-scientific, semi-poetic expositions of natural science to which we have already referred—"The Bird," 1856; "The Insect," 1857; "The Sea," 1861; and "The Mountain," 1868.

It has already been the Translator's good fortune, with the sanction of M. Michelet, to bring two of these before the English public—"The Bird" and "The Sea;" and in England and the United States, they have been as popular in their English garb as the originals were in France. The present volume, "The Mountain," will shortly be succeeded by "The Insect;" thus completing the series.

W. H. DAVENPORT ADAMS.

TABLE OF CONTENTS.

Book the First.

Book the Second.

CHAPTER I.

ZONES OF PEACE: THE MEADOWS.

CHAPTER II.

THE FORESTS: THE TREE OF LIFE: THE GOLDEN BRANCH.

CHAPTER III.

THE AMPHITHEATRE OF THE FORESTS.

CHAPTER IV.

DREAMS OF THE MOUNTAIN AND THE FLOWERS.

CHAPTER V.

DREAMS OF THE MOUNTAIN AND THE FLOWERS: CONTINUED. SWITZERLAND IN MAY 1867.

CHAPTER VI.

THE PAUSE AT THE FOOT OF THE MOUNTAIN: LOVES OF THE ALPINE FLOWERS.

CHAPTER VII.

THE ALPINE PLANTS: THE PROGRESS OF THEIR FLOWERS IN LOVE.

CHAPTER VIII.

THE PASS OF THE GRISONS: THE DEATH OF THE MOUNTAIN.

LIST OF ILLUSTRATIONS,

DRAWN BY PERCIVAL SKELTON.

ENGRAVED BY J. W. WHYMPER, R. PATERSON, AND G. A. MORISON.

THE HEAD-PIECES BY CLARK STANTON, A.R.S.A.

*[Those distinguished by an asterisk * are Whole-Page Engravings.]*

PART THE FIRST.

I

THE VESTIBULE OF MONT BLANC.

MONT BLANC is not a thoroughfare. It does not offer on its mid-slope those great highways of the nations by which France, Germany, and Italy are eternally crossing. It stands apart. One must go expressly to see and salute the illustrious Hermit whose head dominates Europe.

I had seen the Apennines; I had seen the Pyrenees; the great hospitable mountains of the merchant and the traveller, Mont Cenis and Saint Gothard; the swift magic of the Simplon. I reserved to the last—Mont Blanc.

Recently, to my many labours I had added yet another. From the depths of the protracted epopœia which had so long enthralled me, I had essayed that daring flight, the "Bible of Humanity"—a little book, but a great outburst of heart and will. I too, just like the globe, had upreared my mountain; a watch-tower, a peak of sufficient height to survey the whole earth.

I was careful not to visit the sea in search of repose. I love that strange fairy Power. She possesses the secret of life; but she is so restless! How often has she added her tempests to my mental commotion! I repaired to the immovable Alps to implore tranquillity; but not to those noisy

VIEW OF MONT BLANC, FROM SALLENCHES.

Alps which seem an eternal
revel of cascades and beautiful
lakes. I preferred the great
hermit, the dumb giant, Mont
Blanc. Only in him could I
hope to find enough both of
snow and calm.

When from Geneva you
arrive at Sallenches, after pass-
ing through a commonplace and indifferent country, you are
struck by the grandeur of the scene suddenly displayed before
you. The Arve winds, and all is changed. There is no

trickery in the surprise. On the left, an immense *aiguille*, Varens, of ruinous limestone, partly supported by a belt of firs, rises abruptly over the route, and seems to menace it. On the right, the wooded hills might be taken for the first tier of a sombre amphitheatre, which elsewhere one would call a lofty mountain (it is between 5000 and 6000 feet above the sealevel). Yet, in the rear, and at a distance, dominates, from an enormous elevation, the sad and snow-crowned dome.

You should not visit this scene in those rarely beautiful summer days which cast a deceitful charm over the entire land, which decorate all Nature, and invest the landscapes in an uniform smile. The radiant phantasmagoria of shifting lights would kindle the very tombs! The sun, as photography proves, is a great deceiver. He will give the same aspect to the coldest and barrenest valley of Savoy as to the burning hollows of the Valais, which are, in truth, an anticipation of Italy.

I arrived there on a gloomy day, such as you find in that country during the greater part of the year. I was able to see it in its reality, in its meanness and poverty, crushed by yonder heights, with the Arve, a simple torrent, wandering vaguely abroad. Small gardens, diminutive vineyards, a tolerable number of tall firs, and there, on high, the ice-cold giant.

It is with no small surprise we come upon numerous hotsprings. That the Pyrenees should afford them, that those ancient daughters of fire should lavishly pour out the burning waters, seems natural enough. But that here, beneath this immense shroud of snows and firs, should dully roar the internal heat, is a fact which impresses the mind and awakens thought. We say to ourselves: Behind the mask, the cold decoration of winter, there lies concealed *another*—a *somebody* whom we do not see. The ices (some 1200 feet in thickness, I suppose) are for him a simple garb. An individual of granite is buried within, which was formerly begotten of the

earth—one of its mighty sighs, of those aspirations towards
the light when she was still in shadow. But in its tomb
of snow, this soul remains in close affinity with its profound mother, and ever she revives beneath its genial
expansion.

The Baths of Saint Gervais are gloomy. A noble plantation
of firs skirts a small rapid torrent. And by degrees one finds
oneself in a very narrow ravine, sloping between hills which
are about 600 feet in height. The water is cold, the wind icy.
Yet nevertheless there wells out a hot-spring in this locality.
It has all the effect of a miracle. In the snowy waters a
fisherman accidentally discovered the thermal source. In
former times such a circumstance would have been sufficient
foundation for a religious creed. In the Pyrenees, at Vichy,
Bourbon, and elsewhere, all water is a god ; the god Borbo,
the god Gorgo, and the like. In Savoy, these gods become
saints ; Saint Gervais and Saint Protais.

The scene, with its ascetic nature, seems to say : " Before
making use of the gifts of God, leave here on the threshold
thy sin, the secret malady of thy soul." And this is the
essence of wisdom. But I do not know that the place is calculated to soothe the heart. It is certainly one of those
haunted by spirits. It is closely shut in. On either side the
fir-trees overhang, and, approaching one another, cast strange
shadows round about. Long dragon-like trains of fog are
attracted thither from the Arve, and, delighted with the spot,
refuse to quit it. This winding, ever-receding landscape, promises I know not what. It seems replete with mysteries,
dreams, and illusions. One would wish for more light.

Holy light, be my physician ! I will go to the gloomy
nymph ; but I wish to rule over her. When we emerge from
this ravine, and mount to the lofty Saint Gervais, we find it gay
and laughing. The effect of the contrast is singular. I found

it something more and better than attractive. Its beauty is
most touching, and went straight to my heart.

I did not reside at the entrance which overlooks the course
of the Arve, and commands a distant view of Sallenches, but
at the other end of the village, in a little house without any
prospect,—the respectable house of the Gontards, who discovered the hot-spring by which others have profited. This
house was situated on somewhat lower ground, and near the
torrent, whose noise we heard, but whose waters were invisible.
The church stood by the side, shaded by great old trees, and
surrounded by a very beautiful blossomy graveyard. Further
off, beyond the torrent, some small vineyards stretched up a
lofty ascent, and the bluish smoke of a few cottages, and a
grove of firs, were discernible. It was the end of the world
(*finis mundi*).

The rain falling in front of the fir-trees, the wreathing
smoke, the heavy clouds which rose and dragged themselves
towards us,—were these the components of a very lively picture? Yet we nevertheless experienced a certain quickening
of the spirit. Life seemed to us easier to endure. Was this
the effect of the air (at an altitude of 2400 feet)? Was it
owing to our release from the coarser existence, from the
thoughts of an absent world?

The sombre clouds of the soul take flight on those lofty
summits, and betake themselves to the great floating sea which
I can discern wandering opposite to us,—wandering about
yon fantastic *cirques* which ape the likeness of human beings,—
about the *aiguilles* of Varens and the peaks of Montjoye.

I thought of absent friends, of the languishing society of
the great towns lying far below, of the Seine or the Rhine, of
Holland, of the dense fogs of London. I said to myself,
especially in moments of sudden outbursts of light, " How
great an advantage there is in ascending! Would the world
were here, relieved of its burdens and set free!"

From Paris to Geneva, one has 1600 pounds less atmospheric weight to carry; and from Geneva to this place, 2400! It is the abode of true liberty! On a higher or lower level we breathe less freely.

The charming maiden of the house—tall and straight as a poplar, more lithe than the females of Savoy—and her little brother, a mere child, assisted the young servant in domestic work, and in the purchase of provisions, which it was often necessary to fetch from a considerable distance. We lived a little haphazard, with a faith in Providence like that of the Antonys and the Pacômes, who sometimes expected their bread to fall from heaven.

As soon as the rain ceased, and while I was still at the desk, my second and younger self, curious to see the country, set out on an exploring journey. Turning round the church, she went towards Bionney (this is the road of Notre Dame de la Gorge, which would lead into Italy); but all the interest consisted, rightly enough, in ignoring this, and in venturing into an unknown region. Her companion, still more curious to see what was to be seen, was no better informed. All the landscape was still exceedingly dank. The venerable walnut-trees, which belong, I believe, to the days when the dukes of Savoy carried the Cross to Jerusalem, rendered the road very muddy and miry, and still sprinkled it with drops of rain. It was market-day: the highway was full of animation; each person was driving his cattle, cows, geese, or sheep. A thoughtful and very cunning peasant was leading softly, as one guides a newly-married wife, a couple of pretty little black pigs. These country-people were very courteous, and said, as they passed, "Good-day." The women, old before their time, good-natured, but ugly (they work so hard), regarded with a mother's eye (sometimes, it seems, even moved to tears) the young pale lady, as one regards a sick child. They smiled at the *détours* she made to escape from contact with their cows, avoiding them, and abandoning to them the road, with a superfluous degree of respect. The weather also was, so to speak, half an invalid, being unable to decide between the sun and the rain. The oats lay on the ground, waiting to be dried, before they could be gathered into the garner. It was a poor and scanty crop, and exposed to great hazard.

The rain, however, delighted the meadows, and they flourished immensely. It was pleasant, too, to the streams, and the very smallest of them sung and babbled. Many copious, strong, and rapid brooks seemed, with their loud gurgling, out of harmony with such modest and unpretending scenes. They came from on high and from afar, the indisputable children of an upper world. At a certain bend in the road, this upper world was suddenly revealed on one side, through a narrow angle (the glacier of Bionassey). It shone like a mountain of gold in the sun, a dazzling spectacle! One doubled and accelerated one's steps, to examine it more nearly; but already the shifting gold had changed; it was no more than silver. Ah, the inconstancy of light! The silver became simple snow, and the snow, by degrees, assumed the dull hue of lead.

The return home was saddened by this circumstance, and made much more slowly. The day had already sunk, though it was the middle of summer. She re-entered the house in a serious mood, but with hands full of flowers.

Light was the morning, a little cold, but agreeable and lively. We worked in face of the snows which, this year, in the month of August, powdered our lofty hills. Then we went to visit our neighbours, the fir-trees of the cataract. These grave trees of the North, here planted low down on the ice-cold torrent, and there at a great height near the mountain summits, encircled and protected on the intermediate terraces the more delicate trees—the pears and apples—of the tiny

orchards. We contemplated respectfully those venerable resinous patriarchs, the eldest-born of the world, which in the
more difficult ages endured so many hardships, and to-day still
support and defend so many exposed localities. They seem
the natural brothers of all suffering, deserving, and laborious
populations. We concluded a compact of friendship with
them.

Our forest of firs appeared on the right, on the shoulder
of the hill. We crossed the Devil's Bridge (a common name
in every country). We ascended, traversing the vineyards, to
a small, poor, but hospitable farm. The farmer, a shrewd and
very amiable man of ripe years, had been a commissionaire at
Paris for a considerable period, had returned with some small
savings, and married a pretty woman, not a native of the
country. Their children were fine and healthy, and they
seem to enjoy some degree of comfort, at least in those
years when the wind on high is not too bleak. The scene
was a pathetic one; but would this man, already advanced
in years, live to see his eldest son, a boy of twelve, old enough
to work, and replace him at his mother's side?

The fir-wood was exceedingly beautiful. It presented a
succession of sombre avenues : one with a very fantastic effect
—which alternately concealed and displayed the Baths in the
deep hollow; another, more distant, and bright and lively,
revealed the windings of the valley as far as Sallenches. Far
in the depths, some evidently Celtic ruins seemed, with their
black antiquity, to render the forest, so shadowy in itself, still
darker and more obscure.

On emerging from it, and climbing towards a more open
spot, we saw beneath us Saint Gervais, its valley, and the
road of the glaciers—an extensive, a tranquil, and, to use a
word which sums up everything, a *human* view. There, in
the hollow, lay meadows and brooks; human toil and saw-
mills; tiny harvests of oats, rye, and buckwheat; and cottages

SAW-MILLS, NEAR SAINT GERVAIS.

which nowhere else are of such ample dimensions as those of Switzerland. They climbed the acclivities to a great height. Higher up, the summits were less barren than we had supposed, and, by their pale verdure, showed that the giant was not unalterably severe.

All this scene was rendered solemn and affecting by a close, warm air, the presage of a storm. We seated ourselves about midway up the steep, on the same narrow ridge of stone —silent, and too much at one in our thoughts to need to utter them. The rain was still on its way towards us; in a month or two it would be winter. The mutability of everything painfully affected us. All was soft and calm; we could scarcely see the glaciers, and only by a narrow angle; but their verdurous margin promised nothing reliable.

II.

MONT BLANC.

THE GLACIERS.

ONG before visiting Mont Blanc, I had seen the Grindelwald, an easily accessible glacier, whose approaches are not denuded of all their natural character, and set in regular order, like those of too many other glaciers where artificial effects have been carefully prepared. I had seen it suddenly, and without being forewarned —by an abrupt surprise, without reflection, without recalling any of those vain literary souvenirs which falsify the true impression. I felt it in all the force of its astonishment and horror.

I had quitted in the morning noisy Interlachen, and its vulgar affluence ; and having arrived at the village, I took up my quarters at Grindelwald in an excellent hotel. The dim chamber which I entered presented nothing remarkable ; but the attendants open a window—I turn round. The casement, all flooded with light, appeared to me in its narrow framework overflowing with an undefinable, radiant, moving Something, which advanced straight towards me.

Truly, nothing could be more formidable. It was a luminous chaos, seemingly close to the panes of glass, as if it would fain have entered. The effect could not be grander if a star were suddenly to touch the earth itself, and overwhelm it with light.

THE GLACIER OF GRINDELWALD.

At the second glance, however, I saw that this monstrous Thing was not so near. It had the appearance of being in motion, but halted now and then in a sufficiently profound depth. It rested at my feet. How strange! Though motionless, it seemed moving! It was seized, as it were, on its way—taken prisoner *en route*—and immediately petrified.

Such objects should be seen from a distance. Near at hand, without any empty poesy, nothing can seem ruder, harsher, or more coarse. Figure to yourself a great highway of a dirty white—about half a league broad, perhaps—with

profound furrows and deeply sunken ruts dotted about in
every direction. What terrific car, or what devil's chariot,
has then descended by this road ? Its whole surface is en-
crusted with sugar-loaf crystals, of little brilliancy, from fifteen
to twenty feet in height; some of a whitish colour, a few
shaded with pale blue, others of a bottle-green tint, equivocal
and sinister.

It is evident that this descent was an expansion of an
immense sea of ice, whose rim may be seen on high, cutting
the blue heaven with a straight line. All this, lit up by the
sun, wore an aspect of savage hardness, a grand effect of superb
indifference for us mortals, an air—shall I not say ?—of inso-
lence. I am not astonished that Saussure, though of so calm
and sagacious an intellect, should feel, when he had climbed
the glacier, an emotion of anger. I too felt myself surprised
and incensed by these wild enormities. I said to them,
brusquely enough : " Be not ye so haughty ! Ye last but a
little longer than we do. O mountain! O glacier! what
are your ten thousands of feet compared with the height of
the mind ? "

I wished to examine them more closely ; and descending
from the village, I touched upon their border, and entered.
The openings are variable. At this particular moment the
glacier gaped in narrow mouths, of little elevation, shining, and
polished externally. Within all was gliding, with dangerous
declivities leading I know not where. These slopes, a double
and triple bluish dome, their sharp fractures, sharp even to
the eye, and their transparency, warned me not to trust them.
Nothing was more significant than a charming posy of flowers,
which, for many years, had remained embedded, and showed
itself through the ice in all its living colours. Once swallowed
up within it, you are sure of being well preserved. No image
of death can be more impressive than this long funereal
exhibition, this enforced eternity which sports sadly with life,

this impossibility of returning to nature and re-entering into repose.

The mountaineer does not regard his mountain from the same view-point as ourselves. He is strongly attached to it, and constantly returns to it; but he calls it "the evil country." The white glassy waters which escape from it, leaping and bounding in furious rapidity, he names "the wild waters." The black forest of firs, suspended to the precipices, an image of eternal peace, is his war, his battle. In the roughest months of the year, when all other labour ceases, he attacks the forest. It is an arduous campaign, and full of perils. It is not enough to fell the trees, and start them headlong; their course must be directed. He must watch them on their passage, and regulate the terrible leaps which carry them to the bed of the torrents. The conquered is often fatal to the conqueror, the tree to the woodman. The forest has its mournful histories of orphans and widows. For the wife and the family, a terror full of mourning rests

SHOOTING TIMBER DOWN THE TORRENT.

PATH OF THE AVALANCHE DOWN THE JUNGFRAU.

upon yonder heights, whose woods mingled with snow mark them out funereally from afar by spots of white and black.

Formerly the glaciers were objects of aversion; men regarded them with eyes askant. Those of Mont Blanc were called in Savoy "the accursed mountains." German Switzerland, in its old peasants' legends, doomed the damned to the glaciers. They are a kind of hell. Woe to the avaricious woman—to the hard cold heart which in the winter drives her aged father from the blazing hearth ! As a punishment she shall wander, with a hideous black dog, wander without rest in the regions of ice. In the severest nights of winter, when everybody presses close to the charcoal stove, you may see there on high the white woman, faltering and tottering among the sharp-edged crystals.

In the diabolical valley, where, every minute, thunders and crashes the avalanche from the summit of the Jungfrau, a host of doomed barons and ferocious knights ever dash and hurtle one against another, and shatter their fronts of iron.

The Scandinavian legend, sprung from a high and terrible genius, has given fantastical expression to the terrors of the mountain. It is stored with treasures, which are guarded by frightful gnomes, and a dwarf of colossal strength. In the castle of the icy peaks sits enthroned a pitiless virgin, who, with diamond-blazing forehead, incenses every hero, laughing with a laugh more fell than the keen shafts of winter. The heedless dash onward,—they reach the fatal couch,—and there they remain enchained, celebrating eternal nuptials with a bride of crystal.

This does not discourage men. The cruel and haughty she who sits on the summit of the mountain will ever have her lovers. Always they will yearn to gain her. The hunter says, " It is for prey." The climber says, " It is for the distant prospect." And I—I say, " It is to make a book." And I accomplish more ascents, and descend more precipices— seated at the table where I am writing—than all the climbers of earth will make on the Alps.

The reality in all these efforts is, *we mount for the sake of mounting.*

The sublime is—nearly always—the useless. The famous passage through the northern ice, discovered at the end of three hundred years of labour, will never be of any service (if it be true that the ice-masses change their position). Balloon

3

ascents, hitherto, have been without result. There is little
profit in the ascent of Mont Blanc. The experiments made
on its summit might have been made at a somewhat lower
level. What Saussure sought for seven-and-twenty years,
after due preparation, and hovering around Mont Blanc—
what Ramond sought for ten years, in the same fashion, on
Mont Perdu—was, before all, *to have ascended to the summit.*

Of all the wild lotteries which have perturbed the human
heart, the noblest, certainly, was the hunt after the chamois.
Its peril was its attraction ; it was the chase on the mountain
rather than the timid animal. Men boldly confronted it, face
to face, in its most rugged horrors, where it has both the reality
and the illusion for its defence,—ices, fogs, abysses, crevasses,
the deceitfulnesses of distance, the falsities of perspective, the
unbridled whirl of vertigo. These only acted as a greater
stimulus. Men, in all other things most sage and prudent,
went mad. The raptures of love in nowise might be compared
to the awful delight of pursuing the prey in the abysses, or on
the narrow and impossible ridges, whither the malignant little
fiend amused itself with attracting the madman. The gulf
whirls under his haggard eye. Over his head hovers the
hungry vulture. Ah, what an ecstasy of enjoyment! His
father, a year or two ago, made the leap. It is now the son's
turn. One of them, just married to a maiden whom he dearly
loved, said as much as this to Saussure : "Monsieur, it is
nothing. As my father perished, I too must perish." And
in three months he kept his word.

How the listening group will hang around the hunter,
when by the winter fire he, as the oracle of the district, relates
what he has seen during his wanderings among the glaciers !
How they will tremble when he describes his feelings on
gazing into the ominous azure of the yawning crevasse ! " I
have seen," he will say—" yes, with these eyes I have seen,

beneath vaults of twenty, thirty, sometimes one hundred feet in height, grottoes all sparkling with crystals which almost touch the ground. Ay, crystals,—or diamonds, maybe." Who has not dreamed of such stories? How the heart of the credulous Savoyard palpitates! "Oh, if one could but climb to these heights, one's fortune were made! Sixty years of suffering, of carrying or sweeping, would never accomplish so much. One day's daring, a single venturous expedition, would suffice.—What evil can there be in robbing the devil? It is he, or it is the fairies, who there store up their jewels."

To inspire him with the temerity to ascend beyond the limit of the chamois, these rumours of hidden treasures, and the ignorant fancy which confounds the icy stalactites with the crystal of the rock, crystal and diamond for all I know,— are necessary. Men do not discover what they expect, but they discover—Mont Blanc.

Let us investigate the nature of the terrors which formerly encircled it. Chamounix was ignored, and unknown even in the land to which it belonged. The traveller did not make his way along the lower ground through that long and gloomy valley. It was rather the passing wayfarer who, as he followed the route of Notre Dame de la Gorge (the road to Italy), chanced to be of curious mind, and climbing to the Prarion, contemplated from thence the snowy mass of Mont Blanc. But what a terrible prospect! One is near it, at two paces. It has not, as from afar, the effect of an immense elongated corpse, with other Alps lying at its head and feet. From a close view-point, one sees it in all its loftiness, alone, an immense white monk, buried in its cloak and hood of ice, dead, and yet standing erect. Others see in it a splendour, like the ruin of a dying star, of the pale and barren moon, a sepulchral planet upon the terrestrial planet.

Its vast snowy hood (*calotte*) has the effect of a cemetery, whose monuments are the sombre pyramids which start up in striking contrast with the snow. These time-old daughters of Fire protest against the ice-masses; they say that this white catafalque is nothing in comparison with the shadowy infinite which plunges and stretches far down underneath.

If the traveller goes to the mountain-base by way of Chamounix, he finds himself in an impassable ravine, impassable and gloomy for eight months of the year (do not judge of it at the moment when it is visited for a few days in the height of summer by the noisy crowd). The valley is enclosed and shut in by the barriers of the Prarion and the Tête-Noire, and the stranger is, as it were, imprisoned in it. Chateaubriand has felt that under the foot of the colossus, under the weight of this enormous grandeur, it is with difficulty we breathe.

How much more at ease are we on Mont Cenis, or the Saint Gothard! Their summits, solemn as they may be, are nevertheless the great routes of commerce, the natural highways of all animated life. What numbers of horses, of flocks, even of migratory birds! But Mont Blanc leads nowhere; it is an hermit, apparently, wrapped up in its solitary musings.

A strange enigma among the Alps! While every other peak is eloquent with the voices of innumerable streams; while Saint Gothard, in its expansive generosity, pours out to the four winds four rivers which make so much noise through the world; Mont Blanc, the great miser, grudgingly yields two tiny torrents (which enlarge, it is true, but not until they reach a lower level, and have been enriched by other waters). Has it any subterranean issues? All that we know is, that it for ever receives, yet gives very little. May we believe that this silent treasure is prudently amassing, as a precaution against the future thirst and drought of the globe, the wealth of the hidden life!

As early as 1767, on the Léchaud glacier, numerous grottoes were discovered which had been excavated and rifled by the crystal-hunters. In 1784, a guide, it is said, was fortunate enough to chance upon a great quantity in a fallen mass of *débris*, and brought away three hundred pounds weight of large translucent crystals, of a beautiful purple hue. This event turned the brains of the mountaineers. One of the Balmats (a celebrated family of guides, renowned for their foremost intrepidity) ascended, but found nothing save a terrible tempest which involved him in great peril. The spirits of the mountain doubtlessly sought to discourage the rash and heedless adventurers who would have seized their treasures.

But another spirit was wandering through the world—curious, adventurous, intrepid—the Soul of the Eighteenth Century, which would not be discouraged. More and more eagerly it looked on high; a Titanic ambition fired every mind. In 1783 balloons were invented; Pilâtre and Arlandes were the first among mortals to quit the earth.

The ascent of Mont Blanc, stimulated and encouraged by the scientific, the Saussures and the Paccards,* was

* [De Saussure was not twenty years old when the idea first occurred to him of ascending Mont Blanc; and on his first visit to Chamounix, in 1760, he published it abroad in all parts of the valley that he would bestow an ample reward on any guide who discovered a practicable route. For some years, however, nothing came of his liberal offers.

In 1775, however, four guides of Chamounix succeeded in reaching Mont Blanc by the mountain De la Côte, which rises above the village Des Bossons. This mountain, situated between the glaciers Des Bossons and De Tacconay, abuts on the desert of snow and ice which stretches uninterruptedly to the very summit of Mont Blanc. After triumphing over the obstacles which opposed their progress on the glaciers, incessantly intersected by immense crevasses, the four guides penetrated into a great valley of snow, which seemed as if it would reach Mont Blanc. The weather was favourable, they met with no appalling precipices or yawning crevasses, and all things apparently promised success. But the rarefaction of the air, and the reverberation of the sun's rays on the dazzling surface, wearied them beyond endurance. Succumbing to physical and mental fatigue, they gave up their attempt, although they had met with no insuperable obstacle.

Seven years later, in 1783, a second ascent was undertaken by three guides named Cottet, Jorasse, and Carrier. They failed, through the deadly lethargy which overtook one of them, and compelled the others to carry their comrade back to Chamounix.

In the same year a naturalist, named Bourrit, attained to a point so near the summit that

finally accomplished, in June 1786, by Jacques Balmat, of Chamounix. Balmat discovered the route to the summit, and conducted by it Paccard in August 1786, and Saussure in August 1787.

he resolved to renew the enterprise in 1785, and De Saussure undertook to accompany him. They set out at eight A.M. on the 12th of September; bivouacked at the base of the Aiguille du Goûter; and on the following day reached an elevation of 11,250 feet, which proved their *ne plus ultra*. They were then obliged to abandon their attempt, and Mont Blanc remained unconquered until the 8th of August 1786, when, by a route he had previously discovered. Jacques Balmat conducted his friend and physician, Dr. Paccard, to the summit.]

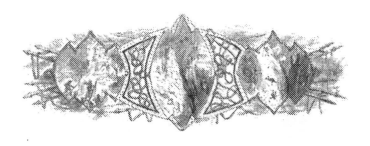

III

EARLY ASCENTS OF MONT BLANC.

THE GLACIERS.

HE glory of M. de Saussure rests, not so much on his ascent, or on his few experiments, but on the noble published record of his adventures, wherein he gives a number of interesting facts, clearly set forth and judiciously appreciated, in reference to Mont Blanc and the Alps in general. We perceive in him, what is rare enough, a man worthy of the name, singularly well balanced in study and character, exercise, and action.

It is singular, curious, and honourable for Switzerland, that land of education, honourable for grave Geneva, that it produced a special man, and preferred him, during a period of forty years, for the discovery of the Alps. In 1741 two English travellers had alighted upon, and laid down the bearings (as if of an unknown island in the South Sea) of, the foot of Mont Blanc—Chamounix. Geneva was all attention. Its illustrious naturalists, the Trembleys and the Bonnets, spoke of it loudly. Bonnet was a kinsman of Saussure, then a new-born infant. His mother (Mademoiselle de la Rive) cherished a vivid impression of what she had heard. To her child was given a persevering, ingenious, and scientific training. A

VILLAGE OF CHAMOUNIX.

mathematician and physician, he taught the science of mathe-
matics when only twenty years old. Well-directed tours
made him a capital walker and skilful climber; in fine, a man
thoroughly inured to mountaineering excursions. He commenced his career in 1760 by ascending to Brevent, a place
whence one obtains the best view of Mont Blanc. He
returned with its image stamped upon his brain. For twenty-
seven years he travelled, every summer, among the Alps,
returning always to the great object for which he had
been bred, and contemplating it ever nearer. It became a
passion with him, and he could dream of nothing else.
"It was a disease," he says. "My gaze never rested upon
Mont Blanc, which is visible from so many points in the
environs of Geneva, without my experiencing a kind of painful
shock."

Why did he make the ascent at so late a date? Why did
he allow others to anticipate him? The family who had so
assiduously prepared him for the enterprise, at the moment

VIEW OF MONT BLANC AND ITS GLACIER, FROM THE BREVENT.

when it should have been undertaken, grew disquieted. This is plain from what happened on his return, as related by himself. All his relations and friends had betaken themselves to Chamounix, where they awaited his descent in an excess of anxiety. And the kinsmen of his guides were not less troubled. Great was the joy when at length they returned from the mountain, and were clasped in their arms. Was that admirable mother present who had so long trained him for the task, and whose perseverance had so greatly contributed to its success? One cannot but regret that he does not inform us.

With a wise slowness, he did not publish his travels for many years afterwards. In this beautiful book, so replete with facts, which will always remain the principal authority on its particular subject, certain important questions, still unsettled, were proposed. The excellent and serious atmosphere, of great moral, but strictly Biblical authority, in which M. de Saussure lived, rendered him somewhat timid. Buffon, at his first essay, had been arrested, and forced to recoil. If De Saussure had found no means of satisfying ancient tradition, he would have wounded his friends, the Bonnets and the Hallers. At all costs it was necessary for him to accommodate the Book of Genesis, to arrange with the Deluge, not to see or not to comprehend any facts which militated against the ancient text. He therefore missed the grand discovery, for which Science had to wait fifty years. The men who lived in the vicinity of the glaciers, the chamois-hunters, wood-cutters, guides, or crystal-hunters, could have told the secret of the whole affair to the savant, just as they had always beheld it, just as one beholds it to-day.

The glacier is not dead, inert, immovable, but *a living thing.* It moves, it advances, it recedes to advance again. It absorbs, but it rejects, and admits no foreign bodies. On the glacier of the Aar, where the incline is very gentle, a rock carried upon the ice accomplished a league in three-and-thirty

years. On the glaciers of Mont Blanc the journey, it seems,
needs forty years. This we know from a ladder left there by
De Saussure. This we know, too, through the tragical catastrophe of one of the Balmats. These heroes of the glacier
have also been its martyrs. It is especially by their agency
that we have discovered its progressive movement. They
have measured it with their bodies. Jacques Balmat was
engulfed in 1834 ; Pierre Balmat in 1820,—and his remains,
cast out at the foot of the glacier in 1861, showed that it
accomplished its descent in forty years. The poor fragments
of bone which are preserved in the museum of Annécy move
the spectator strongly, when he reflects that this heroic family
were not only the first to reach the summit, but by their
misfortunes to establish the law of the glaciers, their regular
evolution, which opens up a new horizon to Science.

As early as 1706 Hottinger had pointed out their alternate
progress and recession. Scheuchzer, of Zurich, had perfectly
described the manner in which the glacier purges itself of its
rocks and of all its incumbrances. The rocks thus rejected
by Mont Blanc from its ample bosom are easily recognized,
being generally composed of a material elsewhere seldom met
with,—that species of gray granite, with greenish points, which
is called *protogene*. Similar rocks were found in the neighbouring valleys, but this was not a fact to embarrass the
scientific observer. But they were also found at a considerable distance ; as far even as the Jura. How were they
transported *thither?* The question was a puzzle. The same
difficulty existed in reference to those which, from their
mineral components, appeared to have belonged to the depths
of the Rhone valley ; to the rocks of the Aar ; and of other
localities.

Some of these boulders, measuring 60 feet in length, and
20 or 30 in height, are evidently of great weight. To assert

that they were rolled into their present positions by currents of water, is to put forward an insupportable hypothesis. Water had never so great a force. And they have not been rolled, it is clear, for they have preserved intact their sharp angles, which in so long a journey would assuredly have been rubbed smooth. "They must have been hurled headlong by the Diluvian currents," says Saussure. A prodigious operation, to carry these rocks right over the Lake of Geneva! For this purpose they would have to fly at the rate of 19,000 feet per second, under the pressure of a mass of water equal to six thousand millions of cubic feet!—The idea appeared ridiculous.

But after 1815, by dint of reaction, Genesis and the Deluge came into favour. To second the Deluge, men called into play the internal fires; they supposed that at the burning eruption of granite, a sudden liquefaction of the ice-masses communicated to the current of the Deluge the frightful power of hurling such huge rocks (60 feet in length!) from the Valais even to the Jura!

If, instead of *imagining*, men had condescended to *observe*, they would have seen that things occurred in the primeval times as they occur in the present. With extreme slowness, but with a sure progress, regular and calculable, the glacier expels its rocks by urging them before it, without any shock, any change or modification of their angles or forms. It transports them as if they were placed, so to speak, upon rollers. And these rollers are the pebbles themselves, which, grinding beneath the mass, drag it slowly onward, accurately polishing the path, and marking the ground with deep, easily recognizable *striæ*, that enable us to follow with ease its exact passage.

This very simple explanation had probably been, from time immemorial, the popular opinion of persons living close to, and constantly seeing, these phenomena. Already, in 1815, it had been adopted by Playfair, who attributed the transportation of boulders to the agency of the glaciers. But then, what became of the Book of Genesis and the currents of the Deluge?

Two men, in the Valais,—the engineer Venetz, and Charpentier, the director of the salt-works,—discussed these questions. The latter, in 1815, on his way to the great Saint Bernard, slept in the hut of a chamois-hunter, who said to him: "These blocks are of too great a size; water could never have transported them. All the valley of the Rhone up to a great height was once occupied by a glacier." A woodman of Meyringen, at a later period, made the same assertion with respect to the glacier of the Grimsel, which formerly extended as far as Berne. An inhabitant of Chamounix also attributed to the glaciers the transport of boulders along the heights of the main route. These blocks, identical in composition with the stone of Mont Blanc, and bearing so plainly on their surface the certificate of their origin, teach all along their course, and with exactness indicate the ancient extension of the glacier.

Did this extension require a terrible excess of cold? Not at all. M. Charles Martins has proved by irrefutable calculations that with a few bad summers in continuation of the winter, with an increase of only four degrees of cold, the limit of perpetual snow would be brought down exactly to the level of the Swiss plain, which it would speedily invade, and gradually convert into a glacier.

No circumstance has profited science more considerably than the familiarity we have acquired with the glacier, by so frequently visiting it, and examining it from above and below. We have arrived at a knowledge of all its belongings from the numerous ascents, and especially the prolonged sojourns which our adventurers have made. Men have lost their reverence for it. They have inhabited the glacier. Messrs. Agassiz

GLACIER OF ROSENLAUI (NOW RAPIDLY RETIRING).

and Desor lived upon one for
whole months and seasons during
five successive years. Its famous
crevasses have been fathomed.
Messrs. Charles Martins and Doll-
fus found some 100 feet deep,
M. Desor one of 1000 feet. Hugi
has sounded the under region.
By dragging or crawling, he has
ascertained how the glaciers differ
in internal structure.   Some were fixed—were solidly attached
to the soil ; others, on the contrary, were completely hollow ;
others rested only on blocks or piles, which must sooner or
later give way.   In brief, their character varies as well. as
their habits.

Did they once occupy the whole world, as Agassiz believes? Have they twice cast over the globe the cold monotonous garb of universal winter? Such, at all events, seems to be the indication afforded by the numerous erratic blocks found in so many countries.

It is the present belief, in the Alps, that for seven years they move forward, and for seven years move backward. If they recede, the summer is hot and the harvest abundant, subsistence easy, and the general ease ensures peace. If they advance, the year is cold and rainy, the fruits do not ripen, the corn-harvest fails, and the people suffer. Revolution is not far distant.

They advanced with horrible rapidity at the great epoch of 1815–16. They advanced in 1849, and by the dearness of food contributed not a little to the downfal of the French Republic. They receded for twelve years in the hot summers which occurred between 1853 and 1865 (according to the observations of M. Charles Martins). Are they now advancing, to afflict us with rainy years, years of sterility, complicated with great events?

They form a formidable thermometer, on which the whole world, moral and political, should ever fix its eyes. The atmospheric changes which they indicate,—phenomena of immense and profound influence,—not only affect the alimentary life, but also our thoughts, our dispositions, our nervous being. It is on the brow of Mont Blanc, more or less overhung with ice, that we may read the future destiny and fortunes of Europe, the seasons of serene peace, and the abrupt cataclysms which overthrow empires and sweep away dynasties.

THE WATERSHED OF EUROPE.

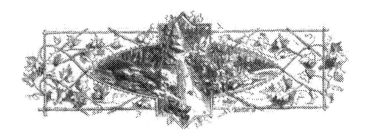

IV

THE EUROPEAN WATER-RESERVOIR.

THERE is nothing worthy of comparison with the Alps. No mountain-system seems to me to approach theirs; neither in the radiation of its felicitously connected and articulated groups, nor in the superb arrangement of its reservoirs, which, from glaciers and torrents, lakes and immense rivers, pour life over Europe.

The Cordilleras or the Pyrenees, with their prolonged line, do not seem a system. The Himalaya, so enormous, as far as I can judge, in the immense separation of its two extremities, between the Scinde and the Ganges, does not so compactly keep its mass together. A great quantity of water, without method or control, is lost in its extensive marshes, and the vast and dangerous jungles which stretch at its feet.

In the Alps, all is harmonious. The noble amphitheatres which send to the four seas the Po, the Rhine, the Rhone, and the Inn (the true Danube), are not so wide apart that one cannot embrace them, so to speak, at a single glance. Most of them at their origin almost touch each other, and are brothers, springing from one and the same mass, the heart of the system, the heart of the European world.

The sublime impression which we receive from these mountains is no fantasy. It is the right and natural intuition of a veritable grandeur. It is the reservoir of Europe, the treasure-house of its fecundity. It is the theatre of the interchanges and lofty correspondences of the atmospheric currents, winds, clouds, and vapours. Water is life begun. The circulation of life, under an aërial or liquid form, takes place upon these heights. They are the mediators, the arbiters of sundered or antagonistic elements. They make their harmony and peace. They accumulate them in glaciers, and then equitably distribute them among the nations.

The strong, wise, and profound saying which has been uttered on this subject proceeds from no man of science, no Saussure. A simple tourist, travelling for amusement, having reached a superb sea of ice in the centre of an imposing mountain-circle, was greatly moved by the scene, and exclaimed, " I have found the *Place de la Concorde* of the world !"

Nothing could be more true, or more rightly felt. The winds of the west and south-west, loaded with the waters and the vapours of the Atlantic, and even of the Pacific, deposit them here, and they are speedily congealed by the breath of the icy north. They would remain as captives if the burning south, in a happy access of fury, did not suddenly re-awaken them, did not constrain them to go forth, in mists, and dews, and showers, to be the joy of the earth.

How beautiful the concord, how noble the harmony ! All that is elsewhere obscure is here illuminated. The Alps are Light. They bring us acquainted with the solidarity of the globe.

Yonder clouds, having travelled from so great a distance, ought after their journey to re-collect themselves willingly, and seek a moment's repose. There is a grand resting-place on the Alps. Surely forty to fifty leagues of glaciers, from Dauphiny to the Tyrol, form a tolerably superb couch. But such is the

levity, such the inconstancy of
these travellers, that the cordial
hospitality of the Alps fails to
detain them. An ingenious
device secures them a little
fixity. Their snow-flakes, half-
melted in the sunshine, having
infiltrated the lower strata, are
hardened by the night frosts,
and become a granular mass.

MISTS ON THE GLACIER.

These grains, or little icicles, possessing a certain degree of
cohesion among themselves, form what is called the *nevé*.
Throughout the summer this *nevé* filters itself through fresh
liquefactions, which deposit the water in the hollow designed

for occupation by the new glacier. Frozen, melted, re-frozen every night (even in the summer season), the *nevé* becomes transformed into white ice, still mingled with air-bubbles. But after awhile the bubbles disappear, and the ice stratifies in azure layers.

Now, then, the vapours are thoroughly congealed. Solid and stratified, they lie in their immovable bed, vowed, apparently, to an eternal and definitive captivity. Others, descending on their surface in snowy flakes, are soon hardened into *nevé*, and covering the azure strata, defend them from the sun. You would think the strata must necessarily increase in size and thickness. The quantity distilled below in the inferior layer seems little when compared with the masses which fall from on high. Yet an equilibrium exists. For sixty years Mont Blanc has remained unaltered. Its summit, says M. Charles Martins, has neither increased nor diminished in height.

In reality, a rude force, which one would suppose to be *in*harmonious, intervenes to complete the harmony. Occasionally the tyrant of the south (Fœhn, Autan, Siroco, Simoun, Vaudère, it has more than twenty names) falls—impatient, terrible, and impetuous—on this gloomy world. With a great roar it summons all the motionless waters which have so much difficulty in rousing themselves from their lethargy. But it is impossible for them to turn a deaf ear to its voice. It insists, it whistles, it thunders.—No delay; no, not a moment's.

The burning demon of Africa loves to strike his great blow at night. You may foresee his approach on the preceding evening. A shifting fog floats about the peaks. The air grows transparent, revealing and bringing nearer every object. A reddish circle surrounds the moon, and the horizon assumes a singular violet hue. The wind roars through the lofty forests; a hoarse murmur proceeds from the torrents. All Nature is seized with expectancy.

In truth, we have everything to fear. Our formidable
benefactor seems bent at first on destroying what he comes to
save.   He shatters, he huddles together, he ravages.   He
hurls enormous blocks from the heights, and rolls gigantic
trees into the channel of the rushing streams.   He seizes and

THE COMING OF THE FŒHN.

carries afar the roofs of the chalets.   A panic terror prevails
in the stable: the cow lows in her fright.   Heavens! what is
going to happen?—The spring is on its way.

The Fœhn makes a jest of the sun.   The latter would
spend fifteen days in melting what the African gale melts in

four-and-twenty-hours. The snow is unable to withstand it. Its influence in two hours melts the burden of the Grindelwald to a depth of twenty-four inches. It terminates the subterrene existence of the mysterious Alpine plants, and puts an end to their long night of eight months' duration. At the bidding of the magician they live again; with intense delight they share the radiance of their brief summer; and their tiny flower-hearts rejoice in a transitory gleam of love. Yes; this furious savage, with its wild dramatic stroke, becomes love's messenger. Nowhere is its power too great but in the valleys, where its warm concentrated breath enervates and oppresses you. The animals are manifestly disturbed; man himself grows agitated; and his wife tremblingly presses nearer to his side. A profound disquiet is visible in all things.

At times the wind of the North, sworn enemy of the Fœhn,* endeavours to overcome it by a sudden surprise; but the struggle is in vain, and it is compelled to succumb. Love still reigns as lord of earth.

How felicitous a metamorphosis! What numerous benefits flow from it! The life and fecundity long slumbering on

---

* ["No wind," says Tschudi, "is better known than this throughout the whole mountain-district of Switzerland. It is not local in its influence, but general; and may be called an European, or, more correctly speaking, an African wind. For as the Polar Circle would seem to be the cradle of the icy North, and the Atlantic of the humid West, so the torrid South is born among the dry and sandy deserts of Africa. It might be supposed that the barrier of the Alps would have afforded a protection against this wind, but on the contrary it endows it with additional force; the hot current of air, instead of rising completely above their summits, becomes chilled by the snow in the lower levels; and thus being condensed, pours furiously into the valleys. These outbursts are most frequent in winter and early spring, when the air from the glaciers is sharpest, and the valleys as yet are but little affected by the solar rays so as to secure a more gradual equalization of the temperature. And for this same cause its violence is greater by night than by day. It is accompanied by atmospheric phenomena of singular beauty, and preceded by a few cold, bleak, and furious gusts, which are followed by a sudden calm; whereupon a vehement scorching wind arises, gathering frequently all the force of a hurricane. It affects animals powerfully. The birds retire from wood and glen; the chamois with difficulty drags itself up the mountain-side; cows, goats, horses, wander vainly in search of fresher air. Man shares in the general discomfort; suffers from a peculiar oppression of the spirits, and a lassitude in every nerve and muscle. In the spring-time, however, its advent is eagerly welcome, as it produces a rapid melting of the ice and snow, and transforms in a few hours the entire aspect of the country."—M. F. Von Tschudi, "Das Thierleben der Alpenwelt."]

the Alpine peaks are now astir. More useful than any river, their dews and mists are spread abroad to fertilize Europe with that delicate irrigation to which we owe the rich meadow-grasses and the green velvety sward. The heavy nitrous rains and the hot electric showers bring out the verdure of the leaf, and stimulate the abrupt exertions of Nature, who, at her first awakening, surpasses and forgets herself in the balmy spring-tide dream.

Happy he who, at the beginning of the great transformation, has the sense and the ear to understand the inaugural concert of all these waters, when millions and millions of springs break forth into song! Springs like to one which I saw yesterday, emerging from the mountain-cleft, diffused through the moss, and in its infant condition little better than simple humidity, yet seemingly saying, "I am," and "I am not;" which this morning was only a silver thread, just enough to quench the thirst of a bird; but this evening how solemn it has become, how majestic, how imperious, and how strong in its loud, full murmur! Its voice predominates over all. It enters into converse with the neighbouring streams. These cherish a mutual intelligency; and voices, and mysterious "asides," and modes of intercommunication, and a certain indescribable kind of dialogue, and a hum of closest intimacy, which seems like an exchange of secrets. Brought into direct communion, they afterwards divide again, and with their prattling flow embrace the islands and the little continents, until they mingle anew in augmented volume, and speed onward with a mighty clamour.

But, lo! before their impetuous course the earth fails suddenly!

What new, strange waterfalls are these? Who shall describe the picturesque forms of all the cataracts of the Alps? The most famous are not the most beautiful. I know of cer-

5

tain hidden masterpieces, which the tourist never visits, and which seem to conceal from the world their tender, languid graces. I can particularize them at this very moment; I will recline and take my rest beside them. An omnipotent attraction retains me near their mysterious flow. Tschudi, in his book on the Alps, has no passage more eloquent or more sympathetic than his description of their water-falls (see especially his first chapter, and that on the *Merle d'Eau*). But how can words express or pictures represent their infinity, their iris of colours, their shifting prisms, and eternal illusions ?

An admirable phrase has been thrown out in reference to them, worth a host of elaborate descriptions. We owe it to the gentle, loving, and devout Madame Guyon.* In her banishment at Annecy, among marshes and canals, and on the fever-haunted borders of the lake, she could see but little of the grand movement of the Alpine waters—brook and torrent, cascade and river. But her heart divined it in its entirety.

* [Jeanne Marie Bouvier de la Mothe, Madame Guyon, illustrious in literary and religious annals as a Quietist and a poet, was born at Montargis, April 13, 1648. After a marriage of much unhappiness she was left a widow, with three children, at the early age of eighteen. In her youth she had manifested a strong religious feeling, which her life-sorrows undoubtedly tended to develop and strengthen; and settling herself at Thonon, on the Lake of Geneva, she devoted herself wholly to good deeds. Her disregard, however, of mere forms and ceremonies, brought upon her a suspicion of heresy; and to clear herself from the imputation, she made known her religious views in a work called "The Torrents"—the title being suggested by Amos v. 24: "Righteousness as a mighty stream" (or torrent). In July 1686 she removed to Paris, where her adoption of Quietism, or the doctrine taught by Molinos—which may roughly be described as a Christian version of Platonic philosophy—gave umbrage to ecclesiastical authorities; and she was imprisoned, in 1688, in the convent of Sainte Marie. Here she wrote some of her finest poems, and acquired the friendship of Fenelon, who eventually embraced her religious creed. She was afterwards imprisoned at Vincennes, Vaugirard, and in the Bastile; nor did she obtain her release, owing to Bossuet's implacable hostility, until 1702. Her undeserved misfortunes neither shook her constancy nor prevailed over her courage; but they broke up her constitution, and she died in 1717, at the age of sixty-nine. Her remains were interred in the church of the Cordeliers at Blois, and a monument erected to her memory; but a more enduring monument is to be found in her works, which, pervaded as they are by a strange atmosphere of mysticism, breathe a spirit of the purest and tenderest piety. Many of her poems have been translated by Cowper.]

She felt in all its force the noble secret that lies at the bottom of all life. And in her book upon "The Torrents" she exclaims, with simple sublimity, "These waters! in very truth, they are souls!"

THE TORRENT AT MONTREUX.

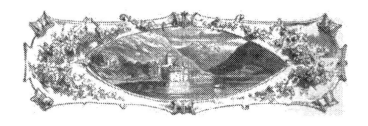

V.

SWITZERLAND:

ITS LAKES AND RIVERS.

THERE are in Switzerland, according to geographers, one thousand lakes. No other country possesses these superb mirrors in such magnificence. Every land afterwards visited by the traveller appears to him gloomy and, as it were, *blind*. Its lakes are the eyes of Switzerland, and their azure surface doubles for it the sky.

Even in those desolate places which seem the very limit and extreme of Nature—in the sombre vicinity of the glaciers —you will discover a radiance in the little solitary lakes which moves you powerfully. One you find encircled with a rampart of ice; another with peat moors and green meadows; a third decorates itself with a fringe of larches, which, glassed in the silver-gray waters, colour them with their emerald images, and with their annual foliage recall—not without a certain charm, whether gay or sad—the happy vegetation of the lower world.

These lakes—these dumb confidants of the glaciers, which achieve through their agency a passage out of the darkness— were regarded by our Celtic forefathers with terror and worship. They seem full of mystery; a savage charm in-

THE MOUNTAIN-MIRROR (LAKE OF LUCERNE).

LAKE ENSIGN, CANYON OF VAUD.

vests them. He who has once beheld for ever remembers them. I do
not feel greatly surprised at the
efforts of a courageous fish to revisit
them every year, in the season of
love's potent impulses. The salmon
from the Northern seas, through the
lengthened circuit of the Rhine, and
in defiance of opposing currents,
presses forward victoriously. He
ascends and overcomes the impetuous cataract. Where he
cannot swim, he glides, advancing with a serpent-like motion.
Nor can, it is said, the most formidable falls—even such as
the Reuss, at the Devil's Bridge*—arrest his onward course.

---

* [Thus described by Longfellow, in his "Hyperion:"—"The sides of the mountains are
barren cliffs; and from their cloud-capped summits, unheard amid the roar of the great torrent below, come streams of snow-white foam, leaping from rock to rock, like the mountain
chamois. As you advance, the scene grows wilder and more desolate. There is not a tree
in sight, not a human habitation. Clouds, black as midnight, lower upon you from the

What is the lake's part in the economy of Nature? It receives what the mountaineers call "the savage water," and transforms it into living water. The vitreous streams, so long pent up in the opaque mass of the glacier, charged with a cold, lifeless deposit, and deprived of light and air, are in need of baptism in the air and the sunshine. Even the chamois-hunter dare not drink of them. He will rather chip off a small fragment of ice, and placing it on the rock, swallow the drops as they fall. Nor have plants any greater affection for this same "savage water."

The primeval arrangement of the lakes, in series of basins, located at various levels and in successive reservoirs, through which the waters pass and purify themselves, may still be observed in the Engadine and in the district of Lucerne. "The Lake of Alpnach," writes Tschudi, "lies sunk in the very depths of the valley. Above, on the second terrace, is the picturesque Lake of Sarner; and still higher, on the third, surrounded by lofty peaks, the lakelet, or tarn, of Lungern is still discernible, although half exhausted by an artificial conduit."

Among earth's "things of loveliness" we recognize two as perfect and peerless. In the Lake of Geneva, the Beautiful —a noble and exalted harmony; in the Lake of Lucerne, the Sublime.

Have the secrets ever been fathomed which the Lake of Geneva guards in its mighty depths? Are we certain that its waters are fed only by the Rhone and its forty confluents? Has it no subterranean inlets, no masked ways of intelligence on the side of Savoy, no unknown sources?

---

ravines above; and the mountain torrent is but a sheet of foam, and sends up an incessant roar. A sudden turn in the road brings you in sight of a lofty bridge, stepping from cliff to cliff with a single stride. A mighty cataract howls beneath it, like an evil spirit, and fills the air with mist; and the mountain wind claps its hands and shrieks through the narrow pass. Ha! ha! This is the Devil's Bridge. It leads the traveller across the fearful chasm, and through a mountain gallery, into the broad green, silent meadow of Andermath."]

the case, one would be inclined to suppose
ɜ inexplicable movements, its sudden rises
Even its storms have a character of their
67 I observed how little its swell resembled
otion of other waters. Its waves appeared
*k*e deep lines hollowed out by a chisel.*

LAKE OF LUCERNE (AND MONT PILATE).

In Switzerland—the land of Light—this lake is light
itself; and grand is the sudden effect when, from the threshold of the Valais—from that narrow defile which is choked
up at St. Maurice—the plain all at once expands and enlarges, and you pause upon the edge of a vast sun-kindled
mirror. In the noon-tide it becomes a gorgeous festival,
which at first sight completely dazzles you. But this mobile,

* [In the original, " De profondes rayures de burin"—*i.e.*, the deep lines made by a burin,
or engraver's graving tool.]

6

THE LAKE OF GENEVA—A STORM-SCENE.

living splendour is, to a certain extent, subdued by the harmonious character of the shores. The very mountains of
Savoy, which shoot sheer down into the lake, admirably
accord with the smiling heights of the Pays de Vaud.
Gradually spreading out from the chestnut groves of Evian
to the bold promontory of Lausanne, the magnificent crescent
becomes a golden sea, which extends and shimmers even to
the remote shadows of the Jura.

A process, elsewhere operating only by stages—as from
lake to lake—is here carried out under your very gaze. You
see the troubled Rhine, rushing at first with a foul and tawny
current, then gradually subduing its impetuosity, and assum-

ing a transparent azure. Nowhere is the filtration of the waters more clearly observable, or the purifying operations which they undergo in the bosom of the lakes.

And for man too, no less than for the waters, is the river

EVIAN, LAKE OF GENEVA.

a lofty and a beautiful image of tranquillity. What struggles has it formerly witnessed!* what desperate contests between rugged Switzerland and passionate Savoy! But at length it has pacified them both. Our fortunate interpreter between races and creeds, by its permanent and attractive channels of intercommunication, unites and marries together its opposing banks. It may be likened to an universal religion of nature, wherein every heart unwittingly makes itself understood by the sentiment of a tender humanity.

Not far from the Bridge of Lucerne stands a small, heavy, unwieldy edifice of stone; ay, of stone assuredly, for not a plank has been employed in its construction. It is the

* These souvenirs are too much forgotten. The reader will find them revived in Rudolph Rey's beautiful monograph on Lake Leman. [It is almost unnecessary to say that Michelet here alludes to the prolonged wars in which Savoy and Switzerland were involved in the sixteenth century. The last great event in this exhausting struggle was the *coup-de-main* attempted against Geneva by Charles-Emanuel I., Duke of Savoy. His troops scaled the walls, and actually penetrated into the city, but were ultimately repulsed with terrible slaughter. A.D. 1602.]

treasure-house of the canton, and a true treasure-house ; for
within it lies an iron coffer, and within this coffer a thing
precious among the precious—the banner in whose folds the
gallant Gondoldingen, chief magistrate of Lucerne, wrapped

THE BRIDGE OF LUCERNE.

himself when wounded to the death.   It is still stained with
his blood.   His last wish—his dying words—will one day be
accepted as a law by the whole world : " Let no magistrate
hold his office for more than one year."

But here, in the Lake of Geneva, take note of the abrupt
change that has occurred, and which might induce you to
think yourself in the North.   Among the lofty chestnut trees
a few beeches and sombre firs present themselves, even on the
lowest terrace, and descending to the very margin of the
waters.   And how gloomy is their aspect !   No bank slopes
gently down to them ; no pleasant road winds round them.
There is scarcely so much as a path where, during a high
wind, a pedestrian may walk in safety.

The great Righi on your right, black Mount Pilate on
your left, eye you with their awful stare.   Over the shoulder
of the latter two ice-cold giants—the Silberhorn, and his
sister, the Jungfrau—look down upon Geneva from a distance
of ten leagues.

If a wreck occurs, there is no chance of safety. But it is not only the waters man has cause to dread. All along the shore your glance is attracted by tottering masses of rock, which call to mind the terrific landslip of the Rossberg.*

From crag to crag you next descend into the basin where, sombre and storm-tossed, and seething within its cavernous walls, lies the small but tragical Lake of Uri. It may be compared to a capricious and ferocious wild bull. The famous wars of Switzerland, and its fiercest fights—its *Morats* and its *Sempachs*†—are there incessantly reproduced by the pent-up and hurtling winds. In the morning comes the whistling North; but at noon the treacherous Fœhn surprises the lake, and plunges it in turmoil. The green waters deliver their assault against a rampart of precipitous cliff. Who shall conquer the furious twain?

* [The landslip of the Rossberg occurred in 1806. It buried five villages, and four hundred and seventy-five persons lost their lives. In the year mentioned, on the morning of the 2nd of September, the catastrophe began, some masses of rock falling down the mountain flank. Towards evening larger masses descended, and the peasantry, now alarmed, endeavoured to escape. But suddenly a large portion of the upper bulk of the mountain was seen to give way, and soon came swooping, and crashing, and groaning into the valley, where it formed a ridge one hundred feet in height, and a league and a half in length and breadth. The entire vale of the Goldau was converted into a scene of desolation; and the villages of Goldau, Basingau, Lowerz, Ober, and Unter Rother were almost utterly destroyed. A small chapel, on the site of the village of Goldau, commemorates this terrible calamity; and a religious service is celebrated every year on its anniversary.]

† [The *Battle of Morat*, in which Charles the Bold, Duke of Burgundy, was completely defeated by the Swiss, was fought on the 22nd of June 1476. His discomfiture was due to his utter want of military tactics. He possessed a great superiority in cavalry and artillery; but plunging into a defile, between the mountains and the lake, he allowed them no room to deploy. His loss was tremendous, being variously estimated at from 8000 to 10,000 men, including many famous knights and nobles, whose bones for three centuries formed a ghastly monument on the battle-field, until it was destroyed, in 1798, by a French army, and a stone column erected in its place.

The *Battle of Sempach* was fought between the Swiss and Leopold, Duke of Austria, July 9, 1386. The Swiss mustered 1300 strong; the Austrians, 4000 horse and 1000 foot. The nature of the ground being unfit for the movements of cavalry, the German knights dismounted, and, clad in steel, and armed with lance and buckler, formed apparently an impassable barrier, nor could all the heroic efforts of the Swiss succeed in breaking through it. Despondency was seizing on their ranks, when Arnold von Winkelried, a knight of Unterwalden, suddenly rushing forward, clasped in his outstretched arms as many spears as possible, received them in his bosom, and by his bodily weight bore them to the ground. Into the breach thus effected

THE LAKE OF URI.

Now, in the rear, is gliding the Fœhn, which, a moment
agone, raged and stormed in the front; and following up a
winding gallery, it comes full in its own face, engages in
battle with itself. Then, between it and this other Fœhn
breaks forth a paroxysm of wrath, a frightful and tumultuous

his comrades impetuously rushed; and the heavily armoured knights, being wholly unable to
elude their rapid movements, fell like trees before the blast. The loss of the Austrians was
nearly 2000, including Duke Leopold, and 600 counts, barons, and knights; that of the Swiss
only 200. The anniversary of this great victory, which secured the independence of Switzerland, is yearly celebrated on the battle-field.

Morat has been illustrated by the genius of Byron:—

> " Morat and Marathon twin names shall stand ;
> They were true Glory's stainless victories,
> Won by the unambitious heart and hand
> Of a proud, brotherly, and civic band,
> All unbought champions in no princely cause
> Of vice-entailed corruption."
>
> *Childe Harold,* c. iii., 64.]

chaos. Happy, indeed, the boatman, if he can leap upon Tell's Platform, and contrive, like the Swiss hero, to fend off his skiff with his foot.

FLUELLEN (NEAR TELL'S PLATFORM), LAKE OF URI.

Who would believe that at a somewhat higher level, among the fair and grassy leas, everything grows suddenly tranquil? The Fœhn, when unopposed by any contrary wind, is a southern breeze,—of considerable force, it is true, but grateful to the chestnuts and the vineyards which bloom on the very summit of the Jura. It is in this range we recognize the benignity and true serenity of the mountain patriarch, the venerable Saint Gothard. True greatness is always gentle. And as we ascend it, and turn our backs on the sublime Fall of the Reuss, we perceive at every step a conspicuous increase in amenity of character.

Saint Gothard is, in effect, the centre of the great hydraulic forces of Europe. Not so lofty as many other peaks, it is its colossal bulk which compels the conciliation of the Alps. All the mountains rendezvous at this convenient point. The

THE PARTING OF THE WATERS (LAC LEMON,
VAL DES ORMONTS).

Mont Blanc chain, which dominates over the Leman and the
Rhine; the ranges of Uri,
Glacis, and Appenzell, which
strike towards Constance; and, finally, the Rhœtian mass,
which feeds the Rhine with its three hundred glaciers,—all
concentrate upon Saint Gothard. Yet it retains little: it
surrenders all. It is Saint Gothard which pours out the
mighty European rivers towards the four seas; like to the
sacred Persian mountain, which also sends its streams to
the four quarters of the world.*

* [The four rivers issuing from the bosom of Saint Gothard, a vast mountain-nucleus, forming
the central *nodus*, or knot, of the Lepontine and Bernese chains of the Alps, are the Rhine, the

Each of these individual rivers well merits a detailed history. How many benefits we owe to them! They not only satisfy the thirst of nations; they do more. They protect them. They are the vanguard of empires. They simultaneously restrain war and assist the cause of peace; are at once the highways and intermediate boundaries of commerce.

No one can look upon their fountain-heads without an emotion of awe; nor on the resplendent arch of azure whence they most frequently issue. No one but must admire their impetuosity, their daring, the colossal cataracts in which they boldly precipitate their waters. Then consider the majesty of their repose in the great lakes. Each of them, the profound soul of their birth-land, serves to engender life even by its very defects. That savageness of which we accuse the greatest—the Inn and the Danube—forms, in truth, the safeguard of Europe. We have been saved by their very ferocity. The celebrated "Gate of Iron," * and the rocks so fruitful in shipwrecks, have nevertheless arrested the invincible onset of the barbarians. The Danube formerly interposed its furious floods between us and Turkish despotism.

Reuss, the Rhone, and the Tessin, or Ticino. The Rhine rises on the eastern slope, the Tessin on the southern, the Russ on the northern, and the Rhone on the western; and all within a circuit of two miles from the mountain centre. The highest peak of the mountain is 10,600 feet above the sea-level.

By the "sacred Persian mountain," the Translator presumes M. Michelet means that of Ararat, or Agridagh, which equally belongs, however, to Russia and Turkey. It lies in the southern portion of the extensive plain of the Aras, about 35 miles broad, and consists of two mountains—the Great Ararat, 17,323 feet on the north-west; and, at a distance of about seven miles to the south-east, the less Ararat, 13,093 feet. Tradition, basing itself on a misconception of the Scriptural statement, asserts that Noah's Ark rested on the summit of Ararat. The glaciers on its flanks give birth to four streams, of which the Axares is the principal.]

* [The "Iron Gate," below Orsova, is a steep rocky plateau, about 1400 yards in width, over which the Danube formerly rushed with a furious flood and violent noise, ending with a difficult and dangerous series of rapids, eddies, and whirlpools. It formed an impracticable obstruction to the ascent of large vessels, no boats with more than thirty inches draught of water being able to pass it. But by blasting the rocks the difficulty has so far been conquered, that at certain periods of the year the channel can be navigated by ships drawing eight or nine feet of water.]

THE VIA MALA (CROSSING A TORRENT).

In like manner the darkling
Rhine, when from the "Via
Mala" and the misty Lake of
Constance it has finally diverged
to the northward, how grand a
part does it play as the arbiter
between races and empires—
pressing back one, treading
under foot another! If it absorbs twelve thousand streams
—if it carries even into Holland its vast alluvial masses, some
eighty millions of cubic feet—this is the secret of the immu-
nity which it secures for both its banks. Its mission is to
disregard our labour and our ambition, and to bestow upon
man the boon of everlasting peace.

No less interesting, though more capricious, is the Rhone. At the outset a troubled and impetuous torrent, it inherits the spirit of the Valais ; it exhibits all the characteristics of the wild Savoyards. But when, on its way to Geneva, it comes in sight of grave Lausanne, it seems on the point of growing placid and prudent. It assumes that singular blue, that steely azure, which hitherto no one has been able to explain, and which it does not long preserve. A mountain-rapid in its early course, it becomes a river at Geneva. Re-captured by the fierce waters of Savoy, it again relapses into a torrent.

Such is its versatility. Yellow at its birth, then for awhile blue, it terminates in a gray gloom. Urgent need there is that our river should be reformed and harmonized by the Saône, his amiable and cautious spouse (who brought him for her dower the Doubs). He is wedded at Ainay, before the famous altar of the Gauls—the altar of the Hundred Nations.*

But think you that he remains prudent? Nay. While, on either side of his course, graceful wantons fling themselves into his arms, he dashes forward in a wild, fierce mood. Growing more and more incapable of self-control, he dashes forward, like a beast escaped from its thrall, like a bull of the Camargue. Despite his immense grandeur, he shrinks back as he grows aged into nearly his infantile condition, and dies as he has lived.†

* [In Lyons, the cross of the church of the Abbey of Ainay is supposed to have belonged to the altar (*Ara Augusti*) erected, at the confluence of the Rhone and the Saône, by the Sixty (not One Hundred) nations of the Gauls in honour of Augustus.]

† While writing these remarks on the Rhone, I had before me the admirable Memoir of my friend Doctor Lortet, as able a geographer as he is an accomplished botanist. This justly respected family, the Lortets, has been founded by a saint, the charitable herbalist of the poor. His son is a physician, very popular at Lyons. His grandsons are not unworthy of their lineage. One, following in the paternal footsteps, has already distinguished himself by some important discoveries in vegetable physiology. I shall refer hereafter to his treatise on the Pressia, which opens up some very novel views. Another, the skilful painter of Swiss scenery, is the only artist since Calame who has succeeded in giving expression to the living

verdure and powerful individuality of the Alps. He chanced to be at the Matterhorn on the day of the memorable catastrophe,[1] his impressive sketch of which will have been seen by everybody. Others of his works are dispersed through the mansions of England, where a keen competition exists for their possession.—*Author's Note.*

[1] [M. Michelet refers to the death of Lord Frederick Douglas, Mr. Hadow, and the Rev. Mr. Hudson, with their guide, Michael Croz, on the 14th of July, 1865. During their descent of the mountain, the connecting-rope broke, and the unfortunate adventurers, losing their footing, fell from a precipice nearly 4000 feet in height. The Matterhorn, in South Switzerland, is 14,836 feet above the sea-level.]

VI.

THE HIGH PASSES OF THE ALPS.

"NOWHERE does one more keenly feel the freedom of the soul." This feeling I felt very vividly, when, young and ignorant, I followed up, for the first time, the sacred highways; when, after a long night spent in the low valleys, soaked with a chilling mist, I saw, two hours before dawn, the Alps already rose-hued in the light of morning.

I knew but little of the history of the Alpine countries, nor of that of Swiss liberty, nor of that of the exiles, saints, and martyrs who had formerly traversed the same paths. Yet I did not the less recognize the fact which I have since more thoroughly understood : *this is the common shrine of Europe.*

Yonder virgin peaks of light which bless us with day when heaven itself is sombre still in its metallic blue, rejoice not only the weary eyes of the sleepless ; but they rekindle the heart, they speak to it of bright anticipations, of faith in justice, and reinvigorate it with manly force and youthful resolution.

It is not to the sky that the poor labourer of Savoy first directs his gaze on awaking, or the fevered mariner of Genoa, or the artizan in the reeking streets of Lyon. From all quarters it is to the Alps they first turn their eyes,—to those Mountains of Consolation, which long before day deliver them from evil visions, and whisper to the captive: "Thou shalt see the sun once more."

The ancients raised three altars in the Alps :—

To THE GOD OF NATURE : to the universal soul, to the Spirit which controls the sport of the elements, the winds, the rains, and the tempests.   They named it Jupiter.

To THE HEROIC STRENGTH, which pierced the mountain, and excavated the road.   In other words, to Hercules.

Rome added a temple and a shrine : To THE PEACE OF THE WORLD.

Venerable monuments these, which all mankind ought to have regarded with feelings of reverence.

They were the common property of all nations—even of antagonistic races ; rising far above the strife of transitory dogmas, lofty symbols of the higher faith, inscribed on man and nature, which shall flourish again after the death of the gods.

Assuredly this temple or this altar was well deserved by him who opened up the perilous paths ; who in the terrible regions, hovering between the avalanche and the abyss, had the courage to pause, to plant his foot firmly, and labour at the foundation and security of a passage.   Previously the desert had known but one inhabitant, the Spirit of Terror. On the sliding slope, on the narrow ledge, vertigo confused the sight and dismayed the heart of the most heroic.   To rest and establish oneself in such a locality—to conquer the mountain—needed a superhuman strength, required a Hercules.

The first to attempt this mighty work was the Gaulish Hercules.   At a single stroke he made two nations.   A Gaul sprang to life in Italy, an Italy in Gaul.   On both sides of the Alps breathed the same soul.   A sublime duality this, to

THE PASS OF THE GRIMSEL (WITH VIEW OF THE LAKE AND HOSPICE).

which, I believe, the earth has nothing worthy of comparison
—a potency, as it were, of humanization.

Ingenious Greece asserts that our beneficent Hercules was
so well satisfied with himself, after achieving his unique enterprise—an enterprise so surpassingly advantageous to man—
that he sat himself down, and surveying Italy from Etna to
the Alps, exclaimed, " Am I mistaken ?—I could believe that
I have grown a god !"

And, in truth, the work was a divine one. From that
day the nations mutually supported each other. Through
the Alpine passes they conducted a perpetual interchange of
benefits, as is specially noticeable in seasons of famine.
Saussure describes the emotion of the Swiss at beholding,
when afflicted by a winter of extreme want, the long files of
Italian mules, and hearing the chiming bells, which bring to
them the corn and rice of Lombardy. In return, herds of
Swiss cattle are despatched every season to the support of the
Italians. A constant interchange is maintained, even in the
depths of winter, and in the lower as well as in the higher
passes. The Valais, by way of the Grimsel, barters its wines
for the butter, cream, and cheese of Hasli. In the month of
November, you will see a long convoy of cattle and mules
traversing the glacier of the Matterhorn, when the hard crisp
snow which covers its chasms and crevasses affords the foot a
precarious support.

The mountain is never wholly without life. Its passes
and its hospices are the scene of a great movement. The files
of noisy waggons, the sounds of horn and bells, and car-
riages and herds, the accents of various languages,—all this
breaks up the sublime silence of the frozen giants which
dominate over these regions. Imposing, voiceless personages,
of whom one knows but little, and many of whom, as yet
unexplored, have not even a name.

7

With diamond-crowned and inaccessible front, they take
but little heed of the events which are transpiring beneath
them. Tranquilly they prolong their dream of a hundred
centuries.

Yet under their feet a world is speeding by; the army of
birds which twice every year, in spring and autumn, crosses
the barrier of the Alps.

Of these migrations, I have spoken elsewhere.* I have
told of their dangers and their terrors, but not sufficiently,
perhaps, of the admirable order which regulates this immense
movement, this grand transplantation of a people.

As early as the middle of February, the stork, abandoning
the minarets of Egypt, Tunis, and Morocco, sails northward
to the spires, to the hereditary nests which it has established
in Holland. The Mediterranean sky is suddenly darkened
with the cloud of wings, like a fantastic hieroglyph; but the
prudent birds carefully avoid the lofty central Alps. They
move forward by either extremity of the range—on the west,
by Geneva and the Jura; on the east, by Tyrol or the Engadine.

This cold season of the year sees also the gentle lark in
haste to love and sing; and the passage of the little hero
which nothing affrights, the redbreast; and of the honest
chaffinch, the wise bird of Ardennes, which revisits its forest
before the first leaf blooms.

The swallow does not make her appearance until April,
when she is sure of finding her table spread, and a banquet
ready of flies and gnats. All the singing-birds follow in her
track; and, finally, the poor nightingale, with her great heart
but feeble head, taking up her post below, and trusting herself to the bushes. Already the timid tomtit has escaped, but
at night, the summits too well guarded by day.

* [In " L'Oiseau," of which an English translation (" The Bird "), by the pen which has
undertaken the present volume, is published by Messrs. Nelson and Sons.]

" Happy are the wingèd race !" men cry ; but the passage of the Alps is not to the birds so simple an affair as one might think. At an elevation of eight or ten thousand feet, the rarefied air fatigues them, and they breathe with difficulty. Some cannot endure the cold. Others are unable to withstand the violence of the tempest.

But more than the tempest do they fear their enemies, the wingèd murderers. Many await them on the route,—frightful vultures and eagles. But these are unwieldy birds, which they may, perhaps, elude. The evil is, that others, more sanguinary and more agile, follow up their track—falcons or hawks ; nay more, a horrible legion of nocturnal birds. All that wisdom and strategy can do, they oppose to the danger. Many are gifted with a lively sympathy ; and assembling together, they sail against the wind, so as to leave no scent of their passage. They unite in innumerable hosts. And in the autumn it is a noble spectacle 'to see the cranes and wild ducks,—the latter a bird of surprising intelligence,—forming their compact triangular array ; placing by turns at the extremity the valiant and the strong, who cleave a path through the air, and render its navigation easier for the weak.*

I wish I could ask the birds what are their thoughts at this critical moment. I would fain interrogate them. They durst not halt. But one can easily divine their terror at witnessing the sadness and anxiety of other animals, which, however, are less keenly hunted than themselves. None are

* [Compare with Milton, *Paradise Lost*, bk. vii. :—
                        " Part more wise,
In common, ranged in figure, wedge their way,
Intelligent of seasons, and set forth
Their aëry caravan, high over seas
Flying, and over lands, with mutual wing
Easing their flight ; so steers the prudent crane
Her annual voyage, borne on winds ; the air
Floats as they pass, fanned with unnumbered plumes."]

so melancholy as the large Italian sheep, which in summer climb the Alps. Whether it is that they regret their native hills, whether they are haunted with a vague apprehension of the dangers of an unknown world, they move about with drooping head; they indulge in no sports or diversions; the very lambs are serious.

Let me mention a still more significant circumstance. Near La Contamine, in a defile of Mont Blanc leading into Italy, I saw the liveliest image of fear and inquietude. Some very young mules which had been purchased in the neighbourhood of Sallenches, and separated from their mothers, were being transported to Piedmont, to be again disposed of; transported to that arid Genoese country, which is so wealthy in historical events, but so poor in the herbage of its barren mountains. The charming little beasts were tractable as young horses, but much more cunning. One of them, in a coat of hair which might have been mistaken for a silken fleece, seemed to have been born that very morning. All had a wild bright eye, sparkling yet profound, and already glowing with passion. I had never before seen natures so extremely timorous. The passage of a vehicle,—the dull and doleful route,—everything alarmed them, and they dashed forward headlong, huddled and pressed together, apparently inclined to leap among the precipices. Their little foolish astonished countenances would have seemed comical, had not one felt too much touched by the spectacle.

Innocent and childish still, they gave expression by their strange pantomime to the thoughts which man and the beasts do not utter aloud, but revolve in their own consciousness, when traversing these dreary regions.

When on the Great Saint Bernard, that rugged and ancient Pass, which the bird never essays, the traveller finds at certain points some forty feet depth of snow; when he sees (as

we did recently) the dead-house and the hospice, its permanent exhibition of corpses embalmed in the ice, he feels in
all its force the tragic character of the scene.

In the Simplon, that desolate Italian acclivity,* the extent
of the peril is shown by the excessive precautions taken.
Eight vaulted galleries, six places of shelter, twenty refuges,
serve to reassure the traveller; but they also warn him that
death hangs over his head. Every moment the hoarse
thunder of the avalanche strikes the resounding vaults, and
rolls onward from echo to reverberating echo.

There exists nothing more imposing than the galleries of
the Splügen,† that colossal work of Italian genius. They fill
the mind with mingled terror and admiration. They have
less the aspect of a mountain-pass than of a palace erected for
the Invisible upon the deep abyss. Their windows—graceful
arcades which frame the views of the mountains and the precipices—produce a fanciful effect. The vast landscapes which
succeed one another so rapidly, when seen only by quick and
sudden glimpses, seem to be an illusion of the vaulted corri-
dors. It is like a cloister of spirits.

Not one of these passes but has seen much, and could
relate much. What tragical and touching incidents have here
occurred! What separations have taken place on this frontier line of two worlds! And what heart-rending agonies!
Who shall describe the misery of those who, from this lofty
point, have taken their last look, and sighed their last farewell, of their Fatherland? But it is not the object or

* [*Montée,*—an ascent, a rising pass.]

† [The Pass of the Splügen (6940 feet in altitude) connects south-eastern Switzerland with
the Lake Como district of north-eastern Italy. The road was laid down by the Austrian
Government in 1823. The covered portions of the pass, on the Italian side, consist of three
great galleries, constructed of solid masonry, in the most substantial and ingenious manner.
The old road was constantly overwhelmed by terrible avalanches; from which cause Marshal
Macdonald, when traversing it with a French *corps d'armée*, November 27th to December 4th,
1800, underwent very severe losses both in men and horses.]

province of this book to deal with history. It would sadden Nature.

Therefore I leave in the eternal solitude of Saint Bernard the good and gallant Desaix, banished thither for having won his victory of Marengo.*

I pass over the tragedies of the prolonged persecutions of the Roman Church, in the sixteenth and seventeenth centuries; I cast not a glance at the mournful procession of heretics, independent thinkers, fugitives, who tore themselves from their beloved Italy. To quit its sun, its art, its admirable cities of marble,—which are the true homes, the enchanting cradles of all *humanity*,—was bitterer than death. The North (mire and filth) was then so repulsive! It matters not; they dragged themselves away. One of them—of high ecclesiastical rank, but yet more distinguished by right of genius—having gained the Alps, tore off and rent in twain his fatal sacerdotal robe, and flung it down the Italian precipices, —and with it all his past, all his domestic ties, his country, and his most cherished recollections! Naked, he descended towards the north, towards poverty and freedom.

In return, how many times, in our own days, has the very genius of liberty, the *great Italian* (so often pursued, yet never surprised!), passed and re-passed over these same summits, during the fifty years that he has been engaged in conceiving, creating, maturing, and begetting the Fatherland!†

One day, all this will be recorded. For the present we will relate a single fact, and no more; a fact previously known to none. I cannot deny myself the pleasure of describing in what manner the last sufferer in the cause of religious liberty (M. Muston ‡) was saved by the Alps themselves, some thirty-six years ago.

* [In the final charge, conceived and led by Desaix, which converted the battle of Marengo (June 14, 1800) from a defeat into a victory, he fell mortally wounded. His body was carried to Milan, embalmed, and afterwards interred in the Convent of Saint Bernard.]

† [A reference to M. Mazzini.]   ‡ [Author of a "History of the Waldenses."]

His book on the Vaudois had exposed him in Piedmont
to all the fury of religious intolerance. He fled by the mountains, and through the horrors of winter. His pursuers
pressed him closely. At night he attained the summits
which form the boundary of Piedmont ; and before him lay
no mode of escape but an immense precipice, a frightful
descent, from the very height of the Alps.

His mind was full of stories of the valiant deeds of his
ancestors—of the many winters spent by the great historian,
Léger * the indomitable, in the Alpine caverns—of the heroic
return of the Four Hundred Vaudois who, with Winter
and the Mountain for their allies, defied the efforts of two
monarchs. Muston, with the same courage, trusted himself
to the Alps, confided to them his safety, launched himself on
the precipitous declivity. He fell—but alive—into France—
the *France of July* 1830—and found in her a mother who
clasped him in her arms.

* [Jean Léger, author of the " General History of the Evangelical Churches of the Piedmontese Valleys," born in Savoy in 1615.· After suffering severely from Roman Catholic
intolerance, he escaped into Holland, and died at Leyden in 1670.]

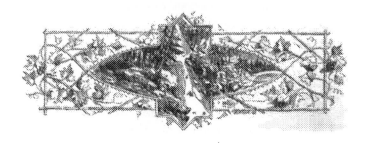

VII.

THE PYRENEES.

THE Pyrenees, daughters of Fire, do not enjoy the youthfulness of the Alps, do not possess their abundant waters. They are rich in metals, marbles, living and vivifying thermal springs. And, above all, they are rich in light.

Their austere, formidable, and unbroken rampart is the barrier between Europe and Africa; that Africa which men call Spain. It is an absolute and direct divorce, for which no graduation prepares us. Notwithstanding the massiveness of the Alps, we can pass with sufficient ease from Italy into Provence, to Lyons. But if you have started from Toulouse over the Pyrenees, and descended their rapid southern slope to Saragossa, you have crossed a world.

With less elevated occasional peaks, they are loftier in the mass than the Alps. Less complex, they become imposing by their majestic simplicity and sublime character.

In a truly beautiful and symmetrical opposition, their two great rivers descend in inverse directions, one to the east, the other to the west; the Ebro to the Mediterranean, the Garonne to the Ocean. But the course of the Ebro is rigidly straight. In the curve of the Garonne is inscribed, and not ungracefully, the fine torrent of the Adour.

THE CIRQUE OF GAVARNI, IN THE PYRENEES.

Their sublimity consists in the radiance, the glowing hues, the fantastic lightnings with which they are incessantly crowned by the rugged southern world they conceal, but which we long to see. In this respect we must acknowledge the Alps to succumb and grow pale before them. In the Pyrenees, the singular green lights of the waters in the *gaves*—meadows of emerald, in striking contrast with their ruins—with the green and red marbles which crop through their black strata of rock, have a distinct character of their own.

A miracle is incessantly repeated on their summits—a continual transfiguration—in a certain airy azure—in the indescribable rose-hue (vanishing between the Dawn and the Morning)—in the purple, the golds, and the flame-colours of the Evening. This marvellous display varies according to the hour, and also in respect to distance ; for at thirty, twenty, or even ten leagues, its aspect is wholly different. You have seized your brush, and think to fix the phantasmagoria. A step further in the plain, and it is all changed. These fairy mountains have assumed quite another physiognomy. Their gay charm of the morning is, at noon, transformed into austerity.

In a hot stormy summer which I spent at Montauban, I had a lofty and extremely large window, like a gallery of crystal, opening on the vast plain of the Tescou and the Tarn, and commanding the line of the Pyrenees from Bayonne to the Pic du Midi, and thence to Roussillon. But at so great a distance I could only distinguish this line at certain hours and on certain days. When the air became transparent, as on days preceding a storm, I could see its floating image. Did I see it ? Or was it a cloud ? No, it was truly the Pyrenean peaks. Only at times they seemed clothed in deeper and wider snow than was really the case. The wide, rich, and beautiful plain (the finest, I think, in the world), by its thousand imposing accidents of field and river, as by its infinite variety, sufficiently warned one of the great space which lay between

us. But the very doubtfulness, the fugitive and deceptive
nature of the vague apparition, only made me the greedier and
more insatiable in reference to its prospect. For entire hours
I would remain absorbed in a dreamy contemplation, which,
far from being cold, was always full of intense emotion. What
visions of the past, what imaginations, what chimeras, we con-

THE PIC DU MIDI.

nected with that uncertain yet real cloud, which re-appeared
but at intervals, with that barrier of a world, and with the
Unknown which stretched beyond!

That Unknown is the land of romance and improbable
adventures, of keen distinct elements which do not graduate
into one another. Between Moor and Goth, between Spain
and Spain, no conciliation is possible, but an eternal conten-
tion prevails — an unlimited battle-field for foolish hopes.
Castles in the air (*Châteaux en Espagne*) float already above
the Pyrenees. That great wall, which decreases in elevation only at its two extremities, has there for its warders
two impetuous spirits,—the Basque and the Catalan,—who
introduce the stranger with marked appropriateness into the
strange country of Don Quixote.

The *ports*, or pretended passes, which, they say, open up

the colossal rampart, are frightful break-neck defiles, where, for six months out of every twelve, neither mule nor man dare venture. The famous "breach" of Roland, which he opened up with his sword *Durandal*,[*] was until recently traversed with extreme difficulty even by the contrabandist or hunted robber. But in addition to these obstacles between the two kingdoms, the Pyrenees, by the rugged hills which serve them as buttresses, effect an almost complete separation of the valleys and populations lying at their feet. The latter form very discordant tribes. Side by side with the Iberian Basques you find the Celtic Gascons; while at either end— Perpignan and Bayonne—abounds the Saracenic immigration.

Innumerable contrasts exist in language and costume. Even at the present day you may see a sufficient number at the fairs of Tarbes. Frequently you will descry in the medley the white cap of Bigorre, the brown of Foix, and the red of Roussillon; sometimes even the large flat hat of Aragon, the round one of Navarre, and the pointed Biscayan bonnet. The Basque carrier arrives there on his ass, with his long cart drawn by three horses; he wears the *berret* of Béarn: but you quickly distinguish the Béarnese from the Basque; the neat and nimble little fellow, so prompt with hand and tongue, from the son of the mountain, who stalks over it rapidly with his long legs—a skilful agriculturist, and proud of the house whose name he bears.

The serious Pyrenees break but once into a smile, at the

---

[*] [According to the old legend, Roland, one of Charlemagne's twelve peers, was killed at Roncesvalles in 778, by the Saracens. To prevent the enemy from gaining possession of his wonderful sword Durandal, which had been wrought by fairies, he smote it upon a rock near where he lay mortally wounded, making a tremendous fissure therein,—the famous *Brèche de Roland*, a deep ravine in the Pyrenees, between 200 and 300 feet wide, shut in by precipitous rocks from 300 to 600 feet high.

"Then would I seek the Pyrenean breach,
Which Roland clove with huge two-handed sway."
WORDSWORTH.]

central point whence issues the pleasant but somewhat capricious river, the Garonne—a river of surprises. The joyous
daughter of a most sullen mother—the black Maladetta *—
she amuses herself at first among the meadows; but a descent
of eighty feet induces her to retrace her course into a basin or
valley where a deep gulf absorbs her, nor restores her to the
day until she has fallen two thousand feet. She is there—we
feel it—there among the rose-bushes, and the fair trees, and
the thousand plants she loves. At length, with a felicitous
effect, she suddenly emerges in a cataract, and seizes upon a
tiny Garonne which has come up from the south. What
adventures await her! And what a marvellous fortune!
Along the route she traverses she creates a world, creates
fertile fields, creates busy towns—even up to the point where,
gigantic, and immense, and forgetful of her mountain birth-
place and her rustic name, she sees the Infinite, *the Gironde.*

The primitive inhabitant of the Pyrenees appears to be the
Basque, the Iberian—the ancient race of a world which preceded the Celt himself. If he has any analogue, however, we
must look for it among the Celts of Brittany, Scotland, or
Ireland. The Basque, eldest-born of the Western races, immovable in his Pyrenean corner, has seen all the nations pass
away before him—Carthaginian, Celt, Roman, Goth, and
Saracen. Our young antiquities excite his compassion. A
Montmorency said to one of them, "Know you that my
family counts a thousand years?" "And we," replied the
Basque—" we have ceased to count!"

* [The Maladetta is one of the loftiest summits of the Pyrenees, 10,886 feet above the
sea-level.]

VIII.

THE PYRENEES.

CONTINUED.

BOTH the sea and the mountain have here their illusions. None are more imaginative than the people of this shore ; lovers of the impossible,—eager seekers after peril,—in the mountain abysses, or the sullen Polar waters. They may traverse their entire extent, however, and yet discover no more dangerous region than their own, the *Côte des Fous.* The secondary mountains which in that dreary quarter erect their summits—some fantastically hewn, others shattered, imminent, and overhanging—wear an unreal aspect. At their foot, the great Landes, peopled at night with visions, were in mediæval times the temples of the Witches' Sabbath.*

---

* [The "Witches' Sabbath" was a nocturnal gathering of witches and warlocks, imps and demons, held at a fixed rendezvous, and presided over by the Arch-devil, in the shape of a large goat. The banquet, consisting of viands that never satisfied the appetite, was lighted up with torches, and followed by eerie music, wild dances, and the lewdest pastimes. The Witch-hills were always places invested with a traditional solemnity or a natural horror. One of the most famous was the loftiest point of the Hartz, the Brocken,—the scene of the *Walpurgis-Night*, in Goethe's "Faust."

" The stubble is yellow, the corn is green,
Now to the Brocken the witches go ;
The mighty multitude here may be seen
Gathering, wizard and witch, below."

Shelley's Translation.]

On ruinous summits washed by the furious ocean-waters sat
enthroned the Prince of the Winds, the dark Spirit of Strife
and Storm, promising great gifts of treasure, for he is an
adept in lies.   Among his sorceresses, most wanton of
all were the Basque—dangerously attractive (says Lancre),
with their dishevelled locks, when, by a diabolical enchantment, the gold of the sunshine glinted through their dusky
brown.

Did not the spell operate to some extent upon our eloquent
Ramond, our enthusiastic wooer of Mont Perdu, which he so
ardently pursued ?   In his youth he had credulously followed
other delusions ; the dreams of Cagliostro, and the worship of
Nature.   At a later period, with a generous and enthusiastic
heart, he took his stand on the threshold of the Revolution,
hoping for the deliverance and happiness of the human race.
Alas ! soon came a harsh revulsion, a severe disillusion !
Thrown back upon himself, proscribed, a wanderer in the
desert, but not overwhelmed, he turned with the same vehe-
mency towards Nature.   He fathomed the enigma of the
globe.   He had already produced a noble work on the
Pyrenees, full of very pregnant observations.   This time
he sought another subject, burning to attain what one
is everywhere conscious of,—the Mountain which incessantly vanishes from our sight, and seems to hide itself in
shadow.

Saussure's enterprise was less difficult.   Mont Blanc was
ever fixed before him, and he knew where to approach it,
and what it was : a dome of granite.   Ramond sought
the secret of a peak which, though composed of limestone, has
soared to as great an altitude even as the spires of granite.
With incredible ardour he pursued this study for ten years
of adventurous explorations and solitary ascents.   In that
warlike epoch the Spaniards, who guarded their frontier

on the Taillon, at an altitude of 10,000 feet, saw below in
the great desolate *cirques*,* or among the precipices, the figure
of the wanderer, and exclaimed, " Who is yonder Spirit ?"

The only beings encountered by Ramond in the deep valleys extending between the two chains of the double wall of
the Pyrenees, were the Spanish sheep, which come every year
from afar in quest of the herbage and the freshness. Their
wild conductors, who in their hearts believe themselves somewhat of sorcerers, are prone to visions. Their sole intimacy
is with their flocks ; with those dreamy animals which know,
apparently, much more than they say. The shepherd thinks
they are souls which, not having been baptized, are not
Christians.

In Spain the shepherd is lord, and devastates the land.
Authorized by the Mesta (a powerful public company), fifty
or sixty thousand shepherds, and their triumphant merinos,†
eat up all Estremadura to Navarre on the one side, and Aragon on the other. With his sheepskin on his back, and on
his legs the *abarca* of shaggy fleece, the shepherd, from a distance, seems himself a wild merino.

I wrote in my " History of France " (prior to 1833) :—
    " It is not for the historian to explain the Pyrenees. It

* [The *cirque* is a local name applied to a semicircular or amphitheatrical wall of mountain peaks. One such is thus described by M. Taine, in his attractive " Voyage aux Pyrenées" :
" A wall of granite crowned with snow is hollowed in front of us into a gigantic cirque. This
cirque is 1200 feet in height, nearly a league in circumference, with three stages of perpendicular
walls, and each stage consisting of thousands of steps or terraces. There the valley terminates ;
the wall consists of a single and insuperable mass. The other summits toppled over, but their
massive foundations never stirred. The mind is appalled by the idea of a stability so unassail-
able, and an eternity so assured. These snow-canopies are spread out on the three stages ; and
on this virginal robe the sun pours its full glory without succeeding in kindling it into lustre.
It preserves its dull, dead whiteness. All this grandeur is austere; the air is frozen under the
rays of the south ; huge humid shadows creep along the foot of the wall. Everlasting winter
reigns here, and the nakedness of the desert."—*Voyage aux Pyrenées*, pp. 357, 358.]

† [The merino sheep is distinguished by its large limbs, and the male by the large spiral
horns, which do not rise above the head. The cheeks and forehead are woolly; the skin of the
neck loose and pendulous ; the fleece long, fine, soft, oily, and woven into silky ringlets. The
breed is valuable only for its wool. It has been successfully introduced into Australia.]

8

needs the science of a Cuvier, a Von Buch, an Elie de Beaumont. Let *them* relate its pre-historic annals. They were present, and I was not, when Nature improvised her mighty epopœia; when the flaming mass of our globe uplifted the axis of the Pyrenees; when the mountains yawned; and the earth, in her Titanic throes, hurled against the sky the black and bold *Maladetta.* Nevertheless, a consoling hand gradually concealed the wounds of the mountain with those emerald prairies which make the Alpine meadows look pale. The jagged peaks were blunted, and rounded into beautiful cupolas. Inferior masses softened down the abrupt inclines, retarded their rapidity, and formed on the side of France that colossal descent, every step of which is a mountain."

Let us ascend, then, not to the Vignemale, not to Mont Perdu, but only as high as the *Port de Paillers,* where the waters divide themselves between the two seas, or rather, between Bagnères and Baréges, between the Beautiful and the Sublime. There you may apprehend at a glance the fantastic loveliness of the Pyrenees, those strange and seemingly incompatible sites which are harmoniously bent together by an inexplicable stroke of faëry enchantment; and that magical atmosphere which alternately removes and brings nearer the objects on which you gaze. But soon succeeds the savage horror of the great mountains which lurk in the rear, like a monster hidden beneath the mask of a youthful beauty. It matters not; let us continue our progress along the entire length of the Gave, by this gloomy defile, and through infinite accumulations of rocks 3000 and 4000 feet in height; through a labyrinth of keen-edged crags, and perpetual snows, and the windings of the Gave, stretching like a barrier from one mountain to another; and, finally, the gigantic cirque and its towers soaring heavenward. At the foot, a dozen springs feed the Gave, which roars under its

BAREGES, IN THE PYRENEES.

bridges of snow, while from a height of 1300 feet falls the loftiest cascade in the Old World.

Nowhere does one feel so powerfully as in the Pyrenees a sympathy with the soul of the earth. It sensibly exists in these profound springs in which its subterranean life mounts up to our lips. No analysis is able to explain their power. We may skilfully mingle and combine all the elements we discover in them, but we produce nothing after all; ever at the bottom lurks some unknown secret. M. de Sénarmont, an eminent metallurgist, says : " Nature has not interrupted the mineral creation. A number of species are not reproduced.

Their elements do not appear to have obeyed the same affinities which we set in motion. Chemical reactions and affinities may be subject, perhaps, to other laws." *

This we perceive to be the case at Baréges, in the Central Pyrenees. We perceive it, too, in Bohemia, in the gloomy funnel-like spring of Carlsbad. These, it is true, are *serious waters (des eaux sérieuses)* and formidable powers. Do not compare them with the innumerable sources, the simple brooks which, traversing mineral strata, simulate the true thermal waters by weak imitations and enfeebled tinctures. The former bestow life, though sometimes they kill the pseudo-invalids who lightly profane them by their silly amusements. You must not play with these. Pleasure-hunters, away! Respect the solemn localities where the powerful Mother communicates with her children.

It is impossible not to comprehend her when you ascend to Baréges. She is there in her awful grandeur, but ready to assist her worshipper; her austere genius is ever present. Whatever indifference you may feel on your first arrival, she soon exerts an influence over you. For the colossal works of the mountain which she herself achieves and elaborates, and which elsewhere are hidden in mystery, are here revealed. It is under the threatening ruin you go in quest of life. The meadows on yonder bank have grown up amidst desolation; houses and flocks now cover the dreary waste. You feel that all is ephemeral; that man is only admitted by favour into this perilous region, into this gloomy laboratory of the mighty forces of Nature.

Her travail is still more visible at Olette; the throes and exertions with which she brings to the surface the spirit brooding in the profound deep. A thousand years it has laboured to manifest itself in all the fulness of its power. Its workings were detected as early as the days of Charlemagne;

* "Annales de Chimie," vol. xxx., p. 129.

and soon after the year 800, a sanctuary to it was consecrated here. Men perceived that a warm soul throbbed in the land, and named it the Exalada. Its presence was known by pregnant signs. On this ascending-scale of mountains a hot spring bubbled on one level; on another, copper mingled with silver. But a tremendous internal convulsion was taking place. Occasional catastrophes terrified and desolated the country. The monks who had founded here the first colony, unable to exorcise the unknown powers, retired to the lower lands.

To the ruins and disasters of that epoch witness is borne by the Rock of Trespasses. The tremor of the earth was incessant. The captive spirit seethed and raged, but could not accomplish its deliverance in less than a thousand years.

It is from Mont Canigou, the hermit-peak of Roussillon, standing apart from the Pyrenean mass, that all these waters flow—as those of Olette, Amelia, Vernet. In its fiery womb it has cherished the life, once so formidable, and now so beneficial.

It has been remarked there (as in Java, and as in the Antilles, at the starting-point of the Gulf Stream) that the more abundant the flow of the thermal sources, the less frequent are the earth's oscillations.* Thirty springs gradually make their appearance, and these the hottest in the world (one is 78° C.). Altogether they afford a daily supply of water computed at 1800 cubic mètres, equal to ten thousand baths. They form, in fact, a river of health, youth, and strength—a veritable stream of life.

The greatest marvel is the different character of these springs. Every temperature, every chemical combination, is represented in them. Within their limited area you find

---

* See the interesting works of Messrs. Renard and Bouis (Olette, 1852), and the *Green Book*, an ancient manuscript, still preserved at Perpignan.

united the waters of the Pyrenees, Cauterets, Bagnères, and
Baréges, while I know not how many others have made it
their rendezvous. And the hidden springs, moreover, which
seethe under foot, demand recognition, and, rising from the
shadows towards the light, seem to say, " At length it is our
turn."

SOURCE OF THE NERVION (IN THE CANTABRIAN PYRENEES).

THE BOLLENTE.

AT ACQUI.

"WORK is my deity. It preserves the world." And, truly, it has preserved *me*. Thanks to it, my life has passed very evenly, has always preserved the same equal tenor, while constantly augmenting its productive force. But for an accident which I met with when about thirty years old, I should know nothing of man's bodily ills.

Absorbed in historical study, in the construction of my enormous pyramid, it was rarely, and only very late in life, that I turned my gaze towards Nature. It was requisite, indeed, that she herself should warn me; should prove to me that one cannot withdraw from her society with impunity. Deeply moved at heart, and touched by a very tender interest, behold me, one morning, plunged into the sciences of life— not as a curious idler in search of amusement—but like a voyager in danger on board his feeble bark, navigating the vague uncertainty he would fain penetrate with his gaze. The enterprise proved of great service to me. An immediate interest, by redoubling one's attention, gives one a second faculty of sight, or at all events enables one to seize some vivid glimpses of things.

Re-assured on one side, I was assailed on another. With

chagrin, with surprise, I had almost said with indignation, in
1853 I found myself ill. For the first time, the world had
had its way. I languished at Nervi, near Genoa. In that
beautiful nook of the Apennines I was, as it were, softly
cradled. The Italian sun, the elastic atmosphere, the basaltic
ledge along which I dragged myself at noon, were my pro-
tectors. On that arid coast, a companion of the lizard, I
consumed myself in repose. Action, for one who has preserved his spirit unimpaired, is a growing, a pressing, an
imperious necessity. Undoubtedly, the idler, who does not
really live, or who has lived too long, and spent his soul upon
the winds, passes through existence with far greater ease.
But he who in mid career, and at full speed, is suddenly
arrested, feels the blow in a very different manner. I was
dying full of life—of ideas, studies, projects—of great works
dreamed of and begun. History, my grand occupation,
claimed me, groaning that it could not complete its task.
Nature claimed me. I had obtained a glimpse of her through
science and happiness. By what savage malignity was she
inspired that, while baring her bosom to me, she should
suddenly cast me from her? Ah, what a terrible irony, while
dashing me to the earth, to say, " Live and enjoy thyself still ! "

Italy has always been the country of great physicians.*
Their infallible oracle imposed upon me an extreme remedy.
This was the sentence : " Let him return into the earth.
Buried under the burning soil, he shall live again."

The salutary and funereal locality, where men inter themselves, is Acqui,† in the district of Montferrat. A narrow,

---

* [They killed Cavour, nevertheless.—*Translator.*]

† [Acqui is the principal town of a province of the same name in the former kingdom of
Piedmont, situated on the left bank of the river Bormida, about eighteen miles from Ales-
sandria. Its warm sulphurous baths are held in great repute, and annually attract a considerable number of visitors. They were much esteemed by the Romans, of whose settlement,
Aqua Statiellæ, some ruins remain.]

meagre, and savage region, which would remain unknown but
for its strategical position, and the wars wherein so many
stalwart men have perished to secure the portal of the Alps.
Iron, sulphur, and silex are the actual constituent parts of
the country. Around it bloom a few scanty groves, and some
small vineyards, which produce a thin white wine, smelling of
the flint. Through the valley flows the Bormida—river or
torrent?—which never runs dry, but whose cataracts and
violent leaps render it, like its sister-rivers of Piedmont, inhospitable and unsocial. Sad and uncouth appear those
profitless watercourses, on which never a bark appears. Sad
and uncouth of aspect, too, the very animals. I saw there a
diminutive bull, which looked at me askant, and without any
cause, leaping suddenly forward, wounded a horse with its horns.

The valley is enriched and ennobled by the ruins of a
Roman aqueduct. Its remains, though still standing, will
one day vanish from the uncertain soil which is inundated
every year by the sudden outbursts of the Bormida, and will
leave this scene in all its naked monotony.

Hot springs abound on both banks of the river. The
town is situated on the left, with its beautiful and famous
baths, the Bollente. These are distinguished by their violent
ebullition, their transparency, and strong impregnation of
sulphur. Their waters flow, or rather dart, with a directness
that indicates the height from which they descend, and the
copiousness of the reservoirs whence they issue. Formerly
they were received by the Roman aqueduct, and carried
across the river to the baths on the opposite side. Neglected
now, in the Jews' Quarter, they follow the fortune of the
town, which was formerly a sovereign-bishopric, but at present
is very thinly peopled. Yet its aspect is interesting, as it
stands in its noble cincture of superb plane-trees, which surround it on one side, and themselves grow few and dreary as
they ascend the bank of the dreary Bormida.

The great mystery lies on the right bank. All the earth
is honeycombed, and the hills deeply undermined by the hot
springs. The secret, in truth, is precisely this decay of the
mountain, which, by incessantly sifting their waters, is incessantly labouring for its own destruction. Three centuries ago,
the Roman Baths were swallowed up in a landslip. And the
same travail is still in operation. At the fall, you perceive
that the entire countryside is in an ebullient condition. Before
you can erect any building, you must confine and stop up
innumerable tiny springs; but though these may no longer
be audible, they are still alive underground, and keep the
earth in a constant state of vibration. In the groves which
embower the baths, at the fountain whither the visitor
repairs to drink the cold waters, on the hills, ay, and everywhere, you have a feeling that some creature, wrongly buried,
is agitating and quaking under your feet.

The Baths are a kind of cloister, divided by partitions on
three sides. The fourth forms a little garden, with shrubs—
is open, and constitutes the entrance. The quarters of the
poor are at a distance, completely separated from those of the
regular boarders; a separation that has only existed for about
forty years, and which, under one aspect, I think is to be
deplored. Were we brought nearer to their wretchedness,
our levity would be less. In spite of ourselves, we should
be rendered more mindful of our common human destinies.
Our venerable manager, the Chevalier Garrone, was particularly careful in assuring himself of the quality of the rations
allotted to them. We were much moved by the spectacle of
this worthy soldier, a man of tall stature, returning every
morning with a decoration in his button-hole—the testing-
spoon he had carried with him—nobly adorned with the
insignia of charity.

They were well fed; but their lodgings, on the other hand,

were close and cheerless. The narrow and naked courts were
without trees, without shade in this burning climate. Nevertheless, we were told that they recovered more quickly and
in greater proportion than the well-to-do patients ; a fact
explained by their temperate and regular life. "They recovered : " the word caught my attention. It secures them a
true privilege ; the water, the spring is theirs. Nature has
created it for those who know how to profit by it.

Ah, said I, if, instead of this close confined lodging, one
could see a double amphitheatre stretching along both banks
of the river, an immense twofold hospitable piscina to which
whole peoples might resort, would it not become a centre
for the future brotherhood of the Italian nations ? It is
here that the great invalid, Italy, might recover from her
heavy infirmity, and throw off her spirit of isolation and
divorce.*

The Baths are accessories ; and an accessory, too, is the
cold water drunk by the patient. The main point of his treatment is the hot mud in which he must be buried.

It is not a foul mud. Its base is silex and broken pebbles,
reduced to a state of impalpable powder. It owes its blackish
tint to a mixture of iron and sulphur. In the small confined
lake where this mud lies concentrated, I admired the powerful
travail of the waters, which, having prepared and sifted it in
the mountain, and afterwards coagulated it, struggling now
against their own handiwork, and endeavouring to force a
way through its opaque mass, upheave it with slight commotions of the earth, and pierce through it in diminutive jets
and microscopic volcanoes. One jet may be only a series of
air-bubbles, but another is permanent, and indicates the constant presence of a stream which, obstructed elsewhere, has
succeeded, after incessant friction, in accomplishing what

* [Written, says Michelet, in 1854.]

seems to be the desire and effort of these tiny souls, delighted with a glimpse of the sun.

I fixed on this black living earth a serious gaze. I said to it: "Dear common Mother! We are one. From you I came, and to you I return. Tell me then, frankly, your secret. What is your hidden toil in the profound shades, whence you send me this warm, powerful, rejuvenescent soul, to make me live again? What do you there?"—"What thou seest; what I am doing now under thine eyes."

She spoke distinctly, in a somewhat low but a gentle, and plainly a maternal voice.

Men exaggerate her mysteries. Her work is simple and obvious in these regions, where, so to speak, she performs the function of the sun.

I had arrived on the 5th of June, and was still in an extremely feeble condition. I had had a fainting-fit in descending from my carriage. I slept for twelve successive hours, and awoke somewhat recovered. A beautiful chamber, with a terrace, opened up to us the limited but agreeable perspective of a little wood, transected by some fine hornbeam hedges which formed an approach to it. Vegetation was scanty, and all around spread a strong odour of sulphur.

A powerful odour of life! The water of some of the neighbouring springs intoxicates you like wine. This intoxication of the air and the waters stimulates and reawakens the senses long before the physical energies are recruited. You forget that you are ill. On the 9th the spark of life revived in me, and already I thought myself living.

Night was a scene of faëry. The atmosphere of love and sulphur intoxicated our fire-flies. The winged creatures, nimbler than those of the North, flashed through their glowing dances in the drear obscurity of the grove, which seemed all the blacker as a background to these sportive showers of

diamonds. They varied infinitely in their flames, sparkling
when they encountered one another, but sometimes growing
pale and faint with languor or desire.

They are not alone. Even in this solemn locality, where
so much true and bitter suffering exists, nature, in the absence
of noisy pleasures, acts the more powerfully, and with little
mystery. Blind human fire-flies seek one another for a moment, flutter to and fro, and then fly away without a thought.
Our more concentrated life kept us somewhat apart. We
preferred in the evening to follow the bank of the Bormida,
whose wave kindled in a glorious sunset; or, better still, to
ascend the heights by the old Roman road. From thence
you discover the town confronting you on the opposite bank;
you trace the meanders of the river; you may even catch a
glimpse of the Viso, which crowns the landscape, but does not
invest it with grandeur. On the other side of the hill the
panorama disappears; you see nothing but the narrow and
rugged valley of the torrent, the Ravanesco, and, far away, the
cemetery, and a few deserted houses.

One day, on this hill—it was the festival of the Fête-Dieu
—we had a sad rencontre with a funeral procession. Inter-
ments here are made late in the evening, and with all possible
haste, the last rites being shortened to the utmost that they
may not depress the sick, and especially the convalescent in
their little amusements. A young man was buried who, like
them, had forgotten the motive of his coming. This unexpected spectacle, at so beautiful a time of the year—clouding
the soft and tender impressions of an Italian summer—destiny,
death, the Alps—so many grand and lofty ideas—threw me
into a reverie: they said, that for the vain seductions of the
world there is but one remedy—Love. It is their barrier,
their limit. In its tender inquietude lies the true wisdom.

On the 19th of June, being in a thoroughly prepared condition, I was at length interred, but only up to my waist. In my magnificent shroud of white marble I underwent the first application of the black mud, which, unctuous as it is, does not soil the skin, being at bottom nothing more than sand. Another marble bath by your side receives you afterwards, and cleanses you in an instant.

Signor Tomasini, the *fangarolo* who applied to my body its coat of mud, was a clever, intelligent, and agreeable person. He was even lettered, and had studied philosophy. We conversed together. He informed me that in winter he gained his living by the chase, snaring small birds, for there was no other game. He owned a little land, worth about 25,000 francs. One of his sons would inherit it after him. For the other, it was his ambition to make him a notary. He did not lament his destiny. His only anxiety arose from his rivalry with the ancient *fangarolos*, whose office had hitherto been hereditary. Having only discharged the duties for about twenty years, he was hated by them as a new-comer.

On the 20th of June the earth encroached further upon me, rising up to the stomach, and covering me almost entirely. On the 21st I wholly disappeared. My face alone was left free that I might breathe. I could then perceive all the ability of my sexton. He was a skilful sculptor in the Egyptian style. I saw my body (the face excepted) very cleverly moulded in this funereal clothing. I could look upon myself as already an inhabitant of the realm of shadows.

It was a strange disguise. And yet there was nothing in it to cause any great astonishment. Should I not be similarly interred in earth in a brief period, in a few short years? Between the one tomb and the other how feeble the difference! Is not our cradle, the earth, whence sprung our race, a cradle also for our resurrection? Let us hope it. We are in good hands.

At first I felt only a very indistinct improvement. My

mental condition was akin to that of dreaming.   After several days' experience, I distinguished successive stages differing each from the other in character.

For the first quarter of an hour all was calm.   Thought, still free, questioned itself.   I examined my malady, and traced it to its origin.   I could only reproach my own ill-regulated will, my excessive efforts to revive by my unaided powers the life of the human race.   The dead with whom I had so long held converse invited and attracted me towards the other shore.   But Nature still detained me upon this.

During the second quarter her influence increased.   The idea of death disappeared in the profoundness of my absorption.   The only image which I could then cherish was that of Mother Earth—*Terra Mater*.   I felt her very plainly, caressing and pitying and warming her wounded child.   Without? Ay, and internally also.   She interpenetrated my frame with her vivifying principles, entered into and blended with me, insinuated into my being her very soul.   The identification between us grew complete.   I could no longer distinguish myself from her.

From this point up to the last quarter of an hour, that part of my body which she did not cover, which remained exposed—my face—was restless and importunate.   The buried body was happy, and it was I.   The head, which remained unburied, lamented, and was no longer I ; at least, I thought so.   Such was the perfect marriage, and more than the marriage, between me and the Earth !   One might more fitly have called it "an exchange of nature."   I was Earth and she was Man.   She had taken upon her shoulders the weight of my infirmities and my sins ; while I, in becoming Earth, had assumed her life, warmth, and youth.

Years, labours, anxieties, all remained at the bottom of my marble shroud.   I was completely renewed.   When I emerged, an indescribable unctuous gleam shone upon my body.   A certain organic element, wholly distinct from the minerals, and whose nature we are ignorant of, gives the effect of a living contact, of having communicated with the Unseen Soul, and the happy inspiration which that Soul communicates in its turn.

Though Nature had been forgotten in the fierce toil which so blindly missed true happiness, she was unwilling it should overwhelm me. With infinite gentleness she had again opened her arms to me, and awaited my coming. She had filled me with life and power. May I be worthy of it! (I exclaimed). Thus I exhaust her ample forces, and with a more prolific heart enter into her sacred unity!

Such was the origin of " The Bird," " The Sea," and " The Insect," as well as of " The Renaissance," and of that which created them and creates all things: " Love."

X.

THE UPWARD PROGRESS OF EARTH:

ITS ASPIRATION.

SUCH was the Earth for me in her bounty at Acqui: thus did I see her rise in vapour and liquid through the divine mud which saved me; thus, I thought, does she act in the numerous strata which compose her enormous density.

Her life is *expansion*; expansion which, from her deeply-lying furnaces, permeating her solid mass, works, and transforms, and electrifies her elements, when exalted by the heat, liquefied and aërated, and raises them to the surface, that they may be completely vivified and animalized.

This fact could not be comprehended in its full extent so long as Earth remained inert, petrified by Genesis and the Biblical tradition. But it was clearly understood when Lavoisier taught us the true nature of expansion, and showed how easily the three conditions of matter—the solid, the liquid, the aërial—are transformed into one another. It was clearly understood when Laplace explained and calculated the Earth's relation to the Sun. Whether he be her father, her lover, or both, it is certain that it is he whom she fixedly regards, that she follows him in his mighty movement, as well as in all his works of circulation and fecundation.

In the shadowy time when vapours enveloped her in a veil
of opaque atmosphere, she already felt his influence, and sought
him from the depths of her dream. This obscurity still exists
in her enormous density. How small, how weak a portion of
the Earth enjoys the felicity of seeing him! But what she
did of old, she does to-day and ever. In her innermost depths,
in the most secret blackness of the abyss, the same tendency
prevails, and the same upward movement.

The gloomy Earth of the shadows is animated by a constant desire to become the luminous Earth ; the Earth of love
which he—the Sun—fertilizes.

How many obstacles lie in the way! It was at first supposed by chemists that the Earth's interior was wholly liquid
and igneous, a sea of fire, where from centre to surface everything found a facile passage. The hypothesis has been given
up. It is much more probable that along with these igneous
portions (glowing fiery lakes, perhaps) Earth has her enormous rocks—her rugged, heavy, inert masses of minerals and
metals—which are, so to speak, her bones and her framework,
but which painfully impede her expansive and ardent soul, as
it throbs and palpitates with a longing for the light.

Ah, hard condition of the Earth! She is not the indolent
woman who, once created and gaily adorned, would content
herself with the boast, "It is well: I am beautiful;" but the
unwearying worker, born to toil and struggle. It is better so,
perhaps. She appears so entranced by the light of her father,
that, in the hot strife and struggle against obstacles, love
would make her forgetful, perhaps, of *self*-love, and destroy
her internal balance. She would rise out of herself.

All the tiny atomic labours which we accomplish on her
surface are but pitiful counterfeits of the enormous laboratory
which travails in her depths. What a spectacle, if one could
see the immense operations by which the internal elements
below endeavour to effect their ascent! We may imagine

them, however. Lying prone on the burning seething mud, this miniature presentment of Earth's mighty works, assisting at all the efforts of the inner principle to rise and ascend, I could easily imagine all of which she is capable for the great object of bringing herself nearer to him whom she ever regrets, and towards whom, by all her arts, she everlastingly tends. The mechanical processes, the chemical combinations, filtration, trituration, expansion, eruption, fermentations far exceeding the capacity of the mineral, she accomplishes all—even the impossible. She succeeds in effecting a passage. She ends in mounting upwards. Augmented by powerful influences, she ascends. For life grows by life, obstacle, and collision. Enriched with unknown electricities, this spirit arrives at its goal. What a career ! What changes she has undergone on her way ! If her nucleus possesses a greater density than steel (as Thomson says), if it is a loadstone (as Poisson asserts), the metamorphosis is immense to draw from that steel, that iron, or from granite almost equally hard as iron, so many ductile materials—to mobilize, shatter, liquefy, and vaporize—and from vapours, reduced to the condition of boiling waters, to bring to the surface for our benefit these potent elixirs of life. It is liquid animality. Only the organs are wanting. But it mingles with ours, and is easily converted into our blood. Why not ? Is it not perfectly natural ? It is the blood of our mother, who opens her veins for us.

In a sufficiently brief period, about half a century, we have been able to witness and take our share in two great revolutions. " Which?—those of 1815? of July 1830 ? or February 1848 ?" No; I speak of greater and more important revolutions, which extended to the globe, to the whole earth.

These revolutions of the globe have been in perfect accordance with the political events which simultaneously transpired. They were singularly modelled on the character of the two

generations who succeeded each other in this same half
century.

Men who had been present at the terrible eruption of the
revolutionary volcano, at the catastrophes of the great wars,
at the national outbursts of 1813, at the immense earthquake
in which the Napoleonic empire was swallowed up—could discover nothing else but violent cataclysm in the primeval history of the globe. They examined with the eyes, the same
eyes which had witnessed these political events. The greatest
mineralogist of the age, Leopold von Buch, could only detect
in the mountains the revolutionary action of the central fire,
the convulsions of the travailing Earth. Here in France
he found a fanatical admirer, an indefatigable observer, and
daring theorist, M. Elie de Beaumont, who organized these
convulsions into a system, who grouped and disciplined the
upheaved mountain-masses, dared to trace and calculate the
vast subterranean veins or beds of granite which one discovers
in Finland and re-discovers in Brittany. An audacious enterprise, and one of indisputable grandeur, which the imperfect
condition of science prevented, perhaps, from being feasible,
but which remains as a goal to be reached hereafter, a lofty
future ideal to be one day realized. Yes, the Earth, so far
as relates to her upper strata, will sooner or later be thoroughly
explored.

This daring "revolution of elevations" was directed, we
must not forget, not only against the Bible and the Deluge,
but against the Popes of the age, by Von Buch against his
master Werner, by Elie de Beaumont against his master
Cuvier. It was not the less approved by high authorities;
by the Aragos, the Ritters, the Alexander von Humboldts.
Only one voice dared to contradict it,—that of Constant
Prévost.

This is what Geology accomplished on the Continent, in
the region of revolutions. But immovable England, which

had not experienced our great social convulsions, judged the globe from a different point of view. What had she seen in her own bosom? A progressive constitution, built up gradually without any violent change, a well-balanced government undergoing little modification; a novelty, it is true, this industrious England, which with adequate rapidity, but without crisis, without struggle, step by step, has risen to her present pride of place! All this was accomplished by herself as, in a vast bee-hive, we see laborious industry raising one upon another the cakes of wax and honey. Or as, to employ a grander comparison, we may behold in the Southern Ocean the polypes similarly constructing in peaceful toil the white rose-tinted cinctures of the islands, extending their area, and elevating them to the level of the waters.

The Britannic conquest—a long series of expeditions, establishments, voyages, even residences, and protracted observations—had the happiest effect. It may be described as a colossal inquiry conducted by minute observers. Rigidly attentive, and in appearance phlegmatic; anxious to discover the actual reality; they looked at Nature with eyes on whose retina was already impressed their own England, the ideal of an industrial creation. At the climax of our commotions, towards 1830, when Von Buch and Elie de Beaumont seemed securely enthroned, a grave voice arose, the geology of Sir Charles Lyell. In his powerful and ingenious treatise, Earth for the first time figured as a worker who, with calm, incessant, and regular labour, manufactures herself.

Lamarck, as early as 1800, had asserted that the equable regularity of the processes of Nature,—the influence of the mediums in which she wrought, and the infinite time allowed to her work,—would suffice to explain everything in the world's economy, without supposing any acts of violence, any *coups d'état* of creation or destruction. Who would have believed that England, a country so fanatically Biblical and so long

in the rear of scientific research, would have resumed the
tradition of Lamarck, when neglected and almost forgotten by
France herself? The result was admirable. The voyages of
Darwin revealed to us in the Southern Seas the silent toil of
the innumerable polypes engaged in creating the future Earth;
on whose surface, perhaps, Man shall hereafter reside. And
at the same time the German, Ehrenberg, demonstrated that
the enormous accumulation of the Andes and other mountains is nothing but the buried ruin of a microscopical world
—of shells, silex, and organized limestone—which has softly
and gradually risen, in layer upon layer, during millions of
years.

These, then, are the two schools: the school of war, the
school of peace. The latter is master of the field. The principle of "peace at any price" which, through Cobden's exertions, prevails in the political relations of his country, seems
to animate Dr. Darwin and Sir Charles Lyell. They suppress
the revolutionary in Nature, and decree that the Earth shall
perform all her operations without violent excesses; that
insensibly, through a vast period of years, she shall modify
and transform herself.

This geological theory of peaceful transformations is supported by the general agreement in opinion of the most eminent
naturalists, as Geoffroy Saint-Hilaire, Goethe, Oken, Owen,
and Darwin; who show how the animal, under the varied
influence of its conditions of existence, and by that instinctive
impulse which leads it to choose what is best for it, is made
and modified. The new geology is, in truth, a branch of the
great whole of natural history; it is the investigation of the
movements and changes undergone by that beautiful animal,
the Earth. We study it as we do the elephant or the
whale. Only—and the difference is great—the Earth is as
slow and laggard in movement as it is colossal in size. It
does not change, except by the action of ages. What need

has it of hurry? It seems to know that it has time and all eternity before it.

The reaction in favour of this new school has taken place legitimately, I believe, but not without injustice to its predecessors. Is it easy to put aside the crises, the upheavals, which all men but yesterday admitted to be facts, in concurrence with Ritter and Humboldt? Numerous mountains bear evidence of having undergone violent convulsions; such is our conclusion on first examining them. We must resort to reason before we can dismiss it, and believe in a slow and tranquil action.

Even in the animal life best regulated in its functions crises will occur, sometimes of a morbid, sometimes of a natural character. Is it to be supposed that the Earth-animal has not undergone analogous cataclysms, that in its prolonged life it has had no abrupt and violent intervals?

But, at all events, we may reasonably conclude that in its infancy the days flowed smoothly and peacefully. Encountering no obstacle in a crust as yet non-existent, it could freely follow its natural tendency towards the light and its beloved star. Why suppose that any explosive detonations took place in an hermetically-sealed vessel? This is very clearly shown in the primeval granites, which date from a far remoter antiquity than the volcanic age. A close observer of these formations, the Norwegian Scheerer, says that Earth propelled to her surface her twofold blended life of solid and liquid— the three constituents of granite, silica, mica, and felspar—in a yielding plastic mass, which as it hardened acquired a rounded shape.

And in this you will discover neither scoria, nor cinders, nor vitrified lavas; none of those materials which, at a later epoch, rendered volcanoes terrible. The further we ascend in the infinite ages, the less do we see of any chaotic outbursts or elemental strife. All as yet is tranquil. The eldest born of the universe is Peace.

The corallines of the Southern Ocean now construct their subaqueous world without either turmoil or violence; and we cannot see why any greater disturbance was needed during those primeval movements of the earth towards the heavens which wrought out the granite formations. The elder mountains rose with majestic calm, not in the shape of jagged pinnacles, but of graceful domes. The picturesque valleys of Alsace, the mamelons or "paps" of the Vosges, possess the most beautiful outlines in all creation. They may be described as the feminine bosom moulded in porphyry.

This bosom, not in relief, but revealing itself in the opposite form, though without losing the maternal character, is plainly discerned in the circular valleys, the ring-like basins which, in the early times, the youthful effusion of the Earth opened up. Such is the valley of Cashmere, a genial paradise in the midst of frowning granite.

By a spontaneous impulse Earth has offered to Heaven the calyx of her deep-embosomed flower.

So glittering and richly decked as she is to-day, cherishes she still a recollection of the ancient days when she lived but an imperfect existence? It may well be so. Great was her happiness when unencumbered with obstacles, when the internal impetus mounted upwards in unrestricted freedom, when she saw—though undoubtedly through mist and vapour —when she saw ever and always before her the goal to which her being incessantly gravitated. But now the terrestrial crust obscures her vision.

In our individual life we know all that transpires. We surround ourselves with our labours and acquisitions, and triumph in their continual augmentation. But there are

times when we discover that our individuality is no longer
free; that it is enthralled by the very burden of its wealth.
We feel the oppression under which we suffer, and we groan
beneath it.

May not Earth have experienced something of a similar
feeling? May she not remember a time when she was less
encumbered by her own gains? One can believe that of such
a time she dreams, that she sometimes pants beneath the
gorgeous robe which has become so heavy. And I do not
refer to volcanic convulsions, nor even to those vast regions
which appear, like Greenland, to sink, or, like Sweden, to
rise; but to her internal tremors, which have been compared
to the Ocean tides.

And has she not, even in her solid parts, a tidal circulation also? Does she remain insensible to the proximate
passage of friendly stars? Does she not feel, even in her
obscurest depths, the motions of that adored lover, that
tender parent, the Sun? With the force of her restrained
impulse towards him, her bosom seems, at times, to heave
and expand!—Regret? Aspiration? Ever vain, incomplete,
and powerless, like all things in this world! The aspiration
falls back to Earth, as if after reflection it had overcome its
yearning, though not without a sigh!

XI

THE TWO GREAT MOUNTAINS OF EARTH,

CALLED CONTINENTS.

HUMBOLDT was delighted with an ingenious exhibition,—the Georama. It was a grand spherical spectacle, which lasted for some hours. In the centre stood the spectator, and saw, on every side of him, the Earth, as if it had been reversed. The two magnificent mountains, which geographers call " continents," their beautiful and imposing outlines, the rounded sinuses of the seas, the exquisite girdles of islands which decorate them on either coast, and seem to constitute the Earth's most glowing firecentres of life,—all charmed and gratified. It was impossible to withdraw one's gaze from the picture.

But no representation can do justice to the reality. None can give the proportional heights and depths. None can indicate—the ancient charts attempted in vain to do it—in each region the living and infinitely varied manifestations of Earth's internal forces.

Our senses here betray us. The subject is overpowering, and escapes our comprehension. From a balloon, at a moderate elevation, the aeronaut sees nothing more than a vast geographical map. It is only by solitary thought and effort of the imagination, far from every distracting object, that we can embrace this beautiful and sublime being, infinitely more complex as it is than any creature which has issued from its bosom.

Beautiful is it in its harmonious, its expansive, and yet restrained, aspiration towards light, love, and life.

Beautiful in the superb clothing of its terrestrial crust, like a gigantic haliotis, with its hundred colours and hundred reflections.

So charming, so loving in its plant life, in the marvellous and immense language of its three hundred thousand floral species; so powerful, so energetic in its animal revelation, the innumerable small planets, fashioned in imitation of the great, which traverse the maternal bosom, embellishing it with infinite grace, and all the charms of liberty.

Its beauty of lines and forms is still further animated and adorned by its beauty of movement.

By its concentric movement, the graceful curves it traces around the sun; by its movement within itself, through the continual ascent of its internal forces; by the electric movement which is so perceptible at the equator, and the magnetic currents, so easily recognized at the poles; by its fluid circulation in the ocean currents; by its light and swift aërial circulation, which, by a constant interchange of cloud and vapour, harmonizes its superficial existence.

In the Earth are re-united the two most exquisite forms —the *circle*, the absolute line of beauty; and that grace, that *harmony of duality*, which we admire in superior beings. The form of the circle is admirably adapted to secure the strong unity of its existence, is admirably adapted to facilitate its movement. In its upper portions (which are undoubtedly the most susceptible and the most highly organized) Earth is twofold, presenting two halves, two continents, which its general galvanic and aërial currents incessantly link together and unite.

If Earth had consulted us upon the form it would be best for it to assume, should we have advised it rightly ? Some, in their ideal of a super-harmonic harmony, would have impressed on its surface a circular perfection, a monotonous uniformity, ill fitted to encourage a varied development of life. Others, less mathematical, but more artistic, would have wished, in its twofold condition, like man, it should possess the human forms, two halves, apparently equal—an equality which we find in all its exactness in our statues, but far less accurately in nature. The actual inequality of the two moieties is precisely that which permits action. If the two hemispheres were of exactly the same force, each drawing equally with a perfect equilibrium, the whole would remain immovable. Life would acquire no impetus. Nothing could have a beginning.

Earth's bold and original characteristic—diametrically opposed to our human art, but of a superior instinct—is to present two moieties, which are not only unequal, but of different form, and in different directions, and are, therefore, so much the better adapted to respond to very different wants. The one stretches in latitude from east to west; that is, in the route of the sun and the great electric currents. The paths which it threw open in this direction were those of the human race. The other extends from north to south, nearly touching the two poles, the two points where the magnetism of the globe is most evident, and reconciling perhaps Earth's internal currents.

How useful is this irregularity, to which, more than any other circumstance, is due the fertility of the earth. Its two principal mountains, which we call continents, have contributed, in their apparent discordance, to vary *ad infinitum* the theatre of life; to stimulate, protect, and exalt it in all the expositions, all the diverse conditions of light, heat, and soil.

The sentiment which I feel on seeing my own mother, I also feel when I contemplate her whose vast and prolific bosom has poured forth the nations to the east and to the west. Who is not overcome with reverence, who does not become conscious that he is in the presence of the most venerable object here below, when he beholds the majestic maternity of Asia? From her has assuredly sprung the race which has most successfully given voice and utterance to the profound soul of the Earth. How many thoughts, how many arts have been born of her! The very language in which I write, the words I now make use of, are those which she discovered, not less than a hundred centuries agone, in the remotest East.

I see the sacred mountain—or, I should rather say, the lofty table-lands dominating over the world—where the Man and the Woman together breathed the first hymn to the Morning, the Light, the central source, the good Agni.

Between the plains of China and the rearward plain of Tartary, between the plains of the Euphrates and the hills of Persia, Asia rules from on high the globe. Possessing a hundred more elevated table-lands than America (as Humboldt says) in her enormous central group, she sees beneath her the entire terrestrial surface.

This great mother of life—Asia—with her fertile organs, expands towards the southern wind. It is the South that impregnates her. But how modified is he, how changed and how transformed, when he visits her! His formidable breath, his long line of threatening floods, arrested by Australia, checked by innumerable islands, and compelled to wheel round and circulate through their basins and straits, arrives in a much more softened form, and genial with rich vapours.

When I had the happiness, in 1863, of perusing that glorious poem, the divine Ramâyân'a,* I saw in its pictures (infinitely more faithful than those of all our travellers) all the variety of Asia, how many Africas and Europes she comprehends in her bosom. As we ascend from stage to stage her mountain-girdles, we meet with every condition of climate. The sun is that of the Tropics; but owing to the lofty elevation, we breathe, and are fanned by, the cooling breezes. From summer we mount into spring. That giant, the Himalaya, which is twice the elevation of the Alps, is midway adorned with our vineyards and orchards. It is clothed in fresh-green forests, and even near its lofty crests its clemency still accepts and tolerates the flora which, in Europe, perishes at a level two thousand feet lower.

What delightful days I have spent at the foot of the holy mountain, between Râma and Sîtâ, in front of the sparkling snows, among the gracious waterfalls and the forests loaded with blossom!† There, of the four Indian seasons one of the most beautiful is winter, which, in its delicate severity, is sometimes frosted in the morning with imperceptible crystals;

* [The Râmâyan'a is one of the two great epic poems of India, and deals with Râma, an incarnation of the god Vishn'u. Its supposed author is Valnûki; and it is said that he taught his poem to the two sons of his hero Râma. It evinces from beginning to end a remarkable poetical genius. The language is spirited, the versification polished, the characters are well conceived, and the interest is maintained throughout. It contains about 24,000 verses (or Slokas), divided into seven books (or Kân'd'as), called, the Bâla, the Ayodhyâ, the Aran'ya, Kishkindhâ, Sundara, Yuddhâ- (or Laukâ-), and Uttara-Kân'd'a. An analysis of the poem will be found in Professor Morier Williams's "Indian Epic Poetry."

Sîtâ, referred to in the text, is, in the mythology of the Hindus, the daughter of Janaka, and wife of Râma (or the incarnate Vishn'u). The word means "furrow;" and she was supposed to have risen from a furrow while her father was ploughing the earth.]

† It is impossible to conceive anything more delicious than the verses of this grand poem (see my "Bible," sect. v.):—"Since I have seen the marvels of that magnificent mountain, the holy Mont Tchitra-Koûta, I have never thought of my exile, or of my solitary life. If I might but spend my existence here with thee, my dear Sîtâ, with my brother Lachsmana, I should know no regret! Seest thou yonder sublime crests which soar to the glowing heaven? Some are masses of silver, others of purple or opal, others of emerald green; and yet another thou wouldst call a diamond kindling with sunshine," &c. This description closely corresponds with Hodgson's, in his narrative of his journey to the sources of the Ganges. He confesses his amazement on finding himself face to face with these mountains of diamonds.]

A HIMALAYAN LANDSCAPE.

but the sun—the spring—the glances of Sîtâ, re-animate the fertilizing heat.

Summer is the season of gloom. Earth for a moment dissolves in tears. She sympathizes with all her soul in the widowhood of Râma. The deluges and torrents pouring down the entire range of the Ghauts harmonize well with her sorrow. Fertilizing tears! which not the less succeed in quenching the thirst of the burning plains, in speedily restoring her joy, in bringing back to her embraces her Sîtâ, and all the charming loveliness of her youth.*

Ocean, the lord of Earth, which clasps her close on every side and cradles her upon his waves, would become too formidable if his great eastern and western currents could accumulate their waves, from Europe to India, without encountering any barrier—could fall upon India or Europe with the terrible weight of two vast seas—could strike simultaneously with the double force of the Atlantic and the Pacific. Earth, lying between them, has offered a firm resistance. She has bisected Ocean by raising up from north to south, like a long undulating serpent, the sublime crest of America, adorned with volcanoes and snowy peaks, with their great reservoirs, savannahs, and prairies. Ocean, restrained and kept in order in two basins on either coast, beats and growls under the dominating presence of the superb and fire-kindled dragon, which overawes the seas.

Between its two great moieties the enormous creature is articulated by a thread, a simple thread—Panama,—like the

---

* Nothing has grieved me more than to read quite recently that "India to-day seems old." Oh, what an accusation for man to make, and what a cause of complaint against her masters! What has become of those admirable works which for so long a period maintained the salubrity of her plains and provided for the economization of her waters? However this may be, let us hope on. She is the country of resurrections;—the nursery of life, of which India has always possessed the secret. If Italy has risen from the tomb, why not India? The mourning of Râma will terminate. Sîtâ will return to her more beautiful than ever, and enfranchised by Râvan'a.

filament which links the two halves of the wasp, and endows
that powerful insect with a subtle and extremely delicate
originality.

With this thread is closely connected the dragon's glorious ornament—a circle of islands, scintillating with burning
life.

Its life, its respiration, it exhales incessantly, towards the
west, in that torrent of boiling and sombre azure water which
leaps forth beneath the Antilles; towards the east in these
haughty peaks which smoke for ever and for ever.

The lofty mission of America is to regulate these fires
and waters. With its volcanoes it lightens and relieves
the choking spasms of the Earth, and anticipates her paroxysms. On the snowy ridge of its Andes it arrests and
maintains suspended an entire ocean. Formidable masses
of water (the vapour of the Pacific) rise to so great an
elevation above Peru, that not a rain-drop falls in the
latter country (says Ulloa) in eighty and eight years. But
they must needs ascend; and in their ascent encounter the
dominant and sovereign Cordilleras, which forbid their passage. They pay an enormous tribute; and are not suffered
to move eastward until they have fed the snows which,
with a breadth of twenty leagues, extend their unbroken
barrier for eighteen hundred. These snows gain enough—
ay, and too much. They pour their superfluity upon the
plain in rivers; which, however, are not so much rivers as
seas of fresh water—the Amazon and the Orinoco—with
mighty inundations.

But the mass of vapours which succeeds in crossing the
mountain rampart is still prodigious—as one may see in the
black canopy which they spread over the Atlantic; and in the
sombre Zone of Rains, where, for three hundred days in the
year, rain falls continuously, overwhelming Africa, weakening

it under the Equator, rendering it uninhabitable, and terrifying every species of animal life.*

The American hemisphere performs two admirable functions :—

It is a great mediator.   It has one eye fixed upon Europe, the other. upon China and India.

It is a great channel of intercommunication, always open and hospitable.

Equatorial Africa is so beset with jungle that it is impossible to traverse it.   Europe is so broken up, that it arrests you at every step.   In Asia, all is laboriously difficult ; the very steppes, says Humboldt, are obstructed with mountains. In America all is easy.   The feeblest traveller, without let or hindrance, may roam from pole to pole.   The humming-bird, when it can no longer obtain its insect-food in Canada, flies away to Peru and Chili.   Even the sea is friendly.   The microscopic armies of atomic shell-fish (called *foraminifera*) march every year from the southern world to the northern, along the American coasts, transported through the maternal waters by the regular currents which flow from Cape Horn to the Floridas and beyond, accomplishing, as in a dream, a voyage of six thousand leagues.

Asia seems a thing *absolute*, perfect, and complete in itself; it appears to be an all-sufficing world.   America is a thing *relative*; it yearns after, it urgently needs the globe, and stretches beyond its own individuality.   Is this a sign of inferiority ?   On the contrary, it is this circumstance which raises it high above every isolated region, and makes it truly *human*.

Its northern half, having sprung from our loins, looks always towards us, and patiently watches for the dawn which

* See the books of Du Chaillu, and the recent travels of Spoke, Baker, and others to the sources of the Nile.

rises above our horizon. Despite its youthful outbursts of arrogance, America longs for Europe—its mother in civilization—whence it received the inspiration and all the past of the human race. Towards this mother it turns, as Earth towards the Sun. We have seen its affecting festivals, its intoxication of delight, when the telegraph-cable, by uniting the two shores, promised it a medium of conversation every minute between New York and London. Its hope at this moment is that a natural bridge between the two is in course of construction : the American coast, upheaved at certain points, manifests a disposition to encroach upon the sea ; and the two worlds in the course of time will not be more than four days apart from one another.

XII

MOUNTAINS OF ICE:

THE POLE.

WE have said that the Cordilleras and the Alps, by arresting and freezing the vapours on their summits, act as intermediary poles. The Poles, in their turn, recall our thoughts to the Alps and the Andes. The points of resemblance between them have been discussed. Let us mark also the differences, on which men less frequently insist.

He who ascends the mountain rises towards the light. When, at an elevation of 5000 or 6000 feet, he emerges from the uncertain zone, the shifting ocean of mists and vapours, he sees the peaks and the glaciers soaring above the surge and swelling into the serene Day.

On the contrary, he who voyages towards either Pole, voyages also towards Night; towards a dim, strange world, where so much of light as still survives has all the effect of a dubious phantasmagoria.

But it is Night, not Death. The living soul of the Earth is still plainly conspicuous, in its mighty upheavals, in the ice-piercing mountain-peaks, in the flames which kindle at the two shadowy extremities of the globe. Erebus in the south,

Jan Mayen in the north,* are two solemn and imposing pharoses.

There, in a monstrous mass unknown to our European Alps, ice upon ice, winter upon winter, have accumulated! The ice has doubled and trebled its hard walls of crystal, has conquered the very sea, and imposed upon its waves repose. Agitated both by the currents of the north and the last echoes of the storms of the south, it grows pacified after awhile ; and first assuming an oily, unctuous appearance, gradually congeals, until, at last, it becomes permanently fixed.

In this region the glaciers do not experience the tortures and diverse accidents of their Alpine congeners. Those which belong to the sloping valleys, by an easy spontaneous motion, have reached, and even encroached upon, their neighbour, the Ocean. Those which have fallen into the abyss of some

* [*Mount Erebus* is a volcano in Victoria Land—an extensive Antarctic continent, discovered by Captain Sir James Ross in 1841. The volcano is situated in lat. 77° 32′ south, and long. 167° 0′ east. It emits flame and smoke in splendid profusion, at an elevation of 12,400 feet above the sea. Its sides are clothed in eternal snow, and glaciers descending from it project many miles into the ocean, and form a perpendicular wall of lofty cliffs.

Jan Mayen Island, in the North Atlantic Ocean, lies about midway between the north coast of Iceland and the eastern shore of Greenland. It bears the name of the Dutch captain who discovered it in 1611. In the snow-shrouded conical volcano of Mount Beerenberg, it rises to an elevation of 6870 feet. It was visited in 1856 by Lord Dufferin, who writes :—

"Although, by reason of our having hit upon its side instead of its narrow end, the outline of Mount Beerenberg appeared to us more like a sugar-loaf than a spire—broader at the base and rounder at the top than I had imagined—in size, colour, and effect it far surpassed anything I had anticipated. Its seven glaciers were quite an unexpected element of beauty. Imagine a mighty river of as great a volume as the Thames started down the side of a mountain —bursting over every impediment—whirled into a thousand eddies—tumbling and raging on from ledge to ledge in quivering cataracts of foam—then suddenly struck rigid by a power so instantaneous in its action, that even the froth and fleeting wreaths of spray have stiffened to the immutability of sculpture. Unless you had seen it, it would be almost impossible to conceive the strangeness of the contrast between the actual tranquillity of these silent crystal rivers and the violent descending energy impressed upon their exterior. You must remember, too, all this is upon a scale of such prodigious magnitude, that when we succeeded in approaching the spot where, with a leap like that of Niagara, one of these glaciers plunges down into the sea, the eye, no longer able to take in its fluvial character, was content to rest in simple astonishment at what then appeared a lucent precipice of gray-green ice, rising to the height of several hundred feet above the masts of the vessel."—"*Letters from High Latitudes*," pp. 140, 141.]

ISLAND OF JAN MAYEN.

tremendous excavation, by their descent upon one another, have created along the shore solemn cathedral-masses, pillars, arcades, and vaults, ogives, and flying arches—a whole world of architecture—built sometimes in the air, sometimes on the sea itself, which, while groaning underneath them, submits to their gloomy solidity.

Frost is the architect. But with what materials does he work ? The cloud. Our Alps receive nothing more than the wind brings to them ; but what is this in the neighbourhood of the Pole, of the enormous cloud-realm which *there* rises above the sea ? Still retaining some degree of warmth below the frozen peaks, it evaporates in mists, which at first trail heavily and slowly, but which the upper air soon attracts and rarifies. It is thus the sea incessantly serves and enriches its enemy—the very winter which imprisons it. The snow falls, falls, falls ; as if doating upon it. The sharp cold transforms its flakes into needles—fine needles of ice. They are changed into transparent prisms ; into mirrors which refract the capricious display of the Aurora Borealis.

This terrible and fantastic world seems to bear the fatal and unchanging yoke of a single law—crystallization ; the harsh law of rectilineal forms, angles, and points, which threaten and proscribe the softened outlines of life. The animal power resists its rigour. The amphibia, the phocæ, clad in an armour of fat,—the bird, that most ardent of all Nature's centres of heat,—thrive in the realms of ice. But will the plant, which is so easily wounded, find among all its terrors a shelter, a refuge, a day or a moment of clemency ? Will she dare to venture among them ? One would not think it. For years, in the vicinity of rocks reflecting the pale radiance of Polar skies, man trod upon the luxuriant mosses without distinguishing the tiny miniature plants which lay almost imperceptibly concealed among them.

A couple of centuries elapsed before he discovered their existence.

Arctic voyagers have frequently compared these poor creatures to the flowers of the lofty Alps. But how many different circumstances exist between these regions and heights to modify the conditions of existence! The latitude of Spitzbergen may correspond to the elevation of the mountains. But between the climates are there any other points of resemblance?

The higher we ascend in the Alps, the drier and lighter becomes the air. At the Poles, the atmosphere is heavy with saturating vapours. Through this density how can the light operate, as it operates through a subtle atmosphere freely admitting the passage of the solar rays, and transmitting all their caloric and chemic powers? In the mountains the air retains nothing; the earth appropriates all the light and heat. At Spitzbergen the granite remains inert and frozen.

In winter, perhaps, an equality obtains. But in springtime, when our Alpine plants break through the snow, they are assisted by a laborious sun, which rises early, sets late, ascends high in the heavens, and plunges to the bottom of the valleys. It is the true awakener of the world, a beneficent and joyous sun. Is it indeed the same which I see yonder for so many days and nights, glaring with sulky beam through the fogs, mounting the horizon so painfully, and so quickly disappearing?

On the 21st of April it makes an effort—it sets no more, it begins a four months' day. But how weak and low it is! Little does the earth receive of its warmth, when lighted only by an oblique ray. Its saviour is the Bird; that powerful being which, with its excess of life, vivifies and warms the soil. The tiny soul of the plant blesses it for its prolonged existence.

If the plant cherishes a dream or a desire, it is that it may become a mother. What will it not do to realize this aspira-

tion? But when scarcely able to draw from the indigent
soil its little life, how shall it attain so sublime a luxury of
existence—so lofty a climax of love and generation? In order
that it may secure its triumphant joy, we see it contracting its
proportions, and shrinking into the mere miniature of a plant.
It reduces every organ, while still in its littleness preserving
a just equilibrium. To accomplish its end it would even sink
into an atom—annihilate its body, be no more than spirit.
At this cost it achieves its desire—to possess a perfect life, to
love, and perpetuate its soul.

Four months of light—an interminable day without repose
or sleep—such is life at Spitzbergen. Ought the Alps to
envy it? No more sleep!—how rigorous a law for animals
and plants! We know the fate of Lord Dufferin's cock, which
he carried with him to the Polar Seas. When the days
lengthened, melancholy and anxious—fearing to fail in his
duty of proclaiming the hour at daybreak—he appeared dis-
tracted and perturbed, and occasionally uttered a most unusual
sound. And finally, when night altogether ceased, he was
attacked with delirium, he dreamed half-aloud, and flying
overboard, was drowned.*

This four months' day (very necessary, no doubt, for otherwise winter would invade the world, and once more tyrannize
over it with universal ice and snow) is not less painful to the
beings which it condemns to sleeplessness. The flower without slumber languishes and withers. On the contrary, see in

* ["Shortly after this, a very melancholy occurrence took place. I had observed for some
days past, as we proceeded north, and the nights became shorter, that a cock we had shipped
at Stornoway had become quite bewildered on the subject of that meteorological phenomenon called the dawn of day. In fact, I doubt whether he ever slept for more than five
minutes at a stretch without waking up in a state of nervous agitation lest it should be cock-
crow. At last, when night ceased altogether, his constitution could no longer bear the shock.
He crowed once or twice sarcastically, then went melancholy mad; finally, taking a calenture,
he cackled lowly (probably of green fields), and leaping overboard, drowned himself."—Lord
Dufferin, "Letters from High Latitudes," p. 32.]

the Alps with what happiness the gentian, when its day is
ended, closes its starry eye, to re-open it on the morrow
rejuvenated and refreshed! The melancholy Polar flower is
deplorably condemned to the labour of constant emotion, of
unbroken existence, without time, forgetfulness, or repose.

A gloomy world, which at the first glance seems void and
disinherited, a realm of death! But it is not so; earth's
ordinary life still triumphs there. The two souls of our
planet, magnetism and electricity, enjoy every night their
revels in the Polar wilderness. Their Aurora Borealis is its
sublime consolation.

The aërial and oceanic currents are the vehicle of this
Aurora. The two torrents of warm waters which from Java
and Cuba mount northward to be cooled and frozen; which,
afterwards reviving, return incessantly to the heart that
poured them forth; assist in the magneto-electric correspond-
ence between the Equator and the Pole. Their storms have
a certain solidarity. In summer, when the liquefaction of the
Polar snows and the northern currents refresh our earth, the
magnetic element seems to precede the central electricity.
Hence arise those violent tempests—especially near this centre
—and those outbursts of thunder, which prove so frightful to
our troubled senses.

But, on the contrary, at the Pole thunder is seldom or
ever heard. In its profound winter-night all nature appears
asleep. And yet what region of heaven is more crowded
with storms? Nearly every evening, towards ten o'clock, the
Aurora bursts forth in all its might. Earth and snow and
glacier are suddenly illuminated. Their vivid crests, and an
atmosphere full of icy particles, break and shatter the lustre,
and fling it back in palpitating rays.

This mysterious spectacle was not investigated very closely

until 1838.   M. Bravais in one direction, and in another his
associates, followed it up and observed it from minute to
minute, with the object of afterwards comparing and correct-
ing their observations.   Under a sky of terrible severity they
persevered in their labours for thirteen nights (January 9–22).

At first a gloomy curtain rises, of violet-coloured mists,
sufficiently transparent for the stars to pierce its folds.
Higher up, a gleam, like that of a vast conflagration,
prevails. A gleam! It is soon a glow of light. A grand
luminous arc appears, with either extremity resting on the
sombre horizon.

This arc, as it slowly rises, grows more and more luminous.
From the observations and calculations of Bravais, it would
appear that it mounts to the extreme verge of the atmosphere, to an elevation of above twenty-five, and, perhaps, of
fifty leagues.* Prodigious is the altitude of the region where
the shooting-star and the meteor grow luminous and incan-
descent. Assuredly nothing so grand is seen elsewhere in
this world.

And nothing more solemn. One might say that the
whole earth "assisted" at the spectacle ; it is both spectator
and actor.   In the evening, or several hours beforehand, its
preoccupation is everywhere demonstrated by the magnetic
needle.   Throughout the boreal hemisphere this needle is
moved and agitated, and even veers from one Pole to the
other.   When the phenomenon passes to the southern Pole,
warning of the change is given.

But see how a kind of effervescence breaks forth in that
majestic pale yellow arc, as it accomplishes its peaceable
ascent !   It becomes double, triple—is sometimes multiplied
ninefold.   The arcs undulate.   An ebb and flow of light
traverses them like a drapery of gold, which swells and sinks,
folds and unfolds its splendour.

* See Elie de Beaumont's paper on the Aurora Borealis.

Is this all ?   No ; the spectacle becomes instinct with life. Long lustrous columns and rays and jets are impetuously and rapidly evolved, changing from yellow to purple, and from red to emerald.

Is it a pastime, or is it a battle ?   Our ancient navigators, on first beholding the scene, thought it represented a dance. For a penetrating eye, and a heart more observant of Nature's emotions, it is a complete drama.   One cannot mistake the trembling, and the profound palpitations of captive souls. Then come alternations, appeals, violent replies, affirmatives, negatives, defiances, combats.   Victories follow, and defeats ; and sometimes fierce outbursts of passion, like those of the daughter of the seas—the Medusa—which lightens up the night, when her lamp alternately reddens, languishes, and grows pale.

A deeply-moved spectator would seem to take an active part in this drama—the loadstone.   By its agitations it visibly sympathizes with, and interests itself in, every phase ; giving expression to the various crises, changes, and sudden vicis-situdes of the spectacle.   It appears troubled, affrighted, and, as it were, infatuated.

But no one can be calm when contemplating such a scene. So prodigious a movement taking place in silence seems to be less Nature than Magic.   In the gloomy regions where it is revealed to man, it has a depressing and not an encouraging influence.

What will be the issue ?   Earth is disquieted.   Who shall conquer ?—who shall seize upon these living lights ?   The two Poles.

It is eleven at night ; and the grand moment has arrived for the struggle to end harmoniously.   The lights have con-tended sufficiently.   They understand one another, grow tran-quil, and subside in love.   They soar together in glory. They transfigure themselves into a sublime fan-like image, a cupola of fire ; and become, as it were, the crown of a divine hymeneal.

With the terrestrial and magnetic soul, the queen of the North, the other, the electric, the life of the Equator, has mingled. They embrace, and the two become one and the same spirit.

THE MOUNTAIN OF FIRE:

JAVA.

HAS Earth a heart? an all-powerful organ, in which its energies are made manifest, by which it aspires, and respires, and palpitates in all its many transformations? If such an organ exist, we ought not to seek for it in the shadowy recesses of its central nucleus, where it is overwhelmed by its own mass, but rather at some point where its inner effort finally arrives at the surface, at a condition of free expansion—there, where its soul of desire encounters the great soul of love and fecundation. A marvellous mystery, but not impenetrably shrouded! Earth by its two faces, in its two oceans, freely exposes it to the open day, to the most garish sun, and upon the flashing sea and in the sublime illumination of its great volcanic circle.

This sovereign organ of life, love, and aspiration manifests itself, on the one side, in the Indian Sea, and the burning belt of islands over which Java holds supremacy; on the other, in the boiling caldron of Cuba and Haïti.

It is a heart with two lobes, whose separation is only superficial. They are united by the grand galvanic current of the Equator which binds Earth together. To electricity, what is space or time?

The great sign common to both is the superb artery with which each is furnished, the mighty torrent of hot waters which leaps alive from the double furnace. So direct and so vigorous the flood, that for a considerable period it pursues its course apart, an azure river in the emerald sea, forming a kind of ridge upon its surface. Its warmth is perceptible at the distance of one thousand, and even one thousand five hundred leagues.

The sole difference between these two centres is, that in the Indian Seas the volcanic force is active, while many of the West Indian volcanoes are extinct. In Haïti, they are chained down, and roar like caged lions. The breathing-places of the adjacent continent, or the great river of the Gulf Stream, may perhaps supply their place. These waters, in many localities, afford the volcanoes an interval of repose.

Ritter has well observed that the islands and peninsulas have contributed largely towards the progress of the globe, and have been the organs of its good fortune. It is a strange spectacle to see America and Africa, the three Asiatic penin-sulas,* and the three European peninsulas,* all directed south-wards, as if to attract the electricity which the flood brings up from the south. Earth, at all these points, aspires to the Ocean, which, equally yearning after her, comes to caress and mould her, comes to invest her shores with the gracefulness of its undulating flow. With its warm salt currents it kindles in her bosom a genial emotion. Then, on the other hand, rising and passing into vapour, into fresh water, it dominates over her, it penetrates, refreshes, and rejuvenates her.

Evidently the islands are its favourite regions, and it surrounds and embraces them, watching intently over their

* [In Asia: Hindostan, Indo-China, and Malacca. In Europe: Spain, Italy, and Greece.]

safety. With its electric wave it incessantly stirs up the life within them; one might almost say it whets or sharpens it. The highest faculties of man, and the most ingenious vivacity of his intellect, have been developed in the islands and peninsulas of India, Greece, and Italy. The adverse headlands, straits, creeks, gulfs, bays, Mediterraneans, where the half-captive Ocean sports in happy strife, and by its gentle friction stimulates the vital powers, have been the fertile cradles of humanity.

Usually these regions are volcanic in character. The Greek isles, like those of the Antilles and the Indian Ocean, were neither more nor less than volcanoes. Those who assert that volcanoes are simply an accident, a superficial obstruction maintained by the sea-waters, cannot explain why they are so closely connected with one another, or why they so faithfully respond to one another's movements. The anterior hypothesis, which the good sense of the human race at first suggested, is much more probable. It offers a satisfactory explanation of the obvious systematic regularity of their terrestrial position.

The ancients looked upon them as the natural and indispensable vents of the lower world. When you notice the stigmata of an insect's body, or the lateral openings in the shell of the haliotis, you say at once: "It is through these they breathe; close them, and the animals would be suffocated." And Earth is, in reality, choked when its volcanoes do not properly act. It undergoes those convulsions which we call earthquakes. Their prolonged vibrations by no means indicate, as some authorities have pretended, that they are produced by a landslip, or a simple dislocation of the terrestrial surface. You may clearly detect in them the violent circulation of the internal breath which can find no means of escape —the distension of the pent-up vapour vainly seeking for an issue.

ETNA, AS SEEN FROM TAORMINA.

The submergence of Atlantis, according to Humboldt, is by no means improbable. Earth's convulsions may have been terrible in those intermediate seasons when its indurated crust no longer afforded a channel for the usual ascent of the Plutonic elements, or the radiant upper earth refused to permit the expansion of the earth of shadows, denied liberty of movement to its jealous sister below. It is conceivable that vast catastrophes might then occur, until the globe, by perfecting its organism, created those respiratory organs now named volcanoes. What would be the fate of this planetary being from which we derive all things, if it were not endowed with that indispensable vital apparatus which we see in the smallest of its creatures?

In its respiration—that first and most necessary vital function—Earth has displayed a greater regularity than is noticeable in any other. In the arrangement of the thousand volcanoes which Ritter calls the "Circle of Fire," it follows with approximative accuracy the direction of the compass. That terrible illumination which awakes the terror, also ensures the safety, of the world. The guardians of Asia and Polynesia face those of the Andes. Oceania, honeycombed by innumerable extinct volcanoes, possesses two hundred which are still in activity. The belt winds northward, by Japan, to Kamtschatka, the Polar fires, and the farthest limits of America; then southward, to Mexico and Peru.

Each of these imposing personages has a characteristic physiognomy. Those of China—glaciers pierced by fire—in no respect resemble the Mexican Jorullo,* surrounded by its progeny—a great volcano which begets others. Still less can

* [The Mexican table-land is traversed by what may be called a volcanic vein, or tunnel, from the Gulf of Mexico to the Pacific, at a distance of about sixteen miles to the south of the ancient capital of Montezuma. This vein communicates with a remarkable line of active volcanoes, of which the easternmost is Tuxtla (95° west long.), near the Mexican Gulf. More to the west is "the snow-shrouded cone of Orizaba, with its ever-fiery crater, seen like a star in the darkness of the night," which has obtained it the designation of Cittalapetl, the "Mountain of the Star." Then come Popocatepetl (17,884 feet), Iztacihuatl, and Toluca. On the

they be compared to the monster cone of Quito and its broad
burning bulk of seven hundred square leagues.*

There is no need to exaggerate their horrors. These fiery
giants enclose and cradle in their arms and on their bosom
numerous important towns, or, more rightly speaking, con-
dors' nests—the noble habitations of man—which a certain
warmth of soil renders bland and agreeable, though they are
situated in the immediate vicinity of eternal snows, and
exposed to all the winds of Ocean. Quito, the most elevated
city in the world, peacefully occupies a site which volcanoes
and earthquakes have vexed and undermined; casts its bridges
across the abyss; and without any emotion of alarm hears the
internal fires groaning beneath its feet.

If the eye could at one glance embrace the entire panorama—could survey from the Pacific to India and America
this sublime collocation of volcanoes, undoubtedly the spectacle would be terribly imposing. Nevertheless, it is in its
centre that Earth celebrates its most sumptuous revels, the
magnificent nuptials of Nature.

Within a glorious girdle of islands, and on a sea balmy

western slope, about seventy miles from the Pacific, stands the volcanic cone of Jorullo, which
was suddenly thrown up to an elevation of 1683 feet on the night of the 29th September 1759.
At the same time five smaller elevations made their appearance, while vast chasms yawned
wide across the surface of the plain, and numerous tiny cones ejected volumes of steam and
vapour. The principal crater and many of these smaller "ovens" (as the Indians call them)
are still active.—*See Humboldt's " Kosmos.*"]

* [" The cordillera or ridge which hems in the valley of Quito on the east contains the snow-
capped peaks of Antisana, Cotopaxi—one of the most beautiful of active volcanoes, whose dazzling cone rises to a height of 18,775 feet—of Tunguragua, and El-Altar, the latter once equal
to Chimborazo in height, and Sangay. The western range includes the gigantic Chimborazo,
which may be seen from the coast of the Pacific, and the pyramidal peak of Illinissa, the
wreck of an ancient volcano. The height of Illinissa was measured by the French
Academicians, by very careful operations, directly above the level of the ocean, the latter
being visible from it; and by its means the absolute elevation of the valley of Quito and its
encircling peaks was deduced. North of Chimborazo and near it is the Carguáirazo, and close
to the city of Quito rises the scarcely less celebrated volcano of Pichincha, whilst the Nevado
of Cayambè (19,535 feet) closes the north-east extremity of the valley."—*Mrs. Somerville,
" Physical Geography,*" i., 161, 162.]

with all-potent odours, Love and Death wage their burning struggle. There Java—the deadly, the prolific, the divine Java—obscures heaven with the smoke of its flaming peaks.

It is dowered with fires. Notwithstanding its limited area, it possesses as many as the entire American continent, and all of them more terrible than burning Etna. And to these we must add its *liquid volcano*, its vein of sombre azure, which the Japanese call the *Black River*, and which in its northward course warms the seas of Asia.* It is remarkable for its muddiness; it tastes salter than human blood.

A hot sea—a torrid sun—volcanic fire—volcanic life! Not a day passes but a tempest breaks out among the Blue Mountains, and lightning so vivid that the eye cannot endure it. Electric rains descending in torrents intoxicate earth and madden vegetation. The very forests, smoking with wreathed vapours in the burning sun, seem like volcanoes situated midway on the mountain-slopes.

In the more precipitous regions they are frequently inaccessible, and sometimes so thickly set, so dense, and so gloomy, that the traveller who penetrates them must carry torches even at mid-day.† Nature, without an eye to watch her, celebrates all at her ease her orgies of vegetation, and creates, as Blume informs us, her river-monsters and colossi.

---

* [The part played by the Gulf Stream in the western hemisphere is played by the great Equatorial Current of the Indian Ocean in the eastern. In allusion to the deep indigo blue of its waters, the Japanese call it the " Black River." Set in motion by the south-eastern trade-wind, this current flows westward between the tenth and twentieth parallels of south latitude. On approaching the island of Madagascar it divides into two branches; one of which, striking to the north-west, curves round the north coast of Madagascar, and flows through the Mozambique Channel; then, being joined by the other branch, the united stream doubles the Cape of Good Hope, off the Agulhas Bank, and, under the name of the South Atlantic Current, skirts the west coast of Africa as far as Guinea. There it bends off to the westward, forms the great Atlantic Equatorial Current, and at Cape St. Roque in Brazil again divides. From the southern branch an offset strikes across the Atlantic to the Cape of Good Hope, makes the circuit of the South Atlantic, and keeping away two hundred miles outside the aforementioned Agulhas current, merges into its original basin, the Indian Ocean.—*See* Maury's " *Physical Geography of the Sea.*"]

† Asiatic Journal: " A Tour in Java."

Rhizanthaceæ without stem seize on the foot of a tree, and gorge themselves with its pith and vitality. Travellers speak of one which is six feet in girth. Their splendour, shining in the deep night of the forest, astonishes, nay, almost terrifies the spectator. These children of the darkness do not owe aught of their resplendent colours to the light. Flourishing low down in the warm vapour, and fattened by the breath of Earth, they seem to be its luxurious dreams, its strange weird phantasies of desire.

To win this flora is a perilous work. Many naturalists have unhesitatingly paid for its treasures with their lives. It is impossible to read without emotion, at the commencement of the *Flora Javæ*, the gloomy record drawn up by the botanist Blume of those who had preceded him, and never returned. It is a mournful Odyssey. And their very biographer, whom their fate could not discourage, found himself on one occasion at Nusa, a small island marvellous for its flowers and poisons, in a most pitiable condition. All around him lay dead his trustiest servants, and he was abandoned to his own resources. Some Javanese arrived, and extricated him from his strait. He had seen death face to face, but he felt no regret, for he had conquered this miracle-world of flowers. " Sick, and in great danger," he says, " I write and I print in haste ; for perhaps I may die to-morrow."

Java has two faces. The southern wears already the aspect of Oceania, enjoys a pure air, and is surrounded by rocks all alive with polypes and madrepores. To the north it is Indian still—India with all it inherits of unhealthiness ; a black alluvial soil fermenting with the deadly travail of Nature reacting on herself—with the work of composition and decomposition. Its inhabitants have been compelled to abandon the rich town of Bantam. It is now a mass of ruins. Superb Batavia is a triumphant cemetery. In less than thirty years, from 1730 to 1752, it swallowed up a million of human lives—sixty thousand in a single twelvemonth (1750)! And though it is now less terrible, its atmosphere has not become purified to any considerable extent.

Animals of the ancient world living forgotten in its bosom are remarkable, it seems, for their funereal aspect. In the evening enormous hairy bats, such as are seen in no other regions, hover to and fro. By day, and even at noon, the strange Flying Dragon,* that memorial of a remote epoch when the serpent was endowed with wings, does not hesitate to make its appearance. Numerous black animals exist, which agree in colour with the black basalt of the mountains. And black, too, is the tiger, that terrible destroyer which, as late as 1830, devoured annually three hundred men.

Over these terrors of the lower world rises triumphant the sublimer terror of the volcanoes. To the eye they seem like living persons. The Javanese aborigines endeavoured to appease them, as if they were deities, and erected temples in their honour. (Four hundred ruined shrines have been discovered on a single rock.) They had their altars, and their statues. Fear created Art. The sculptures still extant bear testimony no less to the awe and dread of the Javanese, than to their skill and manual ingenuity.

Each of these fire-giants differs from its neighbour. Each has its separate appellation. Some are named after the Indian gods, or the heroes of the Rámáyana. Others are distinguished by fantastic and hideous titles (perhaps those of

* The Flying Dragon, or Flying Lizard (Draco), is a genus of Saurian reptiles, allied to the iguanas, but characterised by the lateral membranes extending from the fore six false ribs, which support them, parachute-like, in the air, so that they can pass with facility from tree to tree. When not in use the membrane is folded close to the body. The tail is long, the tongue extensile; the body covered with scales. All the species are arboreal in their habits, and feed on insects.

the native deities). The Gunung Tengger* yawns with a
monstrous crater, some 20,000 feet in width, where four
colossal Etnas smoke and boil at the bottom of a frightful
precipice of 2200 feet. Another comes to the light in a
strange desert, incrusted with petrifactions by calcareous
springs, and breaks through a hard crystalline envelope. One
periodically vents its molten matter like a well-regulated
animal. Another boils in sulphurous waters, which, even
when cooled in little ponds, are always distinguished by a
fever and an agitation. And yet another pours out a lake of
milk of phantasmagorical whiteness. Moreover, the whole
country is honeycombed by copious brackish springs, of which
the greatest plays and dances, growling and thundering below.
It plays at ball with enormous pellets of earth, balls of twenty
feet diameter, which burst, break up, and fling abroad the
soil in all directions. The Arjouna and the Rao roll in clouds
of smoke and in rough boiling floods. The Idjen, waking up
one fine morning, poured forth a river.

Such are their caprices, and each one has its own. But,
at bottom, they are less separated from one another than you
would think. Sometimes when one ignites, another also
takes fire ; and not necessarily the nearest, but often a remote
peak. When an earthquake has occurred in one locality, a
volcano in a distant quarter is frequently extinguished, like a
candle which has been suddenly blown out.

[* " There is not a spot of its size on the face of the earth that contains so many volcanoes
as the island of Java. A range of volcanic mountains, from 5000 to 13,000 feet high, forms
the central crest of the island, and ends to the east in a series of thirty-eight separate volcanoes
with broad bases, rising gradually into cones. They all stand on a plain but little elevated
above the sea, and each individual mountain seems to have been formed independently of the
rest. Most of them are of great antiquity, and are covered with thick vegetation. Some are
extinct, or only emit smoke; from others sulphureous vapours issue with prodigious violence;
one has a large crater filled with boiling water; and a few have had fierce eruptions of late
years."—(Mrs. Somerville, " Physical Geography," i., 252). The volcano of Tengger is about
ten thousand feet in height. Its crater is of a circular form, nearly four miles in diameter, and
about eighteen hundred feet in depth. The other principal fire-mountains are Guntur, Galon-
goon, Merapia, Guevo-Upas, Tegkuban-Prahu, Taschem (referred to in the text as containing
a lake), and Tulaga-Bodas.—See Junghuhn's " Java."]

THE VOLCANO OF TAAL.

One of their most distinctive characteristics is, that they
are all columnar. Resting on the ancient basalts which apparently form the base of the island, they too are partial to the
basaltic form. In their channels and deep furrowed surfaces
they roughly imitate the noble architecture of those black
eldest-born of earth, the pillared arcades of Staffa and
Fingal.* An attempt has been made to account for this

* [Staffa is a small island on the Scottish coast, lying to the west of Mull, and remarkable
for its basaltic "Cave of Fingal," situated on the southern shore, and penetrated by the waters
of ocean. Its entrance consists of a range of columns of basalt, spanned by a natural arch,
which has an extraordinary Gothic character; its sides are adorned with pillars; its floor is
the shining, rolling sea. Its dimensions are 288 feet in length, 33 feet in width (at the entrance),
and 59 feet in height from high-water mark to the point of the arch. The depth of water is

appearance by ascribing it to what is simply a variable accident, the water which hollowed out the furrows. But such an agent would not act with this perfect regularity. It would not develop their cones in that curious form which recalls the radiation of the whalebones of an umbrella. Yet this singular uniformity does but all the more conspicuously mark out and individualize their diversities. All are brothers, yet all are different, with a strange, fantastic, and terrible aspect.

Those raging peaks which incessantly growl and thunder are, nevertheless, at bottom, and to some small extent, humanized. Since their last grand cataclysm in 1772 they have wrought no serious mischief. They no longer give way to those paroxysms in which they seemed bent upon hurling heavenward the entire mountain, and in which they covered a hundred leagues of sea with darkness and showers of ashes. Their exploits are limited at present to an outflow of brackish waters and streams of mud. It is true that they rock the isle and make the ground tremble, but to these phenomena the inhabitants are accustomed. Their storms and lightnings breed no more hurricanes. Owing to this unresting activity, Java, though situated under the Equator, is not cursed with the oppressive zone of black gloomy clouds which oppresses Africa, and overwhelms it with eternal rains. Nor is it

25 feet. The reader will remember the fine sonnet in which Wordsworth commemorates his visit to this great natural wonder:—

> "Thanks for the lesson of this spot—fit school
> For the presumptuous thoughts that would assign
> Mechanic laws to agency divine ;
> And, measuring earth by heaven, would over-rule
> Infinite power. The pillared vestibule,
> Expanding yet precise, the roof embowed,
> Might seem designed to humble man, when proud
> Of his best workmanship by plan and tool.
> Down-bearing with his whole Atlantic weight
> Of tide and tempest on the structure's base,
> And flashing to that structure's topmost height,
> Ocean has proved his strength, and of its grace
> In calms is conscious, finding for his freight
> Of softest music some responsive place."]

ravaged by such torrents as descend from the Ghauts. Its
rains, more profitably economized, but rich in volcanic vapours,
engender a fertile salt, the joy of the earth. It absorbs the
volcano, absorbs the storm, and is drunk with life.*

The double chain which forms the backbone of Java is
intersected by numerous internal, concentrated, and sheltered
valleys. Hundreds of lateral valleys, running in an opposite
direction, vary the spectacle. The diversity of surface secures
a corresponding diversity of vegetation. The soil in the lowlands is madreporic, and was recently *alive*. At a higher
level it has a foundation of granite, charged with the fertile
ruins and hot *débris* of the volcanoes. The whole is a vast
ascending scale which, from sea to mountain, presents six
different climates—from the marine flora and the flora of the
marshes up to the flora of the Alps. A superb amphitheatre,
rich and abundant at each gradation, bearing the dominant
plants and those transitional forms which lead from one zone
to another, and so ingeniously that, without any lacuna, or
abrupt leap, we are carried onwards, and endeavour in vain
to trace between the six climates any rigorous lines of
demarcation.

In the low lands, facing India and the boiling caldron, the
mangrove concentrates the vapours. But, towards Oceania
and the region of the hundred isles, the cocoa-nut tree rises,
with its foot in the emerald wave, and its crest lightly rocking
in the fresh full breeze.

The palm is here of little value. Above its bamboos and
gum-trees Java wears a magnificent girdle of forest; a forest
wholly composed of teak, the oak of oaks, the finest wood in
the world, indestructible teak. It boasts also of a gigantic
plane, the superb *liquidambar*.

Here every kind of human food, and all the provisions of

* Bunsen, "Gaz des Volcans."

the five worlds, superabound. The rice and maize, the figs and bananas of India, the pears of China, the apples of Japan, flourish in company with the peach, the pine-apple, and the orange of Europe—ay, and who would believe it?—even with the strawberry, which multiplies its growth along the banks of the streams.

All this is the innocence of Nature. But side by side with it prevails another and a more formidable world : that of the higher vegetable energies, the plants of temptation, the seducing and the fatal, which double the enjoyment while shortening the duration of life.

To-day they reign throughout the earth, from one pole to the other. They make and unmake nations. The least of these terrible spirits has wrought a greater change in the globe than any war. They have implanted in man the vol-canic fires, and a soul—a violent spirit—which is indefinable, which seems not so much a human thing as a creature of the planet. They have effected a revolution which, before all, has changed our idea of time. Tobacco kills the hours and renders them insensible. Coffee shortens them by the stim-ulus it affords the mind ; it converts them into minutes. Thus, Time is dead, and to-morrow we shall have lived.

Foremost among the intoxications of care let us name alcohol. Eight species of sugar, which thrive in Java, abun-dantly supply this source of delirium, of forcible feebleness. Not less abundantly flourishes tobacco, the herb of dreams, which, with its misty vapours, has enshrouded the world.

But, happily, Java also produces immense supplies of its antidote, coffee. It is this which contends against tobacco, and supplies the place of alcohol. The small island of Java alone furnishes a fourth of all the coffee drunk by man ; and a coffee of very superior quality, when it has been sufficiently dried, without any fear of reducing its weight.

It is the evil quality of coffee, however, to weaken the stomach, which is man's renovator and restorer. It subtilizes too much ; it undermines and enervates the aphrodisiac powers. In burning regions, where the strength of the climate or the facility of sensual enjoyment incessantly appeals to the passions—where, under a twofold fire, man melts, and exhausts himself—he calls to his assistance those temporary regenerators, the spices. These acrid stimulants, which scorch the mouth and set on fire the entrails, revive him only to devour him. Formerly Java and its neighbouring islands were only known as spice-islands, and also as abounding in violent drugs and medicinal poisons. Frightful stories were circulated of its deadly plants, whose juice was a mortal venom ; of its Bohon-upas, whose lightest touch was instant death.

He who would fain see the East in all the fulness of its magical, voluptuous, and sinister forces, should explore the great bazaars of Java. There the curious jewels wrought by the cunning Indian hand are exposed to the desires of woman, temptation, and the cost of pleasure. There, too, another seductive agency may be seen : the vegetable fury of the burning and scorching plains which is so eagerly sought after—the exalted perfumes of terrible herbs and flowers which as yet have not been named. Marvellous and profound the night, in its sweet repose, after the violent heats of the day ! But be cautious in your enjoyment of it : as it grows old, you breathe death.

Take note of this : The peculiarity which gives to those brilliant bazaars so funereal an effect is, that all the thronging crowds are dusky, with dark complexions, and all the animals are black. The contrast is singular in this land of dazzling light. The heat seems to have burned up everything, to have tinted each object with shadow. The little horses which gallop past you seem but a flash of darkness.   The buffaloes, slowly arriving, loaded with fruit and flowers—the most brilliant gifts of life—all wear a livery of bluish black.

I am unwilling at this hour to stray too far, or to ramble in the higher grounds, lest I should meet with the black panther, whose green eyes illumine the darkness with a terrific glare.   And—who knows ?—the superb tyrant of the forest, the black tiger, may have commenced its midnight prowl ; that formidable phantom which the Malays of Java believe to be the Spirit of Death.

PART THE SECOND.

———♦♦———

I.

ZONES OF PEACE:

THE PRAIRIES.

"THE struggle for existence!" (Darwin.) This grand and simple formula will inaugurate a new era in natural history. It expresses with wonderful force the violent competition which prevails among myriads of beings (plants and animals), all interested in living: cruel and yet innocent; killing others to preserve themselves.

A struggle, say I, and an innocent struggle; which, inasmuch as it secures the equilibrium and harmony of Nature and her internal peace, is not in truth a struggle, but rather an exchange—a rotation (*roulement*). Under the Tropics the movement is accelerated, and becomes infinitely rapid.* Each creature has its hour, and enjoys it; its share of the elements, and seizes upon it. There is no retardatory power—no reprieve

---

* Thus was created an art—that of profiting by the struggle. Against the productive fury of a too potent land—which, out of deadly vegetation, in a moment engenders forests—India has ingeniously bethought itself of the war of plants. In the spice-grounds a single herb insinuates itself—the lalang—whose power of encroachment is terrific. Nothing can withstand it. It would choke up everything if men had not discovered its sworn enemy, the gambir, a herb of still more terrible character. Like a lion let loose upon a tiger, the gambir seizes on the lalang, exterminates, annihilates it. It is a dangerous ally. But, fortunately, it perishes, exhausted by its victory, and serves as aliment for the rescued soil.

to preserve that which another demands. Minute after minute each one exclaims, " It is my turn! " Set the wheel spinning —let the grindstone revolve. It is a dazzling spectacle : a torrent of sparks shines and passes. And these are *lives*. But the human spark, the Mind, while passing, contemplates.

Here, in the West, the wheel turns less swiftly, the struggle is less furious ; and we enjoy a little more time as witnesses of it. Organic beings here have less need of this internecine destruction : therefore, in the European climates the spectacle is not so grand, but far more gentle. Our plants are less furious in their wars and hatreds : they tolerate each other, and in their mutual forbearance show a higher courtesy. Sometimes they huddle together closely, and choke themselves in the plain and on the humid bank ; but in the higher ground they open out their ranks, and even extend their support to one another from the meadow to the forest.

That simple word *meadow*,—who will understand it out of Europe ? Undoubtedly our meadow-plants are met with in the torrid climates, where they climb the mountain heights ; but yet they are of a very different character—hard, wild, and fibrous. While here, in Europe, what is softer in character than the meadow ?

It has only one rival—the thick, green, velvety carpet made by the mosses. The bare foot of the tenderest woman, of the little child, feels that it is still tenderer than itself, and lovingly caresses it. Its verdure charms the eye. It is at one and the same time gay and sombre—so perfectly smooth and uniform ! When closely examined, we detect in it a world of miniature plants, united for mutual protection, and nourishing others, which are miniatures on a still smaller scale.

If these were stronger, or grew taller, developing from

A PASTORAL LANDSCAPE AT COUR, NEAR LAUSANNE.

mosses into herbs, they would put themselves under the patronage of those noble giants, the Gramineæ, a forest of which we call *sward* or *turf.* The Gramineæ form an incomparable family. Among plants they are the very lightest, their flower flying away with the wind : on the other hand, they are the most important, for they form the food of man. They protect and educate a world of slender plants, destined to play an important part. They harbour, shelter, and prepare the diminutive forest, which will eventually expand into *the* Forest. Yonder powerful tree, with his burden of a hundred years, is very fortunate in having once been the humble companion of the Gramineæ. The sweet little sisters tended and cherished him among them, and saved him from the gale. What would have been his fate had he begun life under the dense shadow of his father, deprived of air and sunshine ?

He has repaid them amply for their tender care ; for now, grown tall and vigorous, he defends and guards them in his turn, and shelters them against the tempests.

An amiable world of mutual succour, of brotherly hospitality ! Mosses, herbs, plants, and bushes,—all are animated by the same spirit of ready sociability, tolerance, and gentleness. We perceive its diffusion from meadow to forest, and from forest to mountain ; we rise in an atmosphere of calm towards a tranquil sphere, where we shall discover, notwithstanding its apparent poverty, certain unknown principles of life.

. I direct my searching glances towards those favoured spots where sunshine and shadow succeed each other in felicitous alternation — towards those thrice-blessed slopes where all healthful life is grouped in order.

And here I see those indigenous plants which once spoke of the future—the vervain and the mistletoe,—plants which defy death. I see, too, the domestic herbs, such as the salvia, which was a great favourite with my father, and in the Middle Ages held a high reputation. I see my cherished perfumes, a hundred times more wholesome than the sugared and equivocal odours of the tropics—as beneficial to the brain as the intoxicating scents of those exotics are dangerous. Ours— rosemary, thyme, marjoram, of mild and homely aspect—are all legends of love ; are the histories of that passion which renders sorrow so sweet, and draws tears from happy eyes (*qui dulcem curis miscet amaritiem*).

The curative virtues of our indigenous plants are easily explained. They embody our very soul, our tenderest and most grateful recollections; they received all our confidences; they are in harmonious sympathy with our blood, our heart, our temperaments. We, the children of temperate and inter- mediate zones, derive a far greater benefit from them than from their analogues, their kindling sisters. That violent pharmacy which was the birth of ferocious times—of the mili- tary age, when the surgeon's knife was everything — that "medicine of death" which acted by sudden cataclysms (*qui va par coups d'état*), preferred them as so many brutal energies of expeditious operation. They healed the black and the yellow races—men of different climates, of different constitu- tion, of habits and regimen wholly opposed to ours, and afflicted by very different maladies. What do I conclude from this fact? That if they saved *them* here, in a temperate clime, they would kill me. Of this their potency assures me.

The dangerous flora of the tropics has imposed upon us its doses, where in an atom an infinity of force is concentrated. The effect is the opposite of all true medicine, whose purpose is to strengthen the weak. But, on the contrary, tropical nature shortens their days, and centres all its joy and its triumph in promoting a rapid succession of animated beings— in rendering swifter the incessant passage, and accelerating the revolution of the wheel of life.

My meadow is not the uniform velvety sward, the smooth mown turf, of an English park, where the tiny herbage, con- tinually shorn and repressed, can never enjoy the brief season of love, the moment of happiness, the instantaneous existence which the ephemera inherits. Daily crushed back in its upward growth, it creeps so close to the earth that it loses all likeness to a plant; it ceases to be aught but a thread in a splendid carpet, a fine point tending towards the light. The

pitiless scythe decapitates it. It is a sad object of pity : our
glances wander from it, and stray more eagerly towards the
wild, free, happy meadow, loaded with flowers. This, in
truth, is a small undulating sea, which goes and comes as the
breeze flows and ebbs. The agriculturist himself, who looks
upon it only as fodder, profits by it, and watches his hour —
the hour when the plant, rich with a twofold burden of love
and growing maternity, yields up at once its fecundity and its
aroma.

We plunge up to our knees in the meadows, in the flowering herbage of their gentle slopes. The grasses with their
floating blossoms, the gilded melilots, the crimson trefoils,
the tiny violet crane's-bills, the orobe with its blood-red clus-
ters, simulate the shrub — imitate in miniature the virgin
forest—and as they struggle under your footsteps, exhale a
grateful fragrance.

These flowers, whose foliage often seems gifted with wings,
are the aristocrats, the rulers, the haughty "dames" of the
meadow. In the hedgerows winds the scarlet periwinkle,
wearing a dainty wreath. In copses where the waters of
spring-time abound in little torrents, flourishes the great
myosotis. In less humid shades blooms the veronica, whose
azure eyes fascinate us, despite of its innocence, its clearness,
and its intensity : it resembles a spirit speaking to the human
soul.

Since we possess in our own lands such a wealth of delicate flowers in harmony with our dispositions, and so subtly
interpreting our European nature, why do we roam over the
whole earth in quest of decorations for our gardens ?

An immensely important fact in the last half century has
changed the face of our Europe—the sudden, reckless, and
uncontrolled invasion of all the exotic floras. The acacia
came before I was born. During my childhood, and at a

time of great desolation, I witnessed the introduction of the melancholy hortensia; in my youth, of the vulgar dahlia; in my manhood, of the fuchsia, and, simultaneously, of a hundred thousand plants. Many have already degenerated. Some, which in their native habitats were of exquisite delicacy, nourished here by manure and fattening soils, have grown rude and bold, and are now wholly ornamental, and suitable only for coarser decorative purposes. To the true French flora—which, though somewhat scanty, it is true, was charmingly graceful, and the lawful spouse of the French *esprit*— have succeeded these concubines, which the cultivator endeavours to develop in size, and to invest in those noisy colours approved by the barbarous taste of the present age. Our enormous parterres, loaded and overloaded, remind one of the heavy, gaily-coloured shawls which have destroyed the genuine Cashmere, and brutalized the arts of the East.

The seasons fail in their due effect—their deep and native poetry—because troubled by the unexpected apparitions of strange flowers, which often come at inopportune times; are ignorant of the periods of our year, and, for example, beam gaily and smilingly in the melancholy moods of autumn. The time is wan and pathetic; but the antipodean flora thinks it is spring, and vexes our souls with its bravery of colour.

The eye, nevertheless, accustoms itself to their fantastic conceit, as the ear becomes habituated to brazen instruments; and thus our ruder senses embrutify the soul, for a certain kind of pleasure which is without taste and without memories.

If Rousseau had been as weary as we are of these exotics, he would not have exclaimed, after an absence of thirty years, " Ah, I recognize the periwinkle !"

Surely a more artistic age will come, when these intrusions shall no longer force themselves upon us, as they now do, with eager and abrupt impertinence. We shall no longer admit a plant without knowing something of its relationships; of the sister-plants which surround it, and form its companions; and even, as far as possible, of all the great local harmonies by which it is encircled. Removed from these, the most beautiful may become ridiculous. The acacia, a charming tree, with its exotic mien and airy foliage, often produces but a very poor effect when contrasted with the impressive gravity of our trees of the North.

FELLING OAKS IN FONTAINEBLEAU FOREST.

A serious matter for France is the decadence of the oak. Who can see without melancholy the utilitarian trees which are taking its place in the woods of Fontainebleau? The meagre, shadowless pine, in whose shade no herbage can thrive—decorating winter with an artificial spring— is but a poor successor to the age-long umbrageousness of that king of the forest which knew and sheltered our forefathers.

How dignified and solemn were the ancient tribes of the

trees and plants of Gaul ! They were connected by close ties
of friendship and relationship.   Of kith and kin among themselves, they were also akin to us.   They knew and expressed
our thoughts, and spoke to us according to our needs.   If in
seasons of trial we went forth among the oaks, they taught
us lessons of energetic resolution.   With all their apparent
roughness, they had a tender welcome for the sorrowful.   The
afflicted saw them—and not without being consoled—in the
embraces of the ivy, in the friendly clasp of the hundred-
pointed holly, which the sombre splendour of its leaves and
the superb winter-purple of its berries invest with so much
loveliness.   Noble teachings of the royalties of grief—of the
strong and serious beauties of a soul contending with and
triumphing over Fate !

II.

THE FORESTS.

THE tree wails and sighs, moaning with a human voice. About 1840 our French soldiers in Algeria, when felling a great number of vigorous trunks, were deeply moved and almost terrified by their groans. And even when untouched they are always grieving, always lamenting their destiny. These sounds have been attributed to the wind, but frequently result from an internal circulation —which is more irregular than we generally suppose—from the impediments which check the progress of their sap, from the dreams of their vegetable soul.

For that the tree possessed a soul—dim and imperfect, perhaps, but a soul like that of every other animated being— the ancients never doubted. It was the creed of humanity for ten thousand years, until the Scholastic Age transformed all Nature into stone. The arrogant conception that man alone can feel and think, that this vast world of creatures is nothing but a world of dumb "stocks and stones," is a modern paradox of the Middle Ages. Science to-day teaches a contrary lesson, and approximates very closely to the creed of antiquity. Every being, it tells us—even the most rudiment-

ary organism—possesses the gift of labour and effort ; the
knowledge that it may ensure and develop its life ; the power,
to use Charles Darwin's phrase, of "selection;" and sometimes a highly ingenious faculty of profiting by the means
which conduce to this result. Each is endowed with its individual capacity of being, and growing, and continuously
renewing its existence.

In towns and schools a vain and empty wit may laugh at
this idea of the tree's soul ; but men make no jest of it in the
desert, or in the cruel climates of the North or South, where
the tree acts as a saviour, and plainly appears the friend
of man.

The Scandinavians believed that primeval man was at first
a tree, which created the universal life, imbibing it from earth,
and heaven, and night.

Has this worship ceased ? Never wholly. A recent
traveller found it existing in the Caucasus, and Chardin met
with it in Persia. At Ispahan, very recently, the plane-tree
was held in reverence : it was loaded with gifts—just as in
Herodotus we read of Xerxes adorning and embellishing his
plane-tree from Asia Minor.

A tree in the desolate steppes—in their monotonous
infinity ! Oh, then a tree becomes a friend ! On the shores
of the Caspian, for three or four hundred leagues, one sees
nothing, one encounters nothing, but midway an isolated and
solitary tree. It is the love and worship of every passing
wayfarer. Each one offers it a something ; and the very Tar-
tar, in default of any other gift, will snatch a hair from his
beard or his horse's mane.*

Every idea must be judged by its fruits. Error never
creates. The idea which gives birth to a world is, beyond all

* See the beautiful and curious Atlas by M. B. Zaleski.

THE TREE IN THE DESERT OF TARTARY.

doubt, *the truth*. This touching and infinitely prolific conception of the brotherhood of the tree has created, enriched,
and dowered the ancient world. It alone bestowed upon that
world the astonishing agricultural power which made and
remade it; which, through a long series of wars and misfortunes of every kind, effected its perpetual resurrection.

The child speaks in legends. In the still young world
two superb legends taught that the tree is a soul:

The *Tree of Life* (this is the Persian idea), a soul beneficent and prolific, which gives birth to the copious springs, the
four rivers flowing towards the four quarters of the world;

And the *Tree of Grief* (this is the Egyptian and Syrian
idea), a captive, vulnerable, and suffering soul, imprisoned
beneath the bark.

The two beliefs had precisely the same effect—in produc-
ing a great reverence for the tree, a religious care for its preservation, a sentiment of vast tenderness towards it. And
the tree has recognized this effect. It has really created and

multiplied our water sources, has refreshed and enriched the Earth.

The Persian idea, no less true than sublime, is this : that the cypress, the pyramidal tree whose point imitates the flame, is a mediator between earth and heaven. It is an incontestable fact that it attracts and collects the too scanty dews and vapours of hot climates. The large-leaved trees—such, for instance, as the plane, which is also held in high honour by the Asiatics—absorb them thoroughly. The one draws down the cloud from heaven, and the other bestows it upon earth. One may feel certain that in their vicinity the treasure so ardently desired, so eagerly sought after, *water*, will flow forth, though at first in a feeble and almost imperceptible rill. But wait! From neighbouring trees comes another streamlet to the succour of the former. Others follow ; until a hundred water-courses are developed, like a network of irrigation, to give life and abundance to the land.

When we read in Herodotus that Persia was traversed by forty thousand subterranean canals, we are astonished, and inclined to doubt. But Sir John Malcolm, in 1800, discovered a far larger number. Twelve thousand have left their traces in a single province, and still bear witness to the marvellous richness of this garden of the East.*

The Egyptian idea is vigorous and impressive. Man, in his wretchedness and crushing toil, returning to his home, told the tale of his sorrows to his tree—poured out his soul into the flower or trunk. Why does the discreet mimosa shut itself up so closely at evening? It is to keep secret the human heart intrusted to it. Heaven! if we should foully cut down the plant, what would become of that heart? So he acquaints none but his dearly-beloved wife with the name

* See my " Bible de l'Humanité."—*Author's Note.*

of the tree in which it is enshrined. And this tree becomes
for her a beloved being, her very god, a god both dead and
alive; and often through her tears she has seen that it, too,
has wept.

I know not a more pathetic story than that of Isis dis-
covering her spouse in a tree, used for one of the columns of
a Syrian palace. I know of no history more affecting than
that of the innocent Satou, falsely accused, imprisoned beneath the bark of a Persean laurel by his wicked wife, eventually becoming glorified, and a Pharaoh; and, for his sole
revenge, placing her on the throne by his side.

The captivities and commerce of slaves, and kidnapping
of children, gave rise to numerous myths and pathetic legends.
Adonis, barbarously mutilated and immolated, survives in a
pine of Byblos, where he weeps eternally. In Phrygia
it is Athis, a tender and charming child, who is heard be-
wailing his fate in the flowering almond. Happily the tree
opens and lets him free. Ah, what joy! Woman, in a
delirium of rapture, bursts into tears; the crowd go mad.
You may judge whether the tree, surrounded with all these
legends, was not loved, and cared for, and caressed in Asia.

The oaks of Dodona still live and speak. But this religion of myth and fable had, at an early period, lost its
hold upon the Greeks. They laughed to see Xerxes enamoured of a plane tree. Despite their graceful story of
Daphne and Cyparis, they held the tree in little honour,
and bestowed but a scant attention upon it. Hence their
springs diminished, and the fertility of their soil decreased.
Then came Moslem and Christian, with a profound disdain
for nature. The forest perishes, and the water dries up.
The Mediterranean, all along its arid shores, exhibits a bald,
bare desert.

The mid-epoch of time, which closes antiquity and opens

up the Middle Ages, an epoch of peculiar pathos, is represented by Virgil. In his poetry the forest is ever dreamy, melancholy, and full of visions. It seems the parent of the Celtic forest. The mistletoe of immortality, which, in the latter, is cut by our Sibyls, by its golden reflection reminds us of the golden bough of Virgil.*

What did this bough? It evoked life. It was equal in potency to the caduceus, which conducted the dead. It led back the departed soul, constrained it to render itself up to our regrets, to reappear before us, at least in vision, to listen to our prayers and our sighs, to answer us, and again to weep with us.

Ah, affecting miracle! But if it be so powerful, would that it could more easily arrest here upon earth the flight of the winged soul, which, when it seeks to escape us, we vainly endeavour to retain in our embrace. In the silent sorrows, the dark forebodings, which we hide from the beloved one, who has not echoed from the depths of his heart the prayer of Virgil: "Oh, that I could find thee, O branch, in the forest!"

A vast forest! A sea of leaves and dreams. How long

* [The golden bough which admitted the adventurer to the region of the Shades, and which the Sibyl revealed to Æneas (*Virgil*, "*Æneid*," lib. vi.):—

> "Deep in a mass of leafy growth,
> Its stem and foliage golden both,
> A precious bough there lurks unseen,
> Held sacred to the infernal queen:
> Around it bends the whole dark grove,
> And hides from view the treasure-trove.
> Yet none may reach the shades without
> The passport of that golden sprout;
> For so has Proserpine decreed
> That this should be her beauty's meed.
> One plucked, another fills its room,
> And burgeons with like precious bloom.
> Go, then, the shrinking treasure track,
> And pluck it with your hand;
> Itself will follow, nothing slack,
> Should Fate the deed command:
> If not, no weapon man can wield
> Will make its dull reluctance yield."

Professor Conington's Translation, pp. 178, 179.]

13

I wandered in its glades! How was my youth spent, if not in gloomy seeking? up to the day when at last I found and seized that golden branch, with which I have summoned departed nations from the world of shadows.

It is the glory of my life to have resuscitated so many forgotten and uncomprehended heroes, to have been the instrument of recovering justice for them, and the redresser of the wrongs inflicted upon them by destiny. This idea returns to me in the sad hours of night, and strengthens my soul. But have I secured without sacrifice this power of evoking the vanished world? How did I obtain this branch? By too great a love of death. In my youth I dwelt among the graves. I was never weary of summoning the spirit from its shades.

And now the time has come when death is less pleasant to me, when I bid it " wait ! "

Have I spoken thus on my own behalf? Yes; for myself. For still I love.

Nevertheless I have accomplished much. So far as regards. my works and labours I have lived three lives. 1 would willingly accept the stroke of destiny, if among these thoughts another did not intrude, another anxiety in reference to the all-vulnerable point which fills my heart with trembling.

O colossal Forest! where of old I discovered the potent bough which revived the worlds, will you not tell me in what remote corner you preserve for me the tiny herb of safety?

You possess, I know it, the secret of life; and to all you give it. Your innumerous leaves, unconquerable in their aspiration, by condensing the floating waters, and pouring them forth upon our fields, fertilize the earth. The dark tree, which men believe funereal, does, on the contrary, attract, with its subtle organs, the live electric cloud, which makes the joy of our globe. Strong in the powerful sap which incessantly

restores your vigour—in the resinous gold which preserves
and heals your frame—you see man pass away before you,
while prolonging your own span of existence to a thousand
years. Yonder tree has flourished a hundred centuries.
More lasting and more solid than all the porphyries of Egypt,
it beheld the first of the Pharaohs, and heard the opening
strains of the Rig-Veda.*

Tell me, I pray you, O venerable priests, O mighty physicians, the mystery of immortality. The rites of a complete
initiation may be found in you, in the forests of the mountain.
As we ascend, we at every step throw off something of the
wretchedness of our lower world.

---

* [The *Rig-Veda* is the first and principal of the four Vedas (from the Sanscrit *rid*, to
know), on which the early religious faith of the Hindus was founded. It is also the oldest
of the four, and by most authorities is believed to be the most ancient literary document in
existence. Like the other Vedas, it contains two separate divisions: a *Sanhitâ*, or book of
Mantras (hymns); and a *Brâhmana*, which may roughly be described as a rubric or ritual,
partly explanatory and partly directorial. According to Colebrooke, a *Mantra* (from *man*, to
think) is an expression of praise, thanksgiving, or adoration towards the deity. When em-
bodied in a metrical form, and intended to be recited aloud, it was called *R'ich* (*r'ich*, praise)
—whence the word *R'igveda.—See Colebrooke's " Miscellaneous Essays."*]

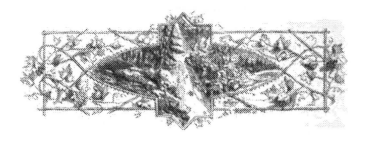

III.

THE AMPHITHEATRE OF THE FORESTS.

N the lowermost terrace of the grand amphitheatre of the mountains bloom the lofty chestnuts, forming a venerable vestibule to the forest itself.

Patriarchs are these, and animated by a strong spirit of kinship. Less ambitious than fertile, the central tree is wide of girth ; and though it does not lift its head to any towering height, it flings off, in every direction, five or six sturdy saplings, the happy progeny which compensates it for the wounds it suffers and for the losses it undergoes. Wrinkled and aged as it may be, this parent-trunk still flourishes greenly, and rejoices at the sight of its children. The latter cling to it strongly ; yea, so strongly that frequently they are soldered to its trunk, and parent and offspring grow strangely intermingled.* Hence results a curious and sometimes prodigious creature, which assumes in your eyes a monstrous aspect. Yet it is nothing more than a natural excess, an excess of mutual attachment. The young have found themselves unable to part from the tender mother who so long exhausted herself for their advantage.

* [The reader may be reminded here of the famous chestnut tree of Mount Etna - the Tree of the Hundred Horses (*Castagno di Cento Cavalli*)—the entire girth of whose trunks at three feet above the ground is about 190 feet.]

The chestnut demands air and space. It thrives best in
open clearings. Its leaves, all green with life, and extended
like the human palm, assume apparently a speaking form.
These beautiful hands, as far as they may, seek the light,
expand themselves towards it, imbibe it greedily. But though
in the depth of their abundant foliage they grow superim-
posed upon one another, they are careful to take such order
as will avoid any mutual injury, are careful not to plunge into
depths of gloom, not to conceal the sun. The chestnut loves
a soil of granite, or of calcareous sand, whose warm radiation
it can feel with far-extending roots. It does not dread a
lava soil, to which it takes while it is still heated, penetrating
into its black entrails. With the shining scoriæ it heaps
around itself a furnace which reverberates the warmth. On
the extinct volcanoes of Auvergne it lodges in the very
crater, and even in their yawning mouth, embellishing them
with its verdurous youth.

As it loves volcanoes, so is it partial to ruins. Near
Chiavenna, and at the bottom of its genial valley, a wood of
chestnut trees has taken possession of the frightful landslip
of Monte Conto. They have established themselves upon,
and they mightily flourish over, the sixty feet of *débris* which
now cover the village of Pleurs.

The real dense forest commences, at a higher level, with
the beech. If the shades cast by its thick foliage are too
gloomy, in compensation its aspect is gay and laughing, and
bids you trust yourself to its care, penetrate beneath its lofty
vault, and ascend with it the mighty mountains. You find it
everywhere, from the Apennines to Norway. You meet with
this *fagus* of Virgil, which sheltered Tityrus,* in the lands of

---

* ["Tityre, tu patulæ recubans sub tegmine fagi" (*Virgil*, "*Eclog.*"). It is doubted, however, by many of the commentators, whether the *fagus* of Virgil can be properly identified
with our modern beech.]

the North.   Nowhere is it of loftier stature or blither mien
than in the cloudy isles of Denmark, the native country of
Hamlet.   It is the child of Europe, and in its nature the
most evenly balanced of all trees.   It flourishes in any of our
climates.

Displaying such a wealth of leaves, it is compelled to be
greedy.   Food it seeks on every side, and in all directions it
stretches forth its roots.   And yet it does not play the tyrant
towards other trees.   It permits the growth of the ash on the
brink of the torrents, whose vapours also nourish its second
brother, the beautiful lime.   In sandy soils the birch blooms
by its side, and the aspen, the ever-moving aspen, whose pale
foliage tones with its melancholy the uniform liveliness of the
beech.

It smiles in the forests, as on the blazing hearth it smiles,
where, crackling and sparkling, it emits a cherry-coloured
flame.   From the beech springs all the bravery of the peasant; his rustic *chaussure*, his *sabots**—the inspiring subject
of one of the most beautiful songs of the South.

A complaint against the beech is the richness of its foliage.
With its heavy shades it shuts out day, and lends no loveliness to earth.   Few plants or flowers can thrive beneath its
canopy.   The fern and the white spirea almost alone resign
themselves to its humid shadows.   From this cause it suffers
in itself.   Its shade *makes* shade; a shade dense, multifold,
obscured, incessantly seeking the day.   By the configuration
of its branches you may plainly perceive how they strive
after air and light.   You see that they yearn and aspire
towards it.   Its appearance is that of a person in restless
movement.

Hence is it, undoubtedly, that with all its susceptibility
to cold, it nevertheless ventures to seek the higher levels
that it may breathe more easily.   The result is a series of

---

* [Wooden shoes.]

adventures. The austere and haughty mountain, in its caprices of rigour, represses that audacity of the beech which
leads it to mount too high. Though it waits until May
before venturing to put forth its leaves, it has often to
undergo some rough treatment. The night of May 24, 1867,
was terrible throughout the Alpine region. On the 23rd the
tempest burst over the Lake of Geneva. Frost came in the
night, and immediately upon it a fierce sun. The trees,
which at that season are very delicate, and fermenting with
sap, had expected no such mischance. The walnut was
burnt up until it became a black spectre. The beech turned
red, and assumed its autumnal garb—a splendid garb, it is
true, crimsoning the mountain with those beautiful glowing
tints so justly dear to the artist.

But to have been arrested in the full current of its sap,
suddenly checked in the fruition of its love, was a hard fortune for it. It lapsed into dreams, and appeared to find the
summer insufferably protracted until its waking-time in August. And even in August, what did it gain? The flower?
No. Love? No; but the consolation of a few leaves to
assure it that it was still alive.

The chestnut, at a lower level, and, in higher grounds,
the resinous trees, have better chances, and enjoy a kind of
immortality. The chestnut, incessantly renewing its growth,
and surrounded by its children—mingled with whom, and
cherished by their young life, it lives—has no reason to die.
The firs and the pines are protected against the cold and the
injuries of the wind by the resin which closes up their pores.
Their economical existence lasts indefinitely, for they expand
but slightly, and waste not their strength upon their foliage
(the fir preserves its leaves for ten years). But the beech is
very prodigal. Flinging abroad every spring an ocean of
leafiness, it pours out its life without thought. To misfortunes and severe wounds it has nothing to oppose but its

intensity of being, and the robust strength of its bark, which heals with astonishing readiness. Always young, always gay, it laughs at fate.

The vigorous life of the mountain, the healthy existence of its broad cinctures, maintains in friendship two trees of

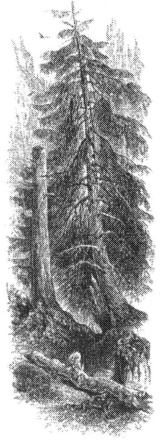

great sociality but widely different character — the green beech and the black fir. The beech laughs, the fir weeps : it matters not. They come together on the same heights. Sometimes they are found intermingled, but more generally as neighbours. They share the domain between them. The beech grows on the southern side, the fir on the northern, on the sunless slopes, plunging down even into the low damp valley, gloomy with its shroud of mist.

It is the great white fir (*abies pectinata*) I speak of, a giant, attired in twofold livery of woe ; white within and black without. The snow rests on the long sombre combs of its far-stretching and vigorous branches ; and if they bend beneath the weight, and groan in their double grief, it does but increase the solemn character of the tree.

THE WHITE FIR.

Is it an immense phantom? There are moments when one would think so. Bristling at times with icy crystals, it resembles a formidable bird expanding its wings of menace. In the countries of the South men look upon it as funereal, but in the North they love it. On the shores of the Baltic, from the sands of Prussia to the Siberian deserts, it affords a lasting refuge and an enduring consolation. Stooping its branches to the very ground, mysterious in its protecting night, it becomes the revered home of beings which could not live under the open sky. In those severe climates how many would perish without its shelter! Mute as the tomb, uniform, infinite, ever resembling itself, it supplies a complete concealment to the wretched wanderer. Safe within its arms, like the squirrel, man will travel seven hundred leagues from fir to fir. The species, which faces the south, and thitherward turns its branches, acts as a guide to the fugitive, and serves him as a compass. How often has it concealed, conducted, and saved the Siberian exile!

Here it is the saviour and true guardian of the mountain, in whose protection the two great labourers, the fir and the beech, both unite. It is there they achieve their splendid mission, the real and proper function of the forest.

You must remember that at great elevations, and in the narrow table-lands, the forest dwindles almost to nothingness; but that at our present stand-point, at the mountain base, or midway up its slopes, it is still of immense extent, and its labour prodigious.

This labour is twofold. First, it receives, arrests, and breaks up the floods from the upper peaks, which would otherwise devastate the mountain.

On the other hand, it incessantly enriches its soil and repairs its losses. It accumulates its wealth of dead leaves upon its surface. It fixes its masses of floating matter. Like

a powerful organ of aspiration, it arrests on their passage the
fogs and the dense mists, and all that in conjunction with them
circulates in the thick atmospheric medium. It summons and
controls these aërial navigators, compelling them to descend.
In this respect the fir acts admirably, as with its pointed
leaves it attracts the cloud. The beech has an absorbent
power over the entire surface of its foliage. How gorgeous
the spectacle when, for a moment, the sun shoots its slanting
ray through the misty mass! You might say the forest
smoked; and, in truth, it does respire.

How pleasant it is to walk in the shade of the firs!
Always clean and free from obstacle, the ground underneath
them affords a noble idea of purity. What can be purer
than the air, with its healthful odours? How soothing a
sense of tranquillity gradually steals upon you! Be not
surprised at it. These trees were not without their value
even in the primeval ages, when they drew off upon their
points the electrical excess which would otherwise have con-
vulsed the world. This is the mission they still discharge.
Our internal tempests, our empty agitations are calmed in
their midst. If the forest is gloomy, if, as men too frequently
say, "light visions haunt every leaf, and cling to every
bough," the dull dreams of the lower world at least are
absent, the ominous phantoms which unwholesome vapours
engender. Life by ascending not only becomes more elastic,
but freer from delusions. The very night grows clear and
translucent. Through the dark dense trees it reveals its
coruscating star, its smiling spheres, the divine light, and the
reality.

I know not how to define the lively energy which takes
possession of us in these higher regions. We lose sight of
the great melancholy fir; for the air becomes too cold, and

AMPHITHEATRE OF FORESTS ABOVE THE LAKE OF GENEVA.

its long arms are too great to battle with the convulsions of the upper air. A more robust tree is needed, with short branches, which will not require to bear so heavy a mass of snow—a courageous tree, a mountaineer, gorged with resin, completely penetrated and protected by it! Such is the picea, that hardy Alpine athlete, which struggles upwards to the most inaccessible steeps, and clings to the very edge of the precipices. It dreads nothing but the mists and humidity of the lower grounds. It will face the cold, but it seeks a wholesome air. With its four rows of stomata it greedily absorbs the sunshine. By climbing upward it gets rid of the strong, stimulating food of the inferior levels, the exciting influences of the fermented life. It enjoys a purer and loftier stimulus —that of the atmosphere and the light—and, at times, the summons of the Fœhn and the electricity of the storm.

The picea does not own the extended wings of the white fir. It sacrifices all extraneous branches, and enriches itself with foliage, which it wraps around every bough, darting and aspiring in every direction, and feeding it with nourishment and strength. All its thought is to rear itself aloft like a pillar, or like the tall mast of a vessel which, braving to-day the mountain gale, to-morrow shall brave the ocean.

These courageous trees lavish no outlay upon themselves —no luxury, no ornament. They have far different cares on the perilous declivities where they climb to the assault. The wind is icy cold, the rock is bare; but still they mount! They stretch abroad, and attach, as best they may, their meagre roots, and with difficulty attain a footing. It is by pressing closely to one another, by drawing up their serried ranks and legions, that they support themselves, and, at the same time, support the mountain.

In the crises of great inundations, the mountain without their assistance would be lost. It bursts open, it yawns

apart; and the furious waters, profiting by these clefts an
enlarging them, ruining and demolishing, pour headlong o
their desperate path towards the valley, where the picea
stand forward to arrest them.   You might imagine that yo
heard the mountain exclaiming
" My children, be firm!"

But lo! from above, a monste
avalanche of snow, and ice, an
rock, pell mell, starts forwar
with a frightful shock, and come
leaping from point to point.   Wo
to the piceas!   It is upon thei
the first fury of the awful tem
pest falls.   They shriek, the
crack.   One moment engulfed

THE FOREST SAVES THE VALLEY.

they have disappeared. Great Heaven, in what condition
shall we see them again? Overturned, with their roots in
the air, and miserably shattered! Oh, lamentable ruin!
However, with their pointed tops they have broken the
force of the blow, as was recently remarked in the Pyrenees,
near Barèges, where, indeed, the avalanche was something
more than a mass of snow. It was a downfall of ice-blocks,
which swept away everything. All the piceas perished, but
they saved the valley.

The resinous trees comprehend more than a genus or
family; they are a vegetable world, whose various forms record for our behoof the ages which have preceded our human
era. Born in the time of the ferns, the cycads, and the
equiseta, they continue to imitate them in certain species.
For example, the ephedra still fashions itself upon the equi-
setum, but by a system of joints attains a greater stature, and
instead of foliage is clothed in scales. The resinous giants,
such as the araucaria and the sequoia,* still astonish the earth

* [The *Sequoia gigantea*, or *Wellingtonia gigantea*, belongs to a genus of the *Taxodium*
family. It was originally discovered in California by a Mr. Dowd in 1852, and first scienti-
fically described by Dr. Lindley. In its full growth its dimensions are truly colossal; some
members of the genus attaining the stature of 450 feet, and a girth of 116 feet. At Calaveras,
in latitude 38° north and longitude 120° 10' west, at an elevation of 4370 feet, flourishes the
famous Mammoth Tree Grove, where, within an area of fifty acres, are found 103 trees of goodly
proportions, 20 of them exceeding 75 feet in circumference; and yet these are only saplings.
The largest tree now standing, "the Mother of the Forest," measures 90 feet in circuit at the
base, 69 feet at 20 feet from the ground, and attains a total height of 321 feet. A similar group
of trees was discovered at Mariposa in 1855. It comprises 300 trunks, and covers a triangular
area of between 400 and 500 feet. Six or seven miles from Frezno is another grove, including
about 500 trees of the same family.

> " Overhead up grew
> Insuperable height of loftiest shade,
> A sylvan scene; and, as the ranks ascend
> Shade above shade, a woody theatre
> Of stateliest view."

The *Araucaria imbricata*, or Chili pine, is a native of the Chilian Andes, on whose western
slopes the column-like trunk frequently soars to a height of 150 feet. Still loftier is the *Araucaria excelsa*, or Norfolk Island pine, a native of Norfolk Island and New Caledonia, which
with a trunk 20 feet in diameter, frequently attains an elevation of 220 feet.]

as she was astonished in her powerful youth, when her trees
were mountains. The sequoias of California, enormous in
girth, and 300 feet in height, are, as Douglas tells us, terrible
in their beauty. At the head-waters of San Antonio, on the
flanks of the Sierra Nevada, exist a hundred of these ancient
giants. One of them, when felled, was proved by its concentric rings to be three thousand years of age.*

They have belonged to every epoch, and they now thrive
in every climate. They accept the most diverse temperatures
and opposite situations. They are found among the cedars of
Libanus, the pines and the cypresses of the luminous East, the
firs of Norway, and the gloomy shades of the North.

In the southern hemisphere, the life of the resinous trees,
which is more concentrated in genial climates, has a very different character. Set free from the hard task of supporting
masses of snow, and enduring the pitiless strokes of the hurricane, they breathe more at ease. The araucaria of Brazil or
Chili bears a leaf like that of our tiny holly. The dammars†
of Amboyna and New Zealand, reeking with hot waters, may
well dilate their lungs. They cast off the thin needle-like form
of the conifers, amplify their foliage, and grow in height and
girth without restraint.

The true stoics are our resinous trees of the North. They
endure the sharpest trials by their power of self-concentration
and their heroic sobriety. It is by such means they have
prevailed over both space and time. Useful and beneficent,
and greatly profiting the world, they ask from it scarcely anything in return.

One is wholly unable to disembarrass oneself of an emo-

* [This may reasonably be doubted, and the best authorities do not estimate it as more
than twelve or fifteen hundred years old.]

† [The *Dammar*, or *Dammar Pine* (*Dammara*), is a conifer, distinguished by its broad
lanceolate, leathery leaves. There are various species, such as the Moluccan Dammar, and the
Kauri Pine of New Zealand.]

tion of gratitude and religious reverence when, wandering alone among the elevated pasturages of Switzerland, one encounters some of these venerable firs which for ages have been preserved as a refuge and a protection for the herd. One perceives in such localities the importance of the tree's mission. One feels that it is the friend and protector of all life. And well does every creature know it ; goats, and sheep, and lambs, and indolent cows, spontaneously resort to its shade to enjoy their repose, each perfectly well acquainted with its own *gogant*—(the name borne by these protecting trees in the Pays de Vaud). There they establish themselves in the summertime, and are at home. Near at hand the cascade murmurs. At different stages of the lofty tree buzzes and swarms a world of squirrels, insects, and birds. All around and about it, at a few paces distant, in the warm sunshine and defended from the wind, flourishes many a charming plant excluded from the fields, and harshly spurned by the labourer as a worthless herb. But the tree forbids nothing. It is the common father of all ; it is, as it were, the good genius of the land.

IV

DREAMS OF THE MOUNTAIN AND THE
FLOWERS.

" **L**ONG before I saw the Alps, my mind had cherished visions of the flowers blooming on their lofty summits, of their delicate and sublime flora.   These daughters of the light do not descend into the plain, or, if they descend, they die.   Therefore, to rise to *them*, to inspect them in their mysterious retreats, became for me, at an early age, a secret and ardent desire.

* * * * * * *

" All of us love flowers—all of us love their colours and perfumes.   But for my part I wanted something more ; I yearned to enter into communion with them, to grow acquainted with their very thoughts.   In my father's garden, it was one of my rare recreations, when a child, to hold converse with them.   They seemed to me little maidens—my younger comrades.   In a low voice I related to them my anxieties and principal grievances.   They listened with much attention ; but being very reserved and modest, said little in return for my confidences.   This mattered not ; I continued faithful to them. It was particularly in the long Sundays, during my mother's absence in the town, that we enjoyed together the greatest freedom of intercourse.   I had leisure then to observe their mode of life, their mute language, to enter into their character. One was active and an early riser; another, slow and indolent. Another, on a certain occasion, fell sick; I hastened to console it with a supply of water or of better mould, inquiring anxiously, 'What ailest thou?'[*]

"Later in life, when, after my marriage, I had a garden of mine own, perfect fireside peace, and, during the absences of my husband, long intervals of leisure, my plants, tended by my own hand only, spoke to me somewhat more freely. They informed me of all their little likes and dislikes, of the state of their health, their occasional fainting fits; in a word, even of their loves. In truth, they might have told me anything, for I should have made no ill use of their secrets. On the other hand, I felt confident in their tender discretion. I would have entrusted them with my dreams, if, in that sweet solitude of work and innocence, I had had time to dream. Where could you find a more natural confessor, or, as I believe, a better counsellor? Poetical and pure, they are nevertheless by no means romantic, but admirably matter-of-fact. However, my days were fully occupied. I was busy with my needle, my household, and my husband (especially during his absence). I had very little leisure even for reading.

"Ever by my side was the storm, the strife of human history, as represented by that great and ardent worker, my husband. Yet, in his extreme tenderness, he took good care to prevent my being mixed up with things so sad and terrible. He spared me the more painful facts, relating to me only what was grand and lofty. Thanks to this forethought of his, I remained myself; I remained young, continuing my childish life with those tiny lives which are the very embodiment of youth. By this he gained. Whatever the toil of the day, he was enabled in the evening to enter a gentler and fairer world; to learn what plant had newly flowered, and examine our

[*] Madame Michelet, "Mémoires d'une Enfant," 1867.

domestic animals, who never failed to make their appearance.

"In this manner we passed through the trials of '51, aggravated as they were by those of '93, whose history he was writing. While exhuming all those dead men and deeds, could he himself have lived without the help of our tender and timid struggle of Nature against History? In our bright wilderness of Nantes, she was present and enfolded him, though never disturbing him with her labours. On one of our saddest days I remember how an unexpected circumstance suddenly changed the current of our thoughts. A splendid blossom, falling from one of our great magnolias, had made its way triumphantly into our apartment, and reigned there mistress of the house. Despite the closed doors, it had invaded the most retired chambers with its penetrating fragrance, which is at once so powerful and so suave, and had intoxicated the atmosphere with a powerful perfume of love and life.

"As in spirit we grew more thoroughly united, how could we work apart? Our union from the first had been apparently profound and complete, yet it increased in completeness of sympathy, and daily became more perfect. I had gained somewhat of his own nature, of that flame which makes or remakes life. Mine was most animated about '56 and '57, in those years whose unparalleled heat (as our Master Schacht asserted) blessed the earth with a decade of fertility. And now behold me, with my feeble mind and mediocre power of expression,—me, who had never dreamed of engaging in composition,—behold me, one morning, pen in hand! But I wrote only for *him*—a few simple notes and unpretending outlines. Of nothing less, however, than my own soul, indistinct with Nature, blended with flowers, and birds, and all innocent things. It tempted him, and he followed in my steps. We

have since laboured side by side, and achieved that delightful journey—too rapid, however, and on too unresting wing—
represented by 'The Bird,' 'The Insect,' and 'The Sea.' They
have seized on the world's heart. Ah, I well know why!

"But I was not very strong, and continually underwent
relapses. I could not rely on a long life. I regretted only
that I was unable to impart to him what I had ever valued
most, what had ever been in my thoughts—my dreams on the
love of flowers. During an illness which I suffered in the
spring of '58, I attempted to write a few words on 'The Death
of Plants;' on that resigned end which gives them back, so
noiselessly and so gently, to the common Mother. In the
summer of '59, when residing on the balmy heaths, among the
odours of the immortelles, between the sea and the Gironde,
I would fain have essayed a beautiful theme—'The Flora of
the Dunes;' a charming subject, which from all time has
blended with the soul of that country-side. This soul animates
every legend which has been recited to me. It is the beautiful daughter of the king drowned in the great sea. But she
flowers again on the shore, and will for ever blossom in the
wild rosemary, full of perfume, of keen subtleness, of sadness,
and regret.

"In that beautiful and solemn vestibule of the Gironde,
what ideas rushed upon my mind! One, at least, I realized.
I gave to my husband (a contribution to 'La Femme,' which
he was then on the point of publishing) 'The Annual Cycle
of the Plant;' the succession of forms which it develops in
course of the year. The plant resembles a wife ever following closely in her husband's footsteps. Fresh in the spring-
time, and the delight of his eyes, in summer she supports
and tenderly nurses him; and when he grows fatigued in
autumn, elevates and inspires him, pouring out upon him joy,
repose, and forgetfulness.

"Nothing awakened more thoughtfulness in my mind than

our winters at Hyères, whither my husband removed me, to
ask of Nature a reprieve, an extension of life.   There, without
stirring from my chamber, I could see the five divisions of the
world in bloom.   The differences of climate disappeared.
Geography in this region is wholly suppressed, and put to the
rout.   It is an enormous Babel of flowers, which confounds
the brain.   One might describe it as the central point from
which Nature distributes plants to all the earth.

"Africa, for instance, is represented by gigantic palms,
loaded with golden fruit; Australia by the eucalyptus, which
in eight years attains a stature of one hundred feet.   But not
less triumphant is Europe, and even Northern Europe.   In
the narrow area of Hyères, the superb palm has all the appearance of an herb by the side of our ancient and majestic elms,
so youthful and so refined in their foliage, so unsurpassable
in gracefulness and a certain delicate austerity.

"This fresh image of the north in our African Provence
exercised a powerful influence upon me when a sudden flame
kindles all along this beautiful shore.   It is a marvellous scene
of faëry; the gardens, and the hedgerows of the driest and
most dusty highways, all break into blossom in a single night.
It is a veritable eruption—a volcanic outburst of flowers.   Yes;
but it is too much for me.   I long and I pray for grace."

V

DREAMS OF THE MOUNTAIN AND THE FLOWERS.

SWITZERLAND IN MAY 1867.

"THEREFORE we took flight, and passed into Switzerland. It is impossible to imagine a stronger contrast. One might have thought one had travelled five hundred leagues. We had never before visited it at so early a period of the year (towards the end of April); and therefore enjoyed the rare advantage of having the twelvemonth all before us, of being present at the complete evolution of the seasons, of watching the appearance of every plant at its proper hour in that magnificent procession which annually takes place. But it seemed in no hurry to commence. The 1st of May, that sweet time which has been sung by the poets of all nations as the festival of life, appeared grave, and reserved, and, I had almost said, reasonable.

"The prudent vines of Geneva and the Vaud as yet had not budded; they dreaded the return of severe weather. Upon the deep but somewhat hard azure of the beautiful lake hovered, in all their winter pomp, the magnificent range of snowy summits. It is thus that you ought to see the mountains transfigured in a hundred forms in the fantastic lustre of their glaciers, and their crystals, still maintaining a communication with their unbroken snows, living among them their grand solitary life, before the coming of the summer and its crowds of vulgar intruders.

"All this was so wise, so grave, that I felt myself in unison with the scene, and experienced, as it were, a profound tranquillity. Upon those still naked declivities, it seemed to me (after the grand tumult of the Provençal spring-time) that I heard not a single sound.

"Though we had a return of frost in May, the season strode onwards rapidly. In sheltered places, moreover, the vine made a wonderful progress. The meadow clothed itself in blossoms. There was a pleasant freshness in the mornings, but the afternoons had already become very warm. These circumstances produced a great harmony of mind and body. My husband felt a notable increase of strength and activity; and I, on my part, gradually revived.

"The simple manners of the country enable young ladies to walk out alone with complete security. Woman enjoys an unrestricted freedom. So in the early dawn it was my delight to steal from the house, and set forth, unattended and in cheerful spirits, for the purpose of bravely climbing to the still fresh green fields, and even to the threshold of the woods. These woods, consisting of fine chestnuts scattered over the smiling sward, had little in them, it is true, of a frightful or gloomy character. As yet, the cattle had not ascended to the higher grounds. I felt an emotion of compassion on seeing them devour, like hay, the most exquisite and even the rarest plants. I was almost on the point of calling cow and horse to account for such a trespass; but, undoubtedly, the poor beasts, accustomed to an insipid fodder, keenly relished the sweet savour and sugared odours of the flowers.

"On the mountain all things seemed asleep. The mightiness of its summit cast it into shadow, while the peaks on the

LAKE OF GENEVA (IN WINTER).

other side of the lake were alone lit up by the sunlight. The birds arose, but with little noise. Below, in the village, the goats were released from their sheds. The little goatherd sounded with rural horn the note of call. From the beginning of spring the goats of Veytaux ascend the mountain daily, and they and I willingly travelled together for a few moments. A handful or two of salt had made us friends. They recognized me everywhere, and without ceremony solicited their usual gift.

"I know not why, but my steps were invariably attracted towards the same place. In the evening I loved its melancholy, in the morning its waking cheerfulness, the surprise of an ever-new landscape. My former tours having been made in the autumn season, when I could find nothing but the wan flower of the saffron, I found the blossoming of the mountain a most attractive sight. I scarcely knew any of the plants, for pictures teach you nothing; you must see them as they are. What a pleasure to wander, alone with one's intense desire, in search of the unknown!

"At Chambabo, near Veytaux, I found a garden already in bloom beneath the chestnuts. For that powerful tree tolerates and suffers the little ones under its spreading boughs. The plants praise it for the shelter it affords them; in winter, covering and concealing them with its accumulated leaves; in summer, nourishing them with its *débris* and rich mould. It prepares for them a fertile soil. Undoubtedly this emboldens them, and many are audacious enough to establish themselves upon its body. But it does not complain; it contentedly accepts these indiscreet plants, which invest its aged trunk with all the gaiety of a posy of flowers.

"The melitis, it is noticeable, will flourish nowhere but at its feet. In its shadow the rampions, on their slender stem, erect their blades of a cold whiteness. Near it, Solomon's

VEYTAUX, LAKE OF GENEVA.

seal waves its snowy bells.   Nowhere else is the columbine
more beautiful, shrining in its purple-violet depths the richness of the warmest gold.   Heavy with dust, its stamens
droop their heads in love's sweet melancholy.   When the
setting sun shoots athwart the blossom with slanting rays, its
purple becomes luminous; you see, as it were, the circulating
blood, and from within to without the radiation of an electric
soul.

"These daily exercises not only delighted, but, at the
same time, tempted me to venture on a further ascent.   It
was precisely their attractions which made me unfaithful.   I
longed to see their Alpine sisters.   The higher slopes were
difficult, it is true, forming a gigantic staircase of three thousand feet, which, through a forest of beech, led to the upper
meadows.   Every morning I made a fresh attempt, in the
constant hope of surprising some daughter of the Alps, which
might have strayed down to the open grounds.   But I never
succeeded, and fell back exhausted.

"All passions increase in strength in proportion to the obstacles they encounter. Night and day came to me the thought of that Flora of the light, that ethereal Flora, which flourished apart from all inferior help, living on a ray, on the pure glance of the sun. Ah, if life has any secrets, is it not there one would surprise them? Are not those sublime eremites entrusted with a hundred confidences which Nature does not deign to reveal to their sisters, the coarser flowers of a lower world?

"Was there not among the upper valleys one of easy access, where my languid feebleness might, without this mortal travail of fruitless ascents, approach the sanctuary of the higher Alpine Flora? To this wish the noble books of Tschudi and Rambert replied,—'There is the Engadine.'

"I was infinitely charmed with their grand and severely simple descriptions. That wild, strange region of valleys, loftier than the majority of mountains, where you find yourself on a level with the glaciers, and may touch them with your hands, those singular flowers whose very existence depends upon nine months of snow, and, before all, the heroic strength of the arola, of that offspring of the ice and frost, produced a vivid impression on my mind.

"However, the Engadine is far off, very far off, at the other end of Switzerland, on the borders of the Tyrol; while a hundred things call us back to Paris, that centre of business and study, of matters too long neglected. And how, in the month of May, ascend to the coldest region in Europe, when the Engadine is still white with snow? A new obstacle! a fresh delay! We must wait until July. What a change in the arrangements we had made for the year!

"To crown it all, the beautiful brunette, who came down from Javernaz to dispose of her flowers, informed us, that even at Javernaz, at that gate of the Valais, situated opposite the *Dent du Midi*, the rains which visited us were congealed into showers of snow. What an ill condition of things did not this augur for the Engadine in a rainy year? Would it enjoy even a momentary breath of summer? Would it not retain throughout its melancholy winter shroud?

"How many reasonable reasons for not attempting the journey! Yet I know not what inner voice it was that whispered me we should not regret it. The greater the apparent difficulty, the more ardent grew my longing. I resolved upon taking my husband into my confidence, and on pouring into his ear a full confession. Frankly I said to him, 'I have a strong desire to see the Engadine.'"*

The fancy of a person who never yields to fancies was deserving of every attention. It was something more than an idea; it was a passion—sudden in growth, it is true, but full of strength. What surprised and moved me was the manner in which her prudence had been tempted. In truth, we were no longer dealing with a caprice which one eludes or diverts, but with a grave and serious matter, nothing less than love itself. All its signs were visible, and especially the gravest—the suppressed agitation of a strong emotion, which develops itself the more strongly while it does but half reveal its force.

I found good reasons for sharing in this feeling. I was very desirous of seeing the sequestered nook which was formerly named "the unknown country of the Alps." I was very desirous of seeing those mysterious lakes which send to the three seas, the Rhine, the Adda, and the Inn (that is, the Danube). I was especially concerned to rediscover, if I could, the subtle ancient France lurking under the mask of stolid Germany—that curious blossom of the snows, which, just now enjoying a transient life, will cease to exist to-morrow.

* [The reader scarcely needs to be told that the preceding pages were written by Madame Michelet.]

I revolved these thoughts in my mind, but said not a word. However, opportunely meeting with a learned Swiss, who was well acquainted with the country, I inquired of him, "Sir, can you point out to me a short road towards the Engadine?"

VI.

THE PAUSE AT THE FOOT OF THE MOUNTAIN.

LOVES OF THE ALPINE FLOWERS (JUNE 1867).

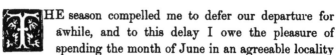HE season compelled me to defer our departure for awhile, and to this delay I owe the pleasure of spending the month of June in an agreeable locality —at Bex, on the threshold of the Valais. There I enjoyed what has rarely, very rarely, fallen to my lot in this world, an interval of meditation.

After the lake, it is a place of repose. The prospect is no longer immense, as at Lausanne, nor over dazzling. You see nothing more of the dramatic struggle of two opposing shores, as between Vevay and Meillerie.* You feel that you have

---

* [Vevay, on the Lake of Leman, ranks second among the towns in the Canton of Vaud, and is most picturesquely situated at the mouth of the deep, wild gorge through which the Veveyse pours its tributary waters into the lake. To the tourist it will be of peculiar interest from its connection with Jean Jacques Rousseau, who has described its bright romantic landscapes with all that graphic force and exquisite colouring he could so skilfully employ. In a small church above the town—a quaint little fane, embowered among trees and vineyards—lie the four English regicides, Ludlow, Broughton, Love, and Cawby. Three miles up the lake lies Clarens, immortalized through its associations with "La Nouvelle Héloïse," and deriving a new and not less permanent charm from the magic of Byron's impassioned verse :—

"Clarens ! sweet Clarens, birth-place of deep Love !
Thine air is the young breath of passionate thought ;
Thy trees take root in Love ; the snows above
The very glaciers have his colours caught,

AT THE FOOT OF THE MOUNTAIN (UNDER THE DENT DU MIDI, BEX).

arrived somewhere, and make up your mind to halt. The Rhone, having escaped from the Valais, and being no longer choked among the rocks, perceives that it has reached the plain, and draws breath before plunging into the lake. The landscape is everywhere subdued in character, though noble and full of majesty. You find yourself beneath the Dent de

> And sunset into rose-hues sees them wrought
> By rays which sleep there lovingly : the rocks,
> The permanent crags, tell here of Love, who sought
> In them a refuge from the worldly shocks
> Which stir and sting the soul with hope that woos, then mocks."

The poet proceeds to describe the scene as—

> "A populous solitude of bees and birds,
> And fairy-formed and many-coloured things,
> Who worship Love with notes more sweet than words,
> And innocently open their glad wings,
> Fearless and full of life : the gush of springs,
> And fall of lofty fountains, and the bend
> Of stirring branches, and the bud which brings
> The swiftest thought of beauty, here extend,
> Mingling, and made by Love, unto one mighty end."

On the opposite shore stands the little village of Meillerie, which is also steeped in "the consecration and the poet's dream," and hallowed by its associations with the genius of two kindred minds, Byron and Rousseau. The rocks which they have celebrated in immortal language have lost somewhat of their beauty, having been blasted by order of Napoleon to afford a passage for the magnificent road of the Simplon. It is at this point, about a mile off the shore, Lake Leman attains its maximum depth (920 French feet).

"Walking from Evian to Meillerie along the banks of the lake," says Lord Lytton, in one of his earlier works, "nothing could be richer than the scene around. The sun was slowly sinking, the waters majestically calm, and a long row of walnut-trees fringed the margin ; above, the shore slopes upward, covered with verdure. Proceeding onward, the shore is yet more thickly wooded, until the steep and almost perpendicular heights of Meillerie rise before you—here gray and barren, there clothed with tangled and fantastic bushes. At a little distance you may see the village, with the sharp spiral steeple rising sharp against the mountain ; and winding further, you may survey, on the opposite shore, the immortal Clarens ; and, whitely gleaming over the water, the walls of Chillon.

"As I paused, the waters languidly rippled at my feet, and one long rose-cloud, the immortalized and consecrated hues of Meillerie transferred from their proper home, faded lingeringly from the steeps of Jura. I confess myself in some respects to be rather of Scott's than of Byron's opinion on the merits of the 'Héloise.' Julie and St. Preux are to me, as to Scott, 'two tiresome pedants.' But they are eloquent pedants! The charm of Rousseau is not in the characters he draws, but in the sentiments he attributes to them. I lose the individuality of the characters—I forget, I dismiss them. I take the sentiments, and find characters of my own more worthy of them. Meillerie is not to me consecrated by Julie, but by ideal love. It is the Julie of one's own heart, that one invokes and conjures up in scenes which no criticism, no reasoning, can divorce from the associations of love. When shall I forget that twilight by the shores of Meillerie—or that starlit wave that brought me back to the opposite shore?"
- *The Student.*]

Morcles, and right opposite the Dent du Midi, but at a happy
distance. The first step to those lofty peaks, adorned with
their green girdle of beech and fir, consists of a breadth of
beautiful hills, crowned by chestnut groves. Above Bex

THE RHONE FLOWING INTO THE LAKE OF GENEVA.

itself, at an elevation of five thousand feet, flourishes, notwithstanding the extraordinary altitude, that favourite haunt of
botanists, the meadow of Javernaz.

Here I enjoyed the happiness of completing my historical
work, and the regret of separating myself from it. Already
I felt its absence, as the absence of one who had wandered
forth into the wide world. But I, I remained at home. It
was truly something, after an exhausting labour which might
have worn out many lives, to recover my own, with my powers

in all their fulness, displaying an increasing fertility, and largely developed by the toil of the ten preceding years.

The time had been of service to me, and I regretted nothing. However, a few shadows mingled with the sunshine. Just as the Dent du Midi,* with its sublime and dusky peak of granite, lends an occasional seriousness to the landscape without completely saddening it, so the approach of old age came as a warning to me, and thoughts of the future forced themselves on my mind. With respect to one secret care, especially, my heart trembled. Had I had a wing like the Alpine bird, the branch on which I rested, trembling, would have made me feel every hour that nothing in this present world is lasting.

" As the sky, so the man." In this manner the uncertain year floated onward, from spring into summer—now a day of sunshine, now a day of shadow, as if unable to decide. Bex, in June, is very warm. Its climate is somewhat weakening, and was not so much tempered as softened by warm rains, which, though very sweet to the meadows and the flowers, were for man too bland and languishing, converting life into a dream.

Nature alone had a voice, and we were constrained to listen. For a moment I quitted the troubled history of humanity, so harsh in the past, and still so harsh in the present! I turned my attention to a less gloomy chronicle, one of more enchanting harmony, and seemingly more suitable to the flowers which surrounded me. On all sides the mountain summoned us. Enthusiasm was not wanting, nor daring projects. Had it not been for the season, we might, perhaps,

* [The *Dent du Midi* is one of the most picturesque summits of the Piedmontese Alps, and from the eastern extremity of the Lake of Geneva its broken, abrupt, and precipitous crags lend a peculiar character to the landscape. Its ascent is usually made from the village of Champéry, one of the loftiest inhabited places in Europe, being 3700 feet above the sea-level. The entire neighbourhood of Champéry is an inspiration for poet and artist, including, as it does, the beautiful scenery of the Val d'Illiez (9 miles in length), and the limestone-valley of the Drance, with its bold crags and noble pine-woods.]

have accomplished great things. But one time we were stopped by the heat; another time, by the rain. Did this grieve me? Not very much, I must confess. Nothing could be more graceful than the warm showers viewed from our balcony. We collected fewer flowers; but then, on the other hand, we lived in closer intimacy with them, questioning them more searchingly, and inhaling their spirit and perfumes.

These fair creatures, so ardently loved and yearned after, modestly came to us, if we did not go to them. The young message-girl of Gryon, an amiable and serious maiden—a

GRYON.

Vaudois of the Valais, and in aspect Italian—frequently brought us the last-born children of the meadows of Javernaz. Unhappy in her family relations, she lived with the plants on the highest pastures, and her real home was with the *gogants* —those firs which are suffered to grow in all their greatness to serve as an occasional defence. There she wandered to and fro, without seeing a living creature, except, perhaps, a venturesome cow, or the great Alpine eagle. This life of solitude, in a region wholly exempt from the commonplace, invested her brown beauty with an undefinable rustic nobleness. Her fine eyes were softened by a certain melancholy languor. She was not without some degree of culture, and even prided herself on her knowledge of Latin. With the common names of the plants she gave the scientific (though, perhaps, a little altered?). But her flowers underwent no change, reaching us in all their charm, freshness, and bloom, just as they had flourished in the meadows.

My sight is good, but not powerful, and ill adapted for examining this little world of imperceptible detail. Even when directed by a guide, I saw but little, and that little imperfectly. But one morning, a master arrived from Javernaz who taught me a new lesson, and proved a decisive revelation to my mind. This interpreter of the flowers was itself a flower, the blue gentian, so grave in its embroidery of black. My attention was arrested by this striking hieroglyphic. I looked at it from my heart. I was touched by it. *I saw!*

I had with me the best books, and many of the most recent. What I had read in the flowers, I afterwards sought to reperuse in their pages. But they spoke far less eloquently, and in a barbarous language. They carefully preserve the names which an ignorant age bestowed on the organs of the flowers; absurd names, which not only retard the advance of the tyro, but for all persons invest the facts of botany with a wearisome and dubious obscurity. They designate the male by female names (anthers, stamens, &c.), and by masculine terms the female (as pistil, stigmata, and the like); while none of them bear any real relation to the forms of the objects they designate.

Why is this ridiculous dialect preserved? Undoubtedly through routine, but partly also to veil these innocent mysteries, and especially to obscure the relationship existing between plants and animals. In some respects inferior to the polypes and the radiata, in others they are superior to them. It was needful to overleap the sacred barrier between the three kingdoms (Animal, Vegetable, Mineral)—the old scholastic division. But what becomes of this barrier nowadays, when we know that for four hours daily certain vegetables become animals?

My first ignorant glance at the official summary published by M. Duchartre in 1866 has taught me an important fact. What know we of the life of assimilation which nourishes plants? Nothing at all. He tells us so in a score of sentences. What of their love, or mode of reproduction? Everything; or, at least, a great deal. He devotes to this subject three hundred luminous pages, crowded with details.

Classification, which occupies another three hundred pages, is based wholly on the characteristics of their generative organs.

Botany, then, to sum up, is nothing more than the science of Love.

A science immediately connected with Zoology, so that the one translates the other. Love is the doubtful region where the animal passes into the flower, the flower into the animal, and sometimes even soars above the lower animal world to identify itself with the higher one of man.

Nutrition is a mystery, but Love is not. There Nature has hidden nothing. It is its work of light, in which it fully reveals itself. No veil is found in it, no difficulty exists in it, except the diminutiveness—frequently extreme—of the lover and the loved. It seems to have taken a pleasure in varying *ad infinitum* the scene, and its little actors, as if to throw a greater light upon the drama.   Three hundred thousand kinds of forms (such is the number of known flowers) have not exhausted its ardent invention, or the visible happiness it feels in the revelation of love.

Behold the manner in which the event is accomplished. One day the leaf in its mirthfulness, rejoicing in the warmth and light, unrolls, and converts itself into a furnace, a genial cradle, and a tender bower, wherein a young world will soon· be born.   From its swollen tissue rises the tiny female (the pistil), a fine and slightly elongated matrix, which is already provided with its ovula, but is virginally closed.   All around it, and upwards to the day, spring numerous little living jets —its lovers, its suitors—who furnish it with a noble court.

Nearly always the tiny male, in his sunward movement, rises higher and further than *she* does.   He is influenced by a twofold attraction; the lustre of that glorious radiance which gilds him and intoxicates him with life, and the mild internal warmth of the tender maternal nucleus which appeals to him from within, and draws him nearer to his beloved object. These are his two temptations.   And ought not liberty,—the mobile life (wherein his airy head floats lightly), and the luminous glory, which seems the very god of the flowers,—ought not these to prevail ?   *Yes*, the science of physics would inform us ; but love says *No*, and the lover does as man would do. He bestows his preference upon his idol ; he inclines towards, he even prostrates himself before her, and frequently with great difficulty, turning away from the beam and the glory towards the obscure depths, in search of his beloved ; and by this one sign proclaiming that she is more to him than all the world, that love is more potent than the sun.

16

VII

THE ALPINE PLANTS:

THE PROGRESS OF THEIR FLOWERS IN LOVE.

IN other flowers it is not the male who outstrips the female, rising higher and stretching further, but it is she who dominates over all. Sovereign and colossal in comparison with her tiny lovers, she seems to mock them with an eternal difficulty.

Such was the spectacle presented by my noble blue gentian, an austere flower with a bitter juice, whose love was impeded by numerous obstacles. The scene was half tragical. From the deep azure chalice, streaked with black at the base, rose majestically the lady, clad in virgin white—not a milky white, but of a far less tender tint, the green sap mingling in it a shade of severity. Her diminutive lovers, feebly coloured of a very pale gold, surrounded her below, pressing her ardently but with vain entreaties. She balanced above them, at an inaccessible height, her double head, or rather her two charming love-lit mouths, girt by a superb frill of very fantastic design.

I compassionated the poor unfortunates over whom she hovered, expanded like a canopy. All access was thus denied to them. However daringly they soared, however they extended themselves, they gained but little by the effort, being repulsed by the borders. She resembled the difficult peak of Monte Viso, which, overhanging on every side, discourages all attempts to climb it, and renders them almost impossible.

But we should do a real wrong to the imperceptible lover, if we thought its passion was in proportion to its size. Desire bestows upon it a tongue. It speaks through its colour, through its warmth. It does not say witlessly, as we do : " My fires, my flame ;" but it changes the temperature around the loved one. So she becomes cognizant of a very gentle flame, which is her lover and love itself. Lamarck was the first to observe this fact in the flower of the arum. In like manner, the glow-worm during the night sighs and shines. The delicate thermometers of Walferdin, if placed inside the blossom, and among the lovers, will enable us to measure the degrees of their passion ; which infinitely surpasses all that we know of animals. In a certain flower (the *capuchin*, or *monk's hood*), the male in ten hours consumes no less than sixteen times its own volume of oxygen. What then must be the case with the flowers of the Tropics, the vegetable fury of Java or Borneo ?

This heat assuredly softens and subdues her, but more is needed. All love has its magic, its secrets, and its arts of fascination. The gifts of birds are their plumage and their song. Animals charm by their grace of movement, through which they exercise a kind of magnetism. In vegetable love this magnetism is represented by the sweet odour of the plant, which forms its all-potent spell. This it is which appeals to the loved one, which fascinates her, and intoxicates her with its essences. It is in truth a divine, a ravishing, and an irresistible language. If we men, who are strangers to this delicate little world, are so sensible of its bland emanations : if women sometimes are deeply moved, and, in spite of them-

selves, perturbed by them; what must be the case with the
tiny *woman-flower*? Penetrated and imbued with the odorous
spirit that surrounds and absorbs her, will she not be conquered beforehand—ay, and more than conquered, transformed.

But, as far as my gentian was concerned, the misfortune
was, that she did not enjoy the seductive magic of perfumes.
Her lovers had not the opportunity of prostrating or subduing
her by their intoxicating magic. Accordingly, their entire
hope lay in the accomplishment of a miracle. It became
necessary that, when utterly burnt up and consumed by
their passion, or by the sun's hot glance, and reduced to a mere
light dust,—they should be torn from the object of their devotion, and borne afar upon the wind. It became necessary
that, floating in the air, their doubtful course should lead
them, by an unlooked-for and admirable stroke of fortune,
exactly towards the beloved one, and that, by a still more
admirable chance, they should sink into her bosom. Now
you would take an oath, or wager more than a million to one,
that this could never occur, but that the haughty virgin would
live and die in solitude.

Only one thing was in their favour,—their enormous
number. In the shape of living dust, divided and multiplied
ad infinitum, they possessed a chance in their very infinity.
Fate might decree that one of them should be happy. And
hence the males resorted to this mode of multiplication.
Millions of lovers and rivals were required, before love could
succeed in making a single husband.

And therefore they would imploringly address themselves
to the wind: "O longed-for breeze, arise and bear us away!"
The playthings of the air—swimming and floating on its
waves—it was certain that nearly all would perish; but what
matter? They yearned at all hazards to rise, that so they

might gain the power of descending. She, the beloved one, could only receive the gift which came from heaven. For myself, I had little hope in their success. The miracle was, however, to be wrought, and God is great.

But would the atom be welcomed which came from above? Of this I was doubtful. Would not the haughty lady, which had hitherto denied herself so firmly, still preserve a rigorous front? I thought so; but great was my error. He found at the threshold—some honey.

And honey is the "yes" of the flowers; it is their universal rite. It welcomes, reassures, and retains the son of destiny when borne thitherwards by so felicitous a chance. It may be translated thus: "Health! enter, for this palace is thine. And thou, conqueror, hast fairly won it!"

What a prodigious fortune for him, for a grain of winged dust, to be restored to this glorious abode, this alcove of white velvet, at bottom sombre and of the richest azure, to unveil the mysteries of the arrogant and sublime maiden, who formerly looked down upon him from such a height!

Few heads would have borne so great a change of fortune. How does he account for the honey, for the unexpected favour with which he is received! Undoubtedly, he interprets it to flatter his own pride, believing that she means to say: "I submit myself to thee, who art my master! Thou comest in the name of heaven. Though I never could have believed that thou wouldst gain me! But thou art strong, and thou art great."

And in his pride, he also believes he hears her whispering: "Friend, how I have waited for thee! How I have dreamed, how I have suffered!"

Whether such were indeed his thoughts—whether this love-potion, this honey, had filled him with intoxication—surprised I saw him (on the field of my microscope) dilate

immensely, and suddenly develop into a giant.   He expanded
a hundredfold ; he was enlarged to three hundred and even a
thousand times his original stature.   For a moment I was
alarmed.   Had he continued affected by this prodigious
impetus, our parts would have been reversed, and it was I
who would have become the atom.

All my wishes, however, were for his success ; and all my
heart seconded him.   And I exclaimed : " Be happy ! Ah,
dear atom, be happy ! Thanks ; glory to the mighty Love,
which bestows upon the flower, as upon man, and the star,
and on all the worlds—the moment of the infinite !"

" But," you say, " who does not see that all this is purely
automatic ; that in thus acting, pistil and stamens, all are
blind ?"

Blinder than the animal ?   Who knows it ?   Blinder than
man himself?   I do not see it.

In the processes of generation, the flower is not only the
equal of the animals, but, in certain species, and in certain
material relations, the equal of the mammal, man.[*]

" But is not instinct concerned in the play of the
mechanical forces ?"   To the cold observer, every being, during the transports of love, would suggest the same doubt.
For all is then obscure and perturbed, hovering on the border-
line between the two worlds of light and darkness.   Love,
especially in its creative moments, is obscurity.   Even in its
sweetest dreams, two elements are constantly blending, which
cross each other, alternate, or grow confused—the elements
of Fate and Will.

Great was the astonishment in Europe when, about 1780,
men were told that the populace of the bee-hive, which had

[*] Compare the works of Robin and Schacht, and the recent " Dissertation," by Lortet, on
the *Pressia*, published in 1867.

been supposed to labour with a fatal and immutable regularity, had just modified the construction of their abodes in adaptation to new conditions. They fortified and complicated the approaches of their hives on the arrival from America of a formidable enemy, the potato-sphynx, which is noted for its greed of honey.

How much greater would be their surprise if men knew that the flowers too have changed their processes ; that new species have effected an innovation, and accomplished an onward movement, unknown to the ancient species? Yet this has actually occurred.

I fell into a stupor of the profoundest astonishment when, by comparing two passages, one in Alphonse de Candolle, the other in Duchartre and Hartwig, I discovered that an immense family of flowers, chiefly Alpine, whose summer existence is very brief, had adopted an entirely novel art of shortening love.

In the vegetable as in the animal world, the female is somewhat slow of movement. It seems that for awhile she hesitates, though not the less does she dream of love, and prepare herself for its enjoyments. And her dreams are adorably simple ! They are the honey of which I have spoken ; and which by gradual expansions is extracted from her very life. She advances a step towards her lover. All this is of little importance ; but see now what has taken place.

The Alps, which are mountains of recent formation compared with many others, abound in campanulas and compositæ, flowers which also seem of recent birth, and which we may believe to have been created on the Alpine chain itself.[*]

These flowers of lofty regions, breathing a rarefied air, rejoice in a pure light which assuredly refines them. But

* A. Candolle, " Géographie Botanique," pp. 1318, 1322, 1323.

their summer is very brief (for many of them not extending beyond five weeks), and by melting their defensive mantles of snow, it exposes them to the cold wind. They have no time to dream—like their sisters, like so many of the older species, which were born before the Alps. Their love and fruition must be immediate, or never. Instinct and necessity precipitated these things. The flower does not wait for her lover, but hurries to encounter him with an innocent honied dart, and seizing upon him, retires, carrying him with it. .

The child comes, the seed is in all haste matured; but to-morrow the snow and the ice will cover the earth. She has just one day to diffuse herself, and for this object wings are necessary. Her mother has therefore provided her with a new and hitherto unknown organ. I refer to the light feathers or plumes, which in a moment, and from all sides, seize upon her, envelop her, and rescue her. If the snow comes, the hidden grain may wait securely, and the safety of the species is put out of peril.

What more could be done by animal instinct? Or, to speak more frankly, what more could human thought accomplish? Certain novel circumstances have created in the flower an unheard-of maternal prevision, and a new art of love.

This is divine, beautiful, grand, and sublime.

It is love, then,—love,—that secures the *universal equality* between beings and species. Let there be no more pride. The same law prevails from the greatest to the least, in the star as in the flower. There are no grades of high or low either in heaven or in love—which, moreover, is heaven itself.

I was occupied with these thoughts, absorbed in them, and, in truth, completely enchanted by them. Evening came on. The last rays of sunset glancing through the woods reached us, not with the splendour of the lake which is flooded by them, but softened by the foliage of our umbrageous hills. Our grand dreamy chestnuts, already looming somewhat duskily, extended around us their catkins of pale golden hue and sweet delicious fragrance (a veritable odour of life, and of a more than vegetable life). They grew yet darker and more shadowy, and we resolved to return to our house through the meadows. It had been my good fortune this year to find the meadow everywhere in flower, and as I ascended to the higher ground, continually to encounter the hay-harvest, than which nothing can be more charming or more touching; for, after all, it is the death of the flowers, which are cut down in their hour of love. However high I climbed the mountains, however far I advanced into the Alps and into the seasons, I still met with the same scene: at Veytaux in May, and at Bex in June; in July, in the Splügen, and the highlands of the Engadine. Thus, in one year, I enjoyed three several springs.

Bex is the kingdom of the grasses. We were lost and drowned, so to speak, in a meadowy sea. In the field we traversed on the evening I speak of, which was already so obscured with the shadows of night that its flowers were no longer discernible, the grass was partly cut, partly standing; some haymakers on their homeward way politely wished us "Good evening," removing their hats in compliment to my wife, and addressing her as "Mademoiselle."

The fragrance of the meadow was neither strong nor weak. It was not that perfume of dry hay which mounts to the brain; nor had it the too damp effect of grass cut down immediately after rain. It was simple, wholesome, genial, but with an innocence — if I may venture to say so — which none of the sweetest worldly odours possess, none of the medicated scents of the rose, or any other plants.

17

We returned home slowly by little narrow footpaths, scarcely discernible in this vegetable sea. My wife went first, smiling, and, I think, happy. I followed her in a half-dreamy condition. Her dress, as it floated to and fro, and beat the odoriferous herbage, diffused delicious airs around me.

VIII

THE PASS OF THE GRISONS.

THE DEATH OF THE MOUNTAIN.

JUNE came to an end, and with it the dream, the indolent study into which I had plunged myself. The amenities of the Valais and its soft warm breath, my immovable journey through the mystery of microscopical loves, would fain have detained me among them, and made me forget my projected tour. But July opened up to us the road to the highlands. Tardy summer at last had melted the snows. Our longed-for Engadine, our land of promise, had become accessible. It had emerged from its prolonged winter. We set out, and not too late. For in July we found it laughing in its early spring. Many flowers were still lingering in expectation of the month of August. Some which in their impatience had risked everything, had been struck hard and frozen. Thus their unique hour is very brief, for the snow recommences in September.

The Grisons* have been Swiss only since 1800; and in

---

* [Few places in Europe are more interesting, from historical associations, than the Canton of the Grisons; anciently a portion of the country of Rhætia, but after the fall of the Swabian Dukes, in 1268, prostrated under the grinding despotism of innumerable petty barons, who each in his small fortalice exercised an independent sway, cruelly oppressing his subjects,

nearly all its characteristics their country is the reverse of Switzerland.

The latter, on a foundation of low plains, is crowned by

plundering helpless travellers, and carrying on an incessant warfare against his neighbours. The only parallel to such a condition of things must be sought in the Scottish Lowlands and the Borders during the evil days of conflict between England and Scotland. For centuries it was patiently endured, nor was the spirit of the sufferers roused to action by the great events which delivered the Forest Cantons from the tyranny of Austria.

At length the storm broke. In 1424, a band of peasants met in the forest-shades of Trûno, to devise some measures for the relief of themselves and their children from an oppression which had become intolerable. They obtained the countenance and support of some of the more enlightened and powerful nobles, as well as of the great ecclesiastical potentates, the Bishop of Coire, and the Abbots of St. Gall and Disentis; and under a venerable sycamore tree, which is still existing, noble, priest, and peasant swore "to be and to remain good and loyal friends and faithful comrades so long as earth held underneath their feet; to stand together with life and substance for the defence of the right, the public peace, the security of the highways, and the freedom of commerce; to protect every member of the bund, lay or cleric, noble or simple, rich or poor, in his rights and possessions; to hold together in war and in peace; to maintain every man his privileges by law, and not by force; to repress all unbridled license; and punish those who refused to obey the law."

Thus originated the Gray League (*Graue Bund*, or, in Roumansch, *Lia Grischa*), so called from the gray home-spun garb of its members. It was afterwards associated with the League of God's House (*Gotteshaus Bund*), which had been formed some few years before (1396), and the League of the Ten Jurisdictions (*Zehn Gerichte*), established in 1428. Having swept the country clear of its petty tyrants, whose memorials may still be found in the ruined towers that crest almost every commanding rock, they proceeded to organize a democratic government of remarkable simplicity. Every village or parish was recognized as an independent commonwealth, with its own mode of government, and peculiar rights. Neighbouring villages then associated themselves in a *schnitze*, or commune, having its general assembly for the regulation of their mutual interests; in this assembly every citizen above the age of eighteen having the right to vote. The historical student will readily apprehend the result: that these communes were incessantly struggling with one another, and incessantly disputing the decisions of the diet of the canton, until the strife was, to some extent, composed by the overruling influence of two great families, those of Planta and De Salis, who eventually got into their own hands the administrative power.

In 1525 the Grisons conquered Chiavenna and the Valteline, whose inhabitants they treated with as little mercy as they themselves had experienced from their ancient chieftains. In 1803 the Grisons became a Swiss canton, which, in 1851, was divided into 14 districts, 39 circles, and 205 parishes. Population in 1861, 91,177.

The language spoken in the Grisons is the Roumansch, or Romance, a corruption or modification of the common or rustic Latin (*lingua Romana rustica*), which the sway of Rome spread over a great part of Europe. It is divided into three dialects, peculiar to the Upper Engadine, the Lower Engadine, and the Oberland, or "country above and below the forest." The first printed book in Roumansch was a translation of the New Testament, by one Tachem Bifrena, published in 1560. The entire Bible has been issued by the Bible Society in Roumansch, for the Swiss Grisons; and in Lower Roumansch, or Engadine, for the inhabitants on the borders of the Tyrol.—*See Professor Diez, "Comparative Grammar of the Six Romance Languages."*]

gigantic peaks. The Grisons are distinguished by less lofty peaks, rising from very elevated valleys. Their province is, in fact, an immense backbone of mountains, where the valley and the plain are themselves of mountainous character, snow-shrouded for six months every year, and for eight months in the Engadine.

The Engadine is the most elevated district in Europe ; so elevated that not only Italy lies beneath it (or at least that part around Chiavenna and Como), but even the lofty Tyrol. From its hundred lakes and three hundred glaciers it pours forth waters on every side, contributing largely to the Rhine, the Rhone, and especially to the Inn, which, soon assuming its well-known name of the Danube, strikes across Europe with a course of seven hundred leagues, to empty itself into the Black Sea.

Switzerland is so privileged a country, where life flows by so sweetly and so free from burden, that all who live within its borders endeavour to become Swiss, and are assimilated in one harmonious mass, in spite of the diversity of populations. Our writers also pretend to confound them. One alone, M. Binet, has justly pointed out that the Grisons (and especially the people of the Engadine) still struggle to preserve their distinctive character, and resist this influence of homogeneity. Their insulated country was, it is said, the refuge of the most ancient of the Italian races, the Etruscan. Their language is Romano-Keltic, in which the Italian terminations do not prevent the groundwork—the roots of words—from being almost always French.*

Our ancient France, with great wisdom, never confounded the Grisons league with the Swiss proper. And they, in truth, turning their back on German Switzerland, always looked towards France and Italy. To these countries their

* See " The Gospels," translated into the Grisons dialect, by M. Menni.

chief emigration was directed. Their relations with the
French, however, in no wise affected, but rather strengthened,
their natural genius, which is wholly Keltic-Italian.

Formerly, this country presented the striking contrast
between a very refined population and a very savage land.
Hither have been driven by hunters and noisy tourists the
poor beasts of the Alps; and here many of them are now
extant? Stags were found in this district as late as 1840.
The bear, a purely harmless animal when not maddened by
protracted want, still lingers out a hermit-life in the forests of
the Lower Engadine. The innocent marmot, nearly exter-
minated in Savoy, still endures in the Grisons; and in its
lofty wastes and wildernesses hisses at your approach. On
the limits of the snow-region you may encounter the partridge,
whiter than the snow itself, which takes to flight at the sound
of your footsteps. Nor is the chamois wholly extinct.

Of yore, too, that superb animal, the mountain-goat,
the king of the horned race of goats, kids, and chamois,
might be met with; but he now exists only in painting, on
the old presses and cabinets of the Engadine. His race has
disappeared. Ere long, perhaps, we shall have to say the
same of the Engadine itself.

Its names are significant; *Curia* and *Chiavenna*, at the
two extremities of the district, furnish us at once with a key
to its history. *Curia** (Coire) is the Court of Justiciary, the
supreme prætorate which Rome established in the mountains,

---

* [*Coire* (in German *Chur*, and in Roumansch *Cuera*) is the chief town of the Grisons. It
occupies a romantic position at the mouth of the grand gorge of the *Schalfik-thal*, and is dominated over by a considerable eminence, which bears on its summit the Bishop's Palace, and the
Dom, or Church of St. Lucius. Its importance is owing to its situation on the great commercial trajects between Italy, and Switzerland and Western Germany—especially the two
famous Alpine highways of the Splügen and the Bernardin. A road of recent construction also
leads from Coire, over the Julier Pass, to the romantic Engadine.

Coire was the *Curia* of the Romans, and the capital of *Rhætia prima*. It has a population
of about 6000 inhabitants.]

and which afterwards the prince-bishop endeavoured to maintain ; though, necessarily, with indifferent success in a country
broken up by nature, ice-bound for six months in the year,
divided into baronies and isolated and strongly democratic
communes.

Chiavenna * ("the key"), a charming Italian town,
situated on the lowest step of those enormous ladders, the
Splügen and the Maloya, opened up or closed the narrow
defiles to three races and three countries, the Germans,
Romanches, and Italians. The Grisons League maintained
that it belonged to them, inasmuch as it was the key to their
dwelling-place. For two hundred years they struggled to
hold possession of this delightful land of wine and sunlight.
Finally they lost it, were driven out of Italy, and have
since succumbed more and more to the oppressive German
influence, which from great central Switzerland advances
and absorbs them—beneficently, let me add ; and so much
the worse !

Coire (or Curia) has an imposing appearance. Seated
beneath those lofty hills of limestone, which Time has torn
and shattered, it looks out upon the gray and misty Rhine,—
a torrent still in its impetuosity, but already a river in breadth
and depth.

Over the lowly commercial town, civilized and Protestant,
where the government of the canton annually assembles,
dominates the ancient sovereignty, as represented by the vast
and opulent cathedral, rich with the treasures of many cen-

---

* [From Coire the traveller proceeds by the *Via Mala*, the grandest and most tremendous of
the Swiss defiles, which penetrates for upwards of a league through the very heart of the
mountains,—with the Rhine dashing over a rocky bed below, and precipices 1600 feet high, and
scarcely 30 feet apart, above,—and by the pass of the Splügen, whose summit is 6940 feet above
the sea, to *Chiavenna* and its vineyards, embosomed among the heights, at the union of the
Val Bregaglia with that of San Giacomo. This was the *Clavenna* of the ancients. By the pass
of the Splügen, to which it is the key, Stilicho, one of the last of the heroes of the Western
Empire, crossed the Alps in mid-winter, as celebrated by the poet Claudian.]

turies. Nowhere else
have I seen a church so
carefully preserved, or
one which has so faith-
fully retained its original
character. At an aston-
ishing height — almost
at the very summit of
the building — is situated
the bishop's princely and
quasi-royal throne. It
has an arrogant look, for
it stands one hundred
feet higher than God's
Perhaps this was pru-
dently designed. Insur-
rection was inscribed as
a lawful right among
the privileges of the

GATEWAY OF THE   CATHEDRAL OF COIRE.

restless Grisons League. The people expressly reserved
their sovereignty, and at times asserted it. They resumed
the authority of the judges, and having exercised for awhile
their revolutionary powers, quietly subsided into their

ordinary condition. Of the three Leaguers, one bore the very expressive name, *Lia dollas dretturas*, the League of Rights or Judgment.

Above all other highways I prefer those grand historical routes which have been trodden by the men of old. For instance, I would rather enter Italy by its ancient, gradual, and legitimate passes, those of Mont Cenis and Saint Gothard, than by the violent leap of the Simplon. In the same manner, when travelling towards the Engadine, I preferred the ordinary road, the Julier. I put aside the other route, the marvellous pass of the Splügen, as an Italian one, which would have dazzled my eyes, and blinded me to what particularly engaged my thoughts,—the antagonism between Switzerland and the Grisons, the special originality of the country into which I was penetrating.

The Julier road may be traversed at any season ; hence the preference which has always been accorded to it. Of far older date than the era of Julius Cæsar, it was named, we are told, from a god of the Kelts, who, on the loftiest point, erected two *menhirs*. The fact that Roman coins have been discovered here only shows that, after the Kelts, the Romans occupied the district, and laid down a regular road.

During the Middle Ages, crusaders, merchants, pilgrims, all followed this route—very solitary for the inhabitants of the Rhine and of Swabia, who were travelling to Venice, the great gate of the East, on their way towards Greece or Egypt, Cyprus, and Jerusalem.

From the Julier road you discover at the first glance that the country is not German. The characteristic trait of the Germans, pointed out by Tacitus in his "Germania," and still in existence, is, that they willingly build their houses in isolated positions. On the other hand, the Velches and the

COIRE, THE ANCIENT CURIA.

Gallo-Italians group themselves in villages; *urban life* is the marked peculiarity of these races.

Approaching from the Zurich side, and by the lake of Wallenstadt, I had observed (and particularly on a beautiful meadow which lies at a considerable elevation above the lake) hundred of *chalets*, all isolated, all built apart, with no desire to secure any neighbours, with no regularity of arrangement, but scattered, on the contrary, in various positions, according to their owners' ideas of taste, usefulness, or fancy. They live there, however, as an aggregate. With them, it is always *the tribe*; just as, for the Italo-Kelt, the ideal is always *the town*.

Throughout the quarter of the Grisons, from Coire even
to Julier, and beyond, into the Engadine, the entire population is collected in villages.   It is the sociable and amiable
instinct of the race ; and also, undoubtedly, dictated by a
sense of security.   A prolonged peace has not changed the
old prudential habit.   The people do not live apart.   The
road which traverses the high ground shows very clearly that
the lowlands, from one village to another, are wholly deserted.
One would say that Spanish brigands, Austrian robbers,
Protestant leagues, and Roman Catholic armies — Rohan
and Richelieu—were still contending for possession of the
country.

The extreme elevation of the district through which you
are passing would not be perceptible, if you were not reminded
of it by the nakedness of many localities, which are without
fruit-trees, or signs of cultivation.   Meagre pasturage and
diminutive cattle.   Scanty forests, plainly damp, which plant
their feet in peat bogs.   Hence the sickly and infirm appearance of the piceas, whose life is exhausted by parasitic plants ;
and which are frequently draped in a false and gloomy pomp
by the gray lichens that enfold them on every side.   In like
manner, in the marshes of Louisiana the cypress woods are
covered with a shroud of Spanish moss.

Wherever five or six houses constitute a hamlet, rises the
tall spire of an ambitious church.   The ancient Catholicism
still weighs oppressively on a great portion of the population.
These churches, Italian in character, are besmeared with
frescoes (and many agreeably so) by passing artists.   Sometimes a single church serves for two closely adjacent villages.
But much oftener, the rival *communes* are prompted by vanity
to have each its independent sanctuary.   These numerous
spires at mid-elevations, and in dominant positions, produce
very frequently a fine effect.   From the heights I noticed a
village which, though it already possessed on the bank of its

torrent an ancient and sufficiently capacious church, had built
itself another midway on the amphitheatre of hills.

Shortly after we have passed the celebrated place·where
the three Leagues of the Grisons sealed their compact by a
solemn oath, in 1471,* the landscape gains in grandeur and
interest. In the lowlands, you will see on either side of you
a noble torrent, furious and foaming, which, as it dashes forward in leaps and abrupt descents, frequently communicates
to your own brain the vertigo of the profound abysses wherein
it plunges. It is evidently of the utmost purity, and very
beautifully tinted with a sea-green hue. How great its contrast, you say, with the gloomy Rhine—the slate-coloured
Rhine we have seen so recently—the gray Rhine of Basle or
Strasburg ! And yet that transparent stream is the Rhine
itself, before it is distained by the black pollutions it receives
in the lower part of its course. But not the less do I find it
difficult to understand how it preserves its purity, carrying
down, as it does, so much *débris* with its waters, and forcing
a passage through the ruined limestone. I saw it flowing
beneath half-demolished declivities, which seemed on the
point of annihilation. I trembled to see four tiny she-goats
of astonishing agility, which, with airy and adventurous
grace, ventured to descend the crumbling steep, arriving,
sometimes by a daring leap, at a little oasis of verdure. So
much danger undergone for only a tuft of grass !

The Rhine is here Italian in character : its German
features have disappeared. The sonorous Italian cadences,
mingled with tones of the old Roumansch, alone are heard :
the savage acclivity, thenceforth without wood or meadow,
makes merry—brightens up, if I may so speak—in this

* [The Grisons League was formed in 1471-72 by the union of three separate confederacies
(see p. 228) or bunden : the Upper, or Gray League (*Ober* or *Graue Bund*); the League of
God's House (*Gotteshaus Bund*); and the League of the Ten Jurisdictions (*Zehn Gerichte*).]

beautiful luminous tongue. It harmonizes admirably, moreover, with the delicate flowers, the grave and exquisite Alpine
flora, which commences at this point. Some pretty children,
with flashing Italian eyes, flung at us both words and
blossoms.

But gradually it all ceased. We saw no more children, no
more plants; nothing but bare rocks and deep silence. In the
finest noon of July, and under the most dazzling of suns, a
gloom hung about our path. The cirque of Julier, which it
skirts, is a vast theatre of ruin and desolation.

THE CIRQUE DE JULIER.

Throughout the whole journey one idea was constantly
recurring to my mind—THE DEATH OF THE MOUNTAIN! The
soil was scarcely held together by the roots of sickly forests.
Some thinly-planted coppices, the poor remains of vanished
woods, vainly endeavoured on the higher levels to arrest the
avalanche. From each vast *lapiaz* (the local name for desolated valleys and ravines) poured down a constant torrent of
earth and rock. If the snow avalanche is not to be appre-
hended along this route, you are constantly menaced with

heavy falls of earth and dust and crumbling *débris*.   You
pass by numerous rudely-constructed sloping barriers of timber, which receive the landslips, and divert them from the
highway.   The scene is far more funereal than any waste of
snow.

These *lapiaz*—common enough in the Alps and the Jura—
notwithstanding their broken surface, assume very frequently
the most fantastically-regular forms.   The crystalline limestone, as it falls away, leaves behind a kind of honeycomb of
stones, like a melancholy hive of sterility.   Where the formation is spath, the more irregular heaps and projections
compose a perfect labyrinth of desolation and ruin.   Hard
shelly fragments and jagged edges of flint make the rock
bristle with their inextricably intertangled fractions, so that
the whole may be compared to the framework of a gloomy
skeleton.

.   On the heights we meet with the "Cemeteries of the
Devil," as the Swiss call these chaotic masses of *débris*, which
resemble heaps of bones—dry and rattling bones—in want of
the repose of the grave.   The too brilliant sun and the inex-
orable light, still parching and illuminating them, cannot
evoke any life or motion.   The hunter and the shepherd avoid
them.   It is impossible to walk therein.   If the cow, terrified
by the storm, dashes in among these gloomy piles, how shall
she be found again in such a maze of stone?   Water filters
through the soil without gathering in springs.   The fissured
rock permits both rain and melted snows to percolate, through
its chinks, its crannies, and narrow funnels, into the profound
crevasses.

At an elevation of 4000 or 5000 feet this dangerous labyrinth is masked by rhododendrons and wild junipers.   Sometimes it cheats and attracts you by a little greensward and a
few flowers; and under this disguise the process of erosion is
the more successfully accomplished in silence, to reveal, one

morning, a desert of hideous nakedness, where nothing shall ever again revive.

How closely does nature resemble man! While writing the above, my soul was horror-stricken with the thought of the moral *lapiaz* which I have witnessed in these days. If Madame Guyon, in the "Torrents,"* the Rivers, and the Brooks, could recognize living souls, how can we mistake them in these arid and hopelessly-devastated chaoses? Many are in the condition of an evil, barren soil; many wound us by contact with their sharp and jagged edges; some—and these are indeed the worst—conceal with a robe of flowers the death that rots within, and disguise the yawning abyss with a smile.

But what will be the end, if this devastation, from the lower grades and the vulgar *lapiaz* of egotism and moral barrenness, should extend further, and if the process of erosion gain upon the immense masses of the people, indifferent to all things, and deficient both in the desire and capability of good? There are moments when one dreads that such will be the case. Despairing cries are uttered from century to century. About 1800 Grainville wrote "The Last Man." Sénancourt, Byron, and others believed in the approaching end of the world. But, for my part, I think it immortal. At unforeseen points, and by unsuspected fibres which prove to be still youthful, it resuscitates itself. Wavering between so many objects in this present age, it still presses firmly forward in the path of science, and hence secures for itself another great chance of renovation. It will refresh its heart at the wellsprings of Mind, and revive its moral flame at the source of Intellectual Light.

Switzerland has seen entire mountains, measuring whole leagues in length, descend bodily from their foundations, and

* [The title of one of her works.]

swallow up valleys and villages.   We are constantly recalling
the terrible landslips of the Rossberg and the Diablerets,
and many similar catastrophes.   From these calamities the
Pyrenees are free.   But perhaps an unresting process of
destruction is still more active.   Violent alternations of cold
and burning heat are there more marked than in the Alps.
The mountain-side being less firmly clothed with ice, is more
seriously devastated by the snows.   To the economizing
action of the glacier succeeds their sudden liquefaction, and
the consequent headlong precipitation of roaring floods.   When
abruptly assailed in spring by the hot African wind, they
pour down in torrents or leap in avalanches : their ravages
affect the lakes, and destroy the superb mirrors which for
ages have reflected the soaring peaks.   Everywhere we come
upon these beautiful, these noble, but somewhat gloomy
basins, blank and void.   As the traveller ascends to Gavarnie
he sees the empty circuits of what were anciently terraced
lakes.   At the most not more than twenty little tarns now
remain in the Pyrenean region.   The granite heart of the
mountain being disintegrated, the mass overtopples, follows
the track of its own snows, and destroys the cirques, just as it
has destroyed the lakes ; and through the channels of the
Ebro, the Adour, and the Garonne, its waters hasten to join
the great seas.

To resume : The cirque of Julier, grand rather than
grandiose, with its summits of sombre gray and its partly
melted snows, explains only too sadly the future dilapidation
of this great Alpine wall.   The snows, it seems to me, are not
glaciers here.   In very few localities are they of a pure white.
Although in the year I am speaking of summer came on
slowly, in many places they were already greatly changed :
here upraised ; there, on the contrary, softening, diminishing,
and assuming a yellowish tint, or just on the point of changing into that dull gray colour which predicts their immediate

liquefaction and downward movement, mingled with quantities of soil. How account for this ruin? Shall we ascribe it to the snow alone? The latter will, in its turn, accuse the wind of the south—the Fœhn, the Sirocco. The Sirocco will say,— "Reproach the desert, for it was the Sahara that sent me forth. What can I do?"

For my part, I absolve wind, and snow, and desert: I accuse none but man.

"Me!" he exclaims. "And what have I to do with yonder lofty summits, which my feet have never trod?"

With the summits?—nothing. But much might be effected on the slopes, and on the lower terraces which support the summits.

The snow undoubtedly loads them every year. In July it will assuredly melt; but its broken mass, divided into numerous streams, would never have acquired the force and violence of the torrent if the forest which of old clothed the declivities had been respected; if the axe had abstained from destroying the living barrier, so long honoured and reverenced by our forefathers.

In the austerest regions, where one would naturally have said, "Nature dies," she planted life. No obstacles discouraged her. Of express purpose she created a robust, powerful, and unconquerable being, which might hardily brave the climate: what do I say?—which might absorb its force into its own austerity. In the cirque of Julier—that miserable waste where everything crumbles into decay, where scarcely three huts are left standing in the midst of ruin, shunning the constant hails of stones and downfall of the soil,—there, I say, formerly flourished a world of trees, perhaps a beautiful forest, which held together and protected the slopes. We saw evident, undeniable proofs that magnificent trees had once thriven there. With admiration I caught

18

sight of two pines—two superb arollas—fraternally standing
side by side, and so close as to touch each other, and without
doubt mingling their roots and nourishing themselves from
the same sources of life.   They occupied the centre of a tolerably wide and palisaded inclosure.   Would this be the cemetery of some five or six unfortunates ·who had once lived
therein?   At least these noble trees are their consolation—are
undoubtedly their belfry, their church.   You understand with
marvellous ease how in such a spot temples might be made of
trees.   Stretching towards heaven their mighty arms, they
resembled the seven-branched candlesticks of the Apocalypse.

The pine is the strongest of trees, but the slowest in
growth.   One cannot determine the date of this wood, which
must have needed centuries for its development.   The two I
speak of lingered on the spot, like a mournful protestation
which said, " Extinct for ever !"

IX.

THE ENGADINE.

EXT to Quito and other loftily-situated towns in the South-American Cordilleras, the Engadine* is, I think, the most elevated of the inhabited regions of the globe. As far as Europe is concerned, it is certainly so : its highest village, Cresta, being 6500 feet above the level of the sea.

A valley in the Little Cantons is only 1000 feet lower ; but being admirably sheltered, it boasts of its vineyards and

---

* [The Engadine (*Engiadina*), or Valley of the Upper Inn, is an Alpine district, about sixty miles in length, with an elevation above the sea-level varying from a minimum of 3234 feet to a maximum of 5600. Into this great valley-reservoir debouch some nineteen or twenty tributary valleys, each possessing its characteristic landscape features, and most of them several thriving and even populous villages. Life is here spent in a very primitive manner; for the Engadine is shut out from the more genial world by barriers of glaciers and snow-loaded mountains, and its climate is so severe that its inhabitants speak of their year as divided between nine months of winter and three of cold weather.

The principal villages are those of Zornets, Tarasp, Samäden, and San Moritz. On the river are situated two towns of some importance—Silva-Plana, 5600 feet, and Martinsbrück, 3137 feet, above the sea.

The Engadine is divided into two portions—the Upper (or south-west) and the Lower (or north-east). It has a population of about 11,000; nearly all—except at the village of Tarasp—of the Protestant faith, and speaking a language called the Ladin, which seems an offspring of the Roumansch, but more nearly resembles modern Italian.

Cresta, referred to in the text, is not within the confines of the Engadine, but on the road between Coire and Silva-Plana. It is one of the loftiest of the Alpine villages, and the traveller here takes leave of the pine. Beyond and above spread vast treeless and desolate pastures.]

SILVA-PLANA, IN THE ENGADINE.

its cultivated fields. The Engadine, on the contrary, traversed
by the northern and southern
winds, is subject to their violent
caprices. The east wind, not less
powerful than the north, visits
it in the direction of the Bernina
glaciers. It is only protected, as far as I can judge, on the
west side.

To appreciate its height, you must approach it from Italy,
ascending the streams from Como to Chiavenna, among the
chestnuts and the vines, and from Chiavenna to Vico-Soprano.
You will there find yourself at the foot of the immense and
abrupt incline of the Maloya, which revolves upon itself, as it
were, through the woods of fir. And when you have traversed

these, you have still a further ascent. At length you attain
the sinister summit, all bleak and barren, and buffeted by
eternal winds. Then, looking behind you, your glance at
once embraces every step of this colossal Jacob's Ladder.

Approaching it, on the contrary, by the *Col de Julier*, you
descend a little, without suspecting that the descent is itself a
lofty mountain. Silva-Plana, an agreeable village, of extreme
cleanliness, with white-looking and apparently well-to-do
houses, receives you, and introduces you to the country under
favourable auspices. Three tiny emerald-green lakes, inclosed
by larch-trees and reflecting their image, shine gaily in the
sun, despite the grave sublimity of the peaks that overhang
them. These lakes, being traversed by running waters, are
very pure, and give promise of a healthy atmosphere. The
ensemble is wanting in grandeur for an Alpine landscape, but
is felicitously proportioned. In the centre of the foreground
smile the spacious and sunny baths of Saint-Moritz. Saint-
Moritz itself—a tolerably populous village, with a few shops,
and some small tradesmen—lies about half-way towards the
base of the Julier mountain. It dominates over, and almost
parcels out, the valley. On either side of it a view is obtained
of a succession of lakes, meadows, and forests.

The larch is of that bright green with which children's
toys are painted. It has a kind of relative gaiety. You are
always a little surprised to find, in localities where neither the
fir nor the robust pine can live, so tender a greenness, such an
air of youthfulness, in a tree which changes its foliage yearly.
But still greater is the astonishment with which we discover
the rarest Alpine flowers blooming in its partial shade ; and as
common here as elsewhere is the Easter-daisy of the meadows.
The superb yellow anemone—the prized object of botanical
research, which can be secured only at the cost of the most
painful ascents—abounds and superabounds under your very

SAINT-MORITZ.

carriage-wheel. Our lady friends
uttered little cries of delight and
admiration. These marvellous
blossoms, growing on an incline
which faced towards the east,
were almost in darkness at five or six o'clock in the afternoon. But they are nowise indebted to the effects of sunshine; they are beautiful in their own beauty. Bending
towards our road, and rendered mysterious by the gloom,
they seemed like eyes—great eyes, fixedly regarding us.

It was a striking scene. This singular and exquisite flora,
which no gold can purchase, which never descends into our
gardens, is only found in these very exposed localities where
so many common plants are unable to flourish.

After passing Saint-Moritz the valley enlarges, assumes a certain grandeur of aspect, and becomes astonishingly severe in its general characteristics. Along the line of lakes two or three villages stretch away one after the other to the horizon, with nothing between them but the desolate meadow. No houses skirt the road. There is no cultivation, no industry. Everywhere prevails a grand and noble silence, such as one encounters on the loftiest mountain summits—on the Righi, for example. But—and this is an important difference—from the Righi one sees all the giants of the Alps massed within the desert region : one has something to speak to ; one salutes the Silberhorn or the Jungfrau. Here the view is meditative, though extensive and beautiful. The **grand** group of the Bernina,* with its numerous .springs and glaciers, is within no great distance, but you catch only occasional glimpses of it. Generally the group is withdrawn behind a curtain of secondary heights. Its bulk is enormous ; and one seeks for it, but knows not where to find it.

Already, as we moved onward, *Celerina*,† which lies lower than Saint-Moritz, and completely in the plain, was shrouded in the obscurity of evening, and in the mists which rise from the numerous waters. A short distance on my right a church, a town, were still lit up with the fires of sunset. This is their second church ; and at first I thought it must be a Roman

* [The Bernina Alps separate the valleys of the Engadine and Bregaglia (north) from the Valteline (south). Several of their peaks exceed 12,000 feet in height; and the principal summit, Niz Morteratsch, reaches an altitude of 13,297 feet. In the valleys are embedded many very remarkable and magnificent glaciers.

The Bernina Pass ascends from Samáden by the Val Pontresina, fenced in on either side by snowy summits, to a point near the Leg Nair, or Black Lake, 7695 feet above the sea. It then descends by Pisciadella into the lovely vale of Paschiavo, beyond which opens out the Valteline.]

† [*Celerina* was the Roman *Schlarigna*. A short distance beyond lies *Samáden* (the Roman *Samedan*), the principal village of the Upper Engadine, where are some old houses formerly belonging to the two great families of the Grisons, Salis and Planta. The view referred to by M. Michelet is entitled " A la Vue de Bernina."]

VIEW OF THE BERNINA.

Catholic building, but the entire country is Protestant. The second church, situated near each village, stands sentinel over the cemetery, and is devoted exclusively to the dead.

At *Samáden*, a little more populous town (it contains, I think, about four hundred houses), are the central post-office, schools, and courts of justice. It is, in fact, the capital of the Upper Engadine, and remarkably well built. Many of the houses are approached by superb flights of steps, with fine balustrades of iron and copper, and picturesque *grilles*, often a century old. The traveller might mistake them for hotels. The handbooks and guides are wrong, however, in calling them the mansions of the wealthy; for opulence is rare, though you may everywhere admire the indications of an honourably and slowly acquired competence, the fruit of prudence and economy. In the course of a twenty years'

:.......... in the great European cities, by constant sobriety, and pr'v. 'ions sustained in the midst of luxurious follies and pleasures, a man acquires and brings back some fifty or sixty thousand francs. He purchases a piece of ground, which costs much and produces little. He builds a good house; and in a country visited by so severe a winter, it needs to be very substantial. Then he shuts himself up and takes his rest; his sole amusement a few flowers, reared with extreme difficulty.

All this is noble and affecting. The seriousness, the extreme care which you discern in everything, becomes impressive in these little places. After toiling yourself throughout a long career, you feel a certain degree of reverence for well-deserved repose, the retirement gained by persistent industry. Samâden has all the gravity of the beautiful villages of Holland, with less wealth, and a simplicity which I felt very strongly. Upon its temple I read in the graceful Roumansch language an inscription peculiarly appropriate to all men who, by their own exertions, have succeeded in winning an honourable position: *A Dio sulet onor ed gloria.* Further on, I found in German, on a noble mansion adorned with flowers (which had even an apology for a garden!), this touching epigraph: "He who has found help in adversity, in fine weather remembers the storm."

On your arrival in this noble village you repair to an hotel, which is far better than sumptuous—it is admirable: so admirable, that the English, great admirers of comfort! sojourn there, and for awhile forget the country. As a rare and singular sign of the excellence of the house, I may mention that I found there *some coffee*—true, genuine, and unadulterated coffee! This I have met with but twice in thirty years of travel: first, near Gavarnie in the Pyrenees; and, second, at Samâden, in the *Hôtel de la Bernina.*

About four o'clock in the morning I rose quietly, and stood
for a moment examining the landscape through my misty
windows.   At the depth of a few feet, amongst moderate
hills, very unequally wooded and diversely lighted, lay the
valley, with its fields and tiny lakes, shrouded in a dense
vapour which crawled and crept along.   The aspect of the
whole was melancholy, grave, and mysterious.   It was, and
yet it was not, summer.   Gradually rose the sun, and I clearly
discerned the position of Samâden, in the centre of its cross-
roads ; one of which—the principal—follows the lakes from
the Maloya to the Tyrol, and the other—the transversal—
rises towards Pontresina, supported on the right by the
mountains of the Bernina.   The town has a small trade in
the cereals of Germany and the wines of Italy.

Walking through Samâden about ten o'clock, I found
myself compelled to put a quantity of questions.   I perceived
three young men, obviously persons of intelligence, conversing
in the street.   They saw me also, but without staring curiously
at me, as is so frequently the case in our small French towns,
much to the annoyance of the stranger.   They replied to my
questions very politely, with much amiability, but in a
manner wholly free from affected eagerness.   They were
about thirty-six years of age, perhaps ; and, from their cautious behaviour, were evidently men of some experience, who
had seen life, and mingled in the world, without losing their
natural amiability of disposition.

These men are moulded by emigration.   Their modesty
secures them general esteem.   I cannot resist the pleasure
of quoting an example, which I borrow from a capital little
book by M. Binet, of Geneva.

Recently, says he, in the village of Sils-Maria, one of my
friends, while looking over the little library of the house in
which he lodged, came upon a manuscript nearly two hundred

years old. It was a memorial of friendship and esteem
brought back from Zurich, by a young student of the valley,
and written by the hands of the professors under whom he
had studied. Along with the signatures of these well-known
men of science, were some armorial devices, carefully painted.
After all this came a few words of sympathy addressed to the
student's family; for this interesting young man, so warmly
loved and esteemed, had been stricken down by death at an
early age.

Established at *Pontresina*,* on the Bernina route, full in
sight of the glacier of Roseg, and having beneath our feet the
meeting of the torrents, we went out for a walk about four in
the afternoon. A fresh but not a cold wind blew from the
west, which a ray of the setting sun, from the height of the
Julier, pleasantly attempered. I was struck by one thing.
Men were at work on the bridge, crossing its tiny parapets
with small timbers, to prevent the abrupt alternation of frosts
and thaws from injuring the masonry. The sight set me
thinking. I felt the terror of that awful winter which
freezes at 40° R., and converts the lake into a rock. This is
Siberian. And what is not Siberian, but still worse, is, that
the sun at certain moments bethinks itself of neighbouring
Italy; and with a sharp, trenchant ray, cutting like a sword,
it strikes hard upon the frozen earth, cleaves it, splits it,
withers and burns up everything.

The highlands have a population of about three thousand
souls. But were it not for their regular emigration, and its
profits, I do not think the country could remain inhabited.
How could it be cultivated? A very clear explanation,

* [*Pontresina* is a village of some importance, owing to its admirable position in the heart of
the finest scenery of the Bernina. From this point tourists ascend the Piz Languard, 10,724
feet, remarkable for the noble Alpine panorama which it commands; the Roseg and Morteratsch glaciers; and the Val de Fain; and proceed, by the Bernina Pass, into the Valteline.]

written by M. Lilly, and transmitted to me through the courtesy of M. Saratz, shows that it would be impossible to rely upon agricultural products. Not only does the snow last seven months, but it frequently returns in the summer when least anticipated. Rye is too hazardous a crop. A little barley, however, is sown. I myself have seen this cereal thriving in a well-sheltered hollow, opening towards the south; but it is rare and uncertain. Hay is cut by the hand more often than by the scythe. It is very short, but, by way of compensation, of exquisite quality, and of a deliciously sweet odour (as is natural, for it consists chiefly of flowers). Hence the milk yielded by the cows is remarkably good, though not very abundant. Butter and cheese are not produced in sufficient quantities, and much requires to be imported. The cattle, well cared for in their stalls and fed upon this dainty fodder, give an excellent breed of young, of beautiful little gray heifers, which are highly esteemed, and fetch a considerable price in the market.

A little work in the woods, and a small amount of cartage, is all that is possible in the Upper Engadine. The law, the fatality of the country, is—Emigration.

Very few families enter the military service of foreign countries. The reproach of furnishing kings with soldiers to make war on their subjects, cannot be levelled at the Engadine. Its population is very refined, and has never yielded any of these rude giants from whom our French monarchs selected their Swiss Guards. A breath of Italy, moreover, is found there; a peculiar aptitude for the arts. When he is ten or twelve years old, the child is despatched to Venice, Milan, Rome, or Naples, where he quickly learns an art peculiar to his country,—a charming art, which is held in high repute among the Italians.

We know that the shepherds, Mozart's compatriots,

practised, among the mountains of Salzburg, the art of
wood-carving, which they had acquired at Nuremburg. The
Tyrolese peasants excel in fabricating toys. Canova, in his
boyhood, when residing at Bassano and Treviso, exercised
himself in modelling butter. Michel Angelo, it is said,
sometimes wrought in snow. The young Engadinois models
and carves in sugar.

In the indolent Italy of the seventeenth and eighteenth
centuries, the life of its courts and gay society—an everlasting
carnival which knew but few variations—was strongly partial
to surprises and small improvisations. At births and mar-
riages, at balls and banquets, posies and madrigals were
rained upon the divinity of the place. It was a fête within a
fête when, towards the close, in great pomp, and to the sound
of instruments, was brought in the superb dessert, the madri-
gal in sugar—temple, grotto, or mountain—with its forest
of flowers and glacier of candy. Quite in the taste of the
"Aminta" and the "Pastor Fido,"* sheepfolds were constructed among these gay devices. All the arts, in truth,

---

* [The "Aminta" was written by Tasso during his residence at the court of Ferrara. In
the character of Tirsi he has portrayed himself, and the whole tone of the pastoral drama
betrays the mental unhappiness which at the time of its composition was preying upon him.
Many passages are graceful, and touched with the light of a fine imagination, though much of
their beauty is due to the influence of the Latin and Greek pastoral poets, Theocritus,
Moschus, Virgil, and Ovid.

The success of the "Aminta" produced the "Pastor Fido" of Guarini, first represented at
Turin in 1585. It was received with general applause, but its direct imitation of Tasso's pastoral
drama could not fail to stir up a rivalry between their respective advocates, which survived
the mortal life of the two poets. "Tasso, it has been said, on reading the 'Pastor Fido,' was
content to observe that, if his rival had not read the 'Aminta,' he would not have excelled it.
To the earlier poem, however, belong more elegance and purity of taste; to the later, more animation and variety. The advantage in point of morality, which some have ascribed to Tasso, is
not very perceptible; Guarini may transgress rather more in some passages, but the tone of the
'Aminta,' in strange opposition to the pure and pious life of its author, breathes nothing but the
avowed laxity of an Italian court. The 'Pastor Fido' may be considered, in a much greater
degree than the 'Aminta,' a prototype of the Italian opera; not that it was spoken in recitative;
but the short and rapid expressions of passion, the broken dialogue, the frequent changes of
persons and incidents, keep the effect of representation and of musical accompaniment continually before the reader's imagination."—Hallam, "Literature of Europe," ii., 251, 252.]

contributed towards the spectacle.   The dessert was sung and
acted; a circumstance which explains how it was that Lulli,
the little confectioner's apprentice, became a musician.

All the skill, all the difficulty consisted in killing Time.
Man's whole occupation was to respond to every caprice, to
break forth in incessant improvisation, to create a new world
from morning to evening, to fashion his pastoral devices and
mimic Alps as quickly as one puts together a bouquet.   But
sugar is rebellious.   Without the sugared *pâtes* all was
impossible.   No moulds were then in use; everything was
fashioned by the human hand—by the daring yet delicate
hand of some young artist, who had a quick perception of the
fashion, of the female fancy, of the kind of objects likely to
extort the prompt exclamation : "Oh, this is fit for a lady !"

Nothing is more complicated than the art of confectionery.
Nothing proceeds less according to rule, or is less dependent
on education.   A taste for it must be *innate*.   It is wholly
the gift of mother Nature;—a happy instinct, a felicitous
divination of the uncertain effects depending on so irregular
an agent as fire !   An astonishing tact is necessary ; a sure
hand, which does not hesitate too much, but halts at the
proper moment and mingles in just proportion ; for a shade
too much or too little, and all is lost !   This point, at once so
narrow and so exact, requires a degree of decision, a flash of
quick intellect, a stroke of adroitness, which is never found
out of France.   The watch of the German goes too slow, that
of the Italian too fast.   They either underdo it or overdo it.
Our Gauls of the Engadine possessed this peculiarly French
gift to the fullest extent.

But the less easily the art is acquired, the ruder are its
stages of imitation.   The master, at certain moments, suffers
all the uncertainties, fears, and paroxysms (if one may use
the comparison) which Benvenuto Cellini experienced in the

famous casting-scene,* when he was overpowered with the fear
that all was lost. Woe to the apprentice at such a moment!
One trembles for the child who looks on, and has no defence.

Really his lot is very hard who, from the freedom of the
mountain air, descends into the confectioner's gloomy den
beneath the paved streets of the city, and breathes the deadly
vapours of its charcoal fires. The elegant and dainty lady
who, in the Rue Vivienne, inhales the odours of the cellars,
has no conception of the wretchedness of the young artist's
life whose skill works out the elegant decorations of her table.

A gleam of light, nevertheless, shines in upon him when
he achieves his first success; when the *pâte*, turned and taken
at the lucky moment, exhibits those warm golden tones
which an ancient (and very observant) gourmand so justly
pronounced "a charm for the eyes." Every painter raves
about them. Rembrandt endeavoured to seize their glowing
red, to kindle with it the gloom of his deep, shadowy furnaces.

A poor simple lad, Claude Lorraine,† who never acquired
any learning, but was always and ever a simpleton, having
carefully contemplated this colour, and keeping it constantly
before his eyes, from a small pastry-cook developed into a
great painter. From his cellar in the north he carried it into
Italy, and worked it up in his pictures, with that strong

[* Benvenuto Cellini, the great Florentine silversmith and sculptor, was born November 1,
1500; died February 13, 1571. The incident to which M. Michelet refers is graphically
described in his extraordinary Autobiography—a medley of fact and fiction, boastfulness and
shrewdness, as interesting as any romance.—See " *Vita di Benvenuto Cellini scritta da lui
medesimo*" (Molini, 1832).]

† [Claude Gelée, more generally known as Claude Lorraine, was born at Château de Cha-
magne, near Charmes, in the ancient duchy of Lorraine, in 1600. Bred as a cook and confectioner, he travelled to Rome, where he was engaged in the service of one Agostino Tassi, a
landscape painter. Here he had an opportunity of learning something of colouring, and by
watching his master, and the intuition of his own genius, he soon attained a wonderful degree
of excellence. His landscapes are *sui generis;* their marked characteristics being a skilful
management of light and a graceful composition of objects. We confess that to us they seem
wanting in a poetical feeling for nature, and in that depth of colour and intensity of sentiment
we find in some of the masterpieces of the English school.

Claude died at Rome on the 23rd of November 1682. England is rich in specimens of his
work, and his landscapes have always been highly esteemed by English connoisseurs.]

passion for the light, that magic of love which fixed the sun (*qui fixa le soleil*).

It is an inexplicable fact that these emigrants, notwithstanding the life they lead in an atmosphere of filth, and among corrupt and deleterious substances, do not seem to alter greatly. The truth is that at the age of twelve or fourteen they carry with them from their native home the fond remembrance of an adored but severe mistress, which preserves them from all harm.

This mistress is the immaculate snow of the virgin Bernina. In cellars, and in ovens heated to a white heat, she rises before their imagination.

This mistress is the scanty but exquisite Flora of the Alps, so infinitely superior to the vulgar floral world of the plains.

It is she who enchains their minds and memory. For twenty or thirty years they dream of her in the gloom of the cities. And after a career of adventures, they return home faithful, and still passionately devoted, to the eternal winter.

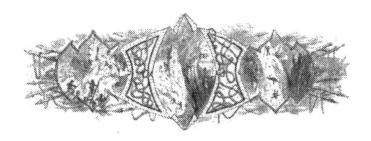

X.

SNOWS AND FLOWERS.

THE proverb of the Engadine,—"Nine months of winter and three of hell,"—excites the stranger's astonishment, for, at so great an elevation, the heat, even in the middle of summer, cannot be very oppressive. In the year of our visit the season was cold, and we had fires kindled in July.

"Nevertheless, however tempting the warm room, or forbidding the external cold, I wrapped myself up, and issued forth. The temptation was too great, when so close at hand lay the rarest botanical treasures. Having already attained an altitude of 6000 feet, I had but to climb another 2000, and find myself without effort in possession of the loftiest Alpine Flora. A courageous lady accompanied me in the ascent, as well as some agreeable friends who proved excellent mountaineers.

"On one occasion, however, I ventured into the desert alone. An undefinable charm of solitude beguiled me. There still exist in the Engadine a number of unknown or forgotten recesses and wild valleys, whose only visitors are the wind and the sun, and which one might suppose to be the secret kingdom of the spirits. It is these I was in search of. I

19

wanted a place and an horizon on which human eye had never
before rested.

"If any person is acquainted with these localities, it is one
man, Colani, son of a famous hunter, and himself, in his old
age, an ardent hunter—of plants. His is a twofold learning,
—tradition and nature; he knows every tree, and every stone;
sympathizes perfectly with the spirit of the country. Every
flower is his beforehand. He captures it at the very moment
of its blooming. Seated by his fireside, he knows the exact
minute when such and such a plant will blossom on some unknown slope of the Bernina.

"Colani was in a hurry to revisit the higher grounds,
which in this laggard year had scarcely been free from snow.
He was more eager than myself to regain possession of the
mountain. The weather was severe. In these elevated
regions the wind changes incessantly. It shifts from quarter
to quarter several times daily. We experienced in summer
the violent gales of a cold spring. There was a frost every
night. And on the evening before our departure, the sun
set—an omen of evil augury—behind a black, shifty, and
fantastic chaos of clouds. Colani foreboded no good, but
remained silent, except when he muttered between his teeth
the names of plants and flowers unknown.

"I rose at four o'clock, and before six was ready to set
out. The sky was gloomy. The harsh wind swept away the
snow which was beginning to fall. It mattered not; we
started. Seated immovable in a small mountain-car, open
in front, I submitted to the attacks of the sharp and subtle
bise, which penetrated and insinuated itself into my body,
as with fine points of steel.

"On my right I saw the massive heights of the Bernina.
Through the shuddering pines I could discern its snow-white
peaks. On the left, a still sadder spectacle, rose a range of

IN THE SOLITUDES OF THE ENGADINE.

naked and inhospitable mountains, not even shrouded in snow.
We advanced but slowly, for the wind blowing right in our
face delayed us. The few wayfarers who passed us on their
road to church, for it was Sunday, were astonished to see 'a
pale lady' journeying in such severe weather.

"We arrived at an inn which, like that at Samâden, calls
itself the Hôtel de Bernina. It is from this point, and not
from a nearer one, that you gain the full effect of the imposing
mountain-chain. The glaciers are seen above, and in many
places reveal to us in all their grandeur their vivid emerald
ridges. They descend upon you ; you become sensible of their
crushing burthen. It makes you shudder only to look at
them.

"On this most melancholy day it was surpassingly grand
to see these giants one by one come forward. The lugubrious
host stood out like white phantoms against the gray sky. A
solitary black spot, the peak of the Bernina, projected itself
like a sharpened spire. On either side of the road the ancient
glaciers had deposited their ruins. You passed through the
midst of the dead.

"Though it was July, the hôtel resembled those places of
refuge created for man's protection against the hurricanes of
winter. There was no one to receive us ; all the gates were
closed ; the large stoves were lighted in the interior, and a
kind of restraint enforced upon life. The hostess took me into
her pity, and loaded me with wrappers. We entered into the
valley.

"There, as if smitten by the finger of a malignant fairy,
the trees suddenly cease. The landscape loses all traces of
an horizon ; is more and more closely pent in between a double
range of lofty mountains. It is not so much a valley as a
narrow corridor ascending to the Col de la Stretta. The
rugged road is very painful to the traveller. Beneath, at a
much lower level, flows a grayish-coloured torrent. The cars

do not venture much further. We had engaged at Bernina
the rustic vehicle of the haymakers, but a field of snow
arrested us. I traversed it on foot with the glee of a daring
and fearless child.

"What a contrast between the earth and the heaven!
From the fierce firmament swooped upon us the fury of
winter. Sleet had replaced snow. A violent wind hissed
around us and lashed our faces. Above our heads gathered
a thicker gloom. But at our feet, on the border of the snow-
field, smiled the most agreeable image of life. The peerless
spring-anemone bent downwards, attired in a fairy garb of
pale lilac. Her hour had already passed. She lay, as it
were, asleep in the dream of a happy moment. Long, soft,
airy, and electric silken folds falling over her head, enwrapped
her maternal bosom. In this first apparition of the Alp I
greeted a sweet and charming soul, which revealed to me the
presence of God in a wilderness of desolation.

"Gradually the world closed in behind us, and the desert
commenced. Solitude is everywhere imposing ; but oh, how
much more on the threshold of dead Nature, and in the immediate vicinity of the everlasting snows!

"My guide with firm step advanced before me ; he had
wandered about the mountain too often to experience anything
of the perturbation of an unaccustomed mind. As ardent in
hunting plants as formerly in hunting the chamois, you could
see bright gleams of rapture in his flashing eyes. He broke
out into paroxysms of silent laughter, and displayed something
of the disposition of the classic Faun, at each capture we
accomplished. These flowers were his prey.

"Despite the melancholy heaven, and the black cold—
life's bitter enemy—they perfumed the air. The daphne,
with a tint which somewhat resembles that of the lilac,
also recalls its fragrance and penetrating suavity. By her

side, the vanilla orchis contrasts the dark purple of its spiral
ear with the pale surrounding herbage. No perfume is more
constant. Even when lying interred in the depths of an her-
barium, it exhales a souvenir of its fragrant soul, which still
seems absorbed in love.

"The great blue gentian, already deflowered, had closed
its urn. On the meadow reigned the brilliant and dazzling
gentian of Bavière. Its intensely azure star trembled and
coruscated. It made the entire joy of the desert on that
pitiful day. It brought back to me the absent sky, doubled
and deepened in its blue loveliness.

"It is a bare, bleak locality. I could not find there the
Linnea which seeks the protection of the arolla. The daughter
of the woods—and dwelling under their shelter—she clothes
the rock with her undulating trains, with her pale rose-hued
bells, which tremble in the lightest breeze. Even the blossoms
which are found at Julier and the Splügen (such as the
myosotis and pediculate rose) do not flourish here. The
declivities are very steep, and deficient in those peat-marshes
which feed the flowers with their fermented waters.

"These contrive to make the best of their destiny by
various prudential measures. The gentians open and close at
suitable moments, and proportion their stems to the cold and
the fury of the tempest—frequently shortening them when
need arises. The thyrsus-like campanula, instead of flinging
abroad its bells upon the wind, folds them around its gentle
self like a sheath, and converts them into a swarm of alveoli.
As to the other plants, the leaves grouped at their birth
around the stem like a ruff or frill, remain close to the ground.
Nurses and housekeepers, they possess their characteristic
prudence. Only their nursling, the flower, on some fine day,
mounts towards the light, drinks it in eagerly, and—dies!

"This rugged situation is nevertheless a refuge. Rolled
headlong by the avalanche, the little emigrant from the lofty

summits frequently falls here, and thinks it has found a securer asylum. It makes itself at home, and takes up its position according to its need of water, warmth, and light. But the cold is not the less severe. The winter follows closely in its track (even in July). Poor little youngling, who has made the perilous journey only to fail in accomplishing its destiny!

" Numerous precocious flowers had already perished, stricken by the cruel wind, which blows more sharply in confined localities than on the mountain summits. The pale soldanella, which it lashed incessantly, had yielded up its flexibility to this savage demon, and gently resigned itself to the rigours of fate.

" Meanwhile Colani had completely forgotten me. He had strayed afar, and was lost in the labyrinth of crumbling rocks. I was alone, and realized at last, what I so much desired, the melancholy of the mountain. But I had not anticipated a silence so gloomy. In the wan, clear obscure of the snowy sky, nothing stirred : not a bird animated the scene—not even a gnat. A whistle—that of a surprised marmot—made me tremble ; and afterwards the desert was more silent than before. There was no murmuring stream, no sound of flowing waters. The torrent rolled below and at a distance. Only the vexed air groaned, or at intervals broke forth into ominous wailings.

" I felt no fear, but the sensation of an absorbed soul, which, alone with itself, traverses the infinite, and returns to its God. With my emotion mingled a strange, sharp, keen desire. I paused a moment. If I had not cherished a human love, why ever again descend to the lower world ?

" Such is the intoxication of these ascents, the attraction of these regions, our need of bird-like flight. But, undoubtedly, heaven is no *nearer* to us even there. It lies within ourselves —in the innocence of our lives and the rectitude of our hearts."

XI

THE DESTINY OF THE ENGADINE.

SOMEWHAT disenchanted with the desert and these lofty prairies, I willingly retraced my road, and returned to the villages. I longed to see men again. We did not encounter any. Our Lower Pontresina, with its post-station and its inns, it is true, exhibited a few human figures. The other on the heights, only five minutes distant, was perfectly solitary. The houses, very neat and comfortable in appearance, were closely shut up—even the windows (and this in July). There were no children, no dogs —not a soul.

I had seen in Holland also some pretty deserted villages. But the small Dutch house, with its marbles and porcelains, its pictures and collections, often with its boat and canal, has not the gloomy austerity of the mansion of the Engadine. Nor has it the rustic nobility of the vast granges which invest the latter with a certain venerable air.

Most of these houses are really fortresses. From the enormous solidity of their walls, we perceive that the enemy lies close at hand—the great winter, a moment checked, but preparing to renew the assault to-morrow. We perceive that the owner—who, on his return to his native place, erected for himself a stronghold—being accustomed to a milder climate,

and having lived in the security of large towns, here in the
desert puts himself in a condition of complete defence.
Having undergone so many trials and adventures, he seems
to have revolved in his mind the problem propounded by
Bernard Palissy in the dangerous times wherein he lived :
" How shall one envelop and inclose oneself in a perfect
repose ? To obtain a secure asylum, ought not our model
to be the carapace or the shell, whose thick volutes are a
guarantee of safety ?"

A perfect shell ought to be entirely closed, ought not to
have a single opening. And here, at all events, it is a very
small one. In this enormous wall, as in the cavity of a rock,
the embrasure narrows internally, and at the bottom of it lies
the window. To speak the truth, this abode is built with a
special view to the interior. It is its own little world, and
requires nothing from without. At the most, a tiny garden
is laid out at the side, where each little square of culinary
herbs is so surrounded by planks as to look like a chest. The
flowers which for nine months have exacted so much attention
appear on genial summer days at the window ; not without a
certain coquettishness, but on the condition of being always
ready to return into their confinement.

The more recently erected houses, whose ground-floor is
raised above the level of the earth, have their principal entrance
on the somewhat ambitious terrace of which I have spoken.
The older mansions, which are very original in character, possess
a great vaulted vestibule, low and gloomy, which to the left
opens upon the grange, to the right upon the dwelling-rooms.
The grange, high and spacious, with great carved trellises of a
fine brown wood, has a very noble effect. The house, centring
therein its life and security for a seclusion of eight months,
has not thought it possible to do too much for the grange ; so
it has all the appearance of a church. Good resinous wood of

a delightful odour is stored there for fuel. Hay, exquisite and delicate, full of living perfumes, makes one almost envy the cattle so excellent a provision. Happy prisoners are they, stationed within a short distance of the family; its companions and cherished purveyors, carefully tended and liberally fed!

Other doors open upon the kitchen, the reception-room, and behind on the inner apartment, which is well protected, with a southward exposure, and is the meeting-place of the family. The wainscotted partitions of reddish larch or indestructible arolla, glittering and highly polished, wear a sombre and yet cheerful tint, which perfectly rests the eye when dazzled and fatigued by the snow.

There is kept the cherished souvenir of the family,—the hereditary chest, finely carved and blazoned with armorial bearings, reposing majestically in its corner. Nobles or not, all have their own crest or emblem, as was formerly the case in France with our burgesses and even our peasants. The portraits of kinsmen and ancestors are honourably displayed on the walls and at the windows.

A good large stove occupies a considerable space in the chamber, and rises to a height of five or six feet; the space above it up to the ceiling being masqued with a trellis-work and very neat curtains. I know not why, but the mystery which it hides was revealed to me. Behind the stove is discreetly concealed a narrow little staircase which leads to the paradise. By this I understand a small apartment where, in the depth of winter, the husband and his wife take refuge, nestle together, and live a marmot-like life right above the stove. But as the latter does not touch the ceiling, it allows only a very agreeable warmth to ascend there.

Such are the sensible, genuine, and choice pleasures of the North, which one might well prefer to all others. So exqui-

site in themselves, they are greatly enhanced by their contrast
with a rugged and terrible external nature. In Russia they
are enervating, and prove fatal to the very race.

Here they are greatly refined. He who has lived, travelled, and suffered, will all the more keenly feel the charm of
this happy domestic interior. I am confident that to-day he
desires nothing from the beautiful south and the brilliant
countries where he laboured so long. He would willingly
resign all the enchantments of Italy for the narrow little staircase which leads to his thrice-happy nest.

The fireside is here the true foundation of life and of
religion itself. The old Roumansch Bible lies on the shelf,
properly reverenced ; and by its side hang pictures of Luther
and Melancthon. But men who have seen so much of the
world are never exclusive, so that sometimes I have known it
accompanied by the Madonna, a copy after Raphael.

The *true* Madonna is the Wife. Who animates the house,
and fills it with life and soul ? Evidently she alone. Not so
worn and weary as her husband, she throws herself into her
marital duties with all the energy of the climate and the
ardour of the Kelt. She is no soft German woman. One
remembers that one is in the country of Jean Colani, the
famous chamois-killer. For a keen eye, a sure foot, an
unerring aim, he had but one rival—his daughter. Wild and
audacious like himself, but madly ardent in her terrible pur-
suit, she despised marriage : she burned away, she moved
onward, " in maiden meditation, fancy free."

Ulysses has travelled, but not Penelope : she may therefore be more disquieted in mind, may find the winter very
long and the country very solitary. Are the few visits they
pay in their sledge enough to satisfy her mind ? For him it
suffices, because he is enamoured of repose. The very winter

which condemns him to rest is the charm that makes him
love the country. He resembles a tree, and is attached to
his home by fibres and roots which are invisible; numerous
as those of the arolla, stretched in every direction—deep as
those of the larch, which penetrate as far into the earth as
they can make their way.

The interior is not the less happy, and the concord, so far
as one can judge, is perfect. The *ménage*, generally excellent
in Switzerland, is here closely limited by the climate. The
husband has laboured industriously, and acquired a little fortune. His wife conforms herself to his tastes. My slight
opportunities of observation have given me the very favourable
idea of a woman wholly devoted to her household, incurious
as to the outer world; like the window-panes, which, often
convex, ridged, and very thick, admit the light, but afford no
glimpse of the passers-by. Just the opposite is the case with
the mirror or *espion*, where the Flemish woman sits at work,
observing all that transpires without. And still more unlike
it is the close, glazed balcony of the little projecting cabinet
which permits the German frau, without rising from her stool,
to gaze up and down the entire length of the street.

Do I mean that this man with his solitary tastes is inhospitable? On no account. The door is not thrice-bolted, as
in Holland and other countries. I was struck—nay, touched—
to see that these people, who have undergone many trials and
suffered sorely, do not remain unfriendly nor shrink from
human companionship. Their welcome to the stranger is sin-
cere; their fireside genial for him who trusts himself to it
with confidence. I judge of this particularly by a painter of
great ability—a Slave, and a man of capricious disposition
and glowing fancy, who lived for several years the Robinson
Crusoe of the craters and glaciers of the Bernina. He was
the object of their thought, of their constant disquietude, and

their most touching cares. They sent him their best wines; they compelled him to desist from his excursions in inclement weather; they took care of him in the winter. He found in the village a truly fraternal hospitality.

There is one thing which tends to paralyze and render inactive the people of the Engadine : they believe that their race and language will before long disappear.

Is it nature which threatens this calamity?

They have no cause, it seems, to apprehend that the glaciers which anciently occupied their country will again reconquer it. Of these many a story is told, but all referring to remote times. The Morterasch formerly engulfed the chalets. The Roseg owes its name, they say, to a very pitiful legend. Every year, before dawn, the priest of Pontresina repaired thither to celebrate the *Messa di Rosodi*, or "mass of dew"—that is, of the morning; a mass for the souls of the victims swallowed up by the Roseg.

These disasters are rare. The gradual course of destruction and the sure diminution of life are much more to be feared. Several species of birds, as M. Saratz tells me, have quitted the Engadine in the last fifteen years (since about 1850). A very subtle and sagacious creature—the magpie— which is found more or less over all the world, had always cultivated this country; but it has lately taken its decision. It has even quitted the Lower Engadine, where the climate is comparatively milder, and transported elsewhere its industry.

The wild goat has perished; the chamois grows rare. Where could we find to-day the two thousand seven hundred animals killed in the course of his career by Jean Marchiet— the elder Colani—the King of the Mountain? The successor in this dynasty—our present Colani, who is still young, having but recently come to the throne—is a king without a kingdom. His subjects, the chamois, have perished and disappeared. He is thrown back upon the plants, has become a collector of flowers, and supplies from his treasures both the Old and New Worlds.

But what a different life! What a melancholy change! From an heroic career having descended to the profession of science, he has sunk into a simple botanist; yet even in the new existence to which he has confined himself he has dared to undertake the botanical conquest and subjugation of Germany. The solitary wild, at an elevation of 8000 feet, is no longer a secure asylum. Rare and unique plants have disappeared, to lie interred, in a mummy condition, in those great cemeteries which men call museums.

Is this an image of the Engadine? Will it survive? Will it become a desert? or a portion, vulgar and prosaic, of the German provinces?

Germany herself, that fertile mother of sciences which we all love and admire, is powerfully original. But, to speak frankly, her outer members are imbued with vulgarity. Her excessive and disproportionate culture everywhere enslaves and levels the *genius loci*. It is a wonderful system of gardening, singularly complex and scientific, which kills all the little flowers, however exquisite, that flourish with the spontaneity of nature.

Throughout the whole canton of the Grisons, which is the largest in Switzerland, there are but forty thousand persons speaking the language of the country. In the Upper Engadine two languages are spoken. But it is the German which prevails in the schools and churches, and will gradually absorb the new generations.

Languages die out. Humboldt relates that in some country, on the banks of the Orinoco, whose name I forget, he saw a parroquet, a hundred years old, which spoke in an unknown tongue. It was that of a tribe which had long disappeared. An old man said to him, "When the bird and I are gone, no one will remain to speak that language."

The citizens who vote, regulate the affairs, and elect the members of the legislature of Coire, are not very numerous (only twenty-three, I was informed at Saint-Moritz). The others, simple inhabitants, taking no part in political life, give but little thought to the future, and feel no particular pride in founding lasting families. I met with very few children.

It seems as if already it were the past which this country contemplated. I do not believe that anywhere else the dead receive so much consideration. Its numerous churches communicate to the country a peculiar melancholy charm. Pontresina has its own cemetery, lying on the mid slope of the mountain; Celerina its own, on an isolated knoll, which produces a great effect. Diametrically opposite to the custom of Germany, which has so often *set its dead to dance* (*les morts en danse*),—to that of Italy, which makes many a strange exhibition of its ossuaries,—the Engadine has given to the dead the place of supremacy, the noblest abodes, and the royalty of rest.

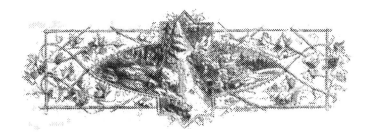

XII

THE AROLLA.

DECAY OF THE TREE AND OF MAN.

PONTRESINA, with its ancient name signifying "the Bridge of the Rhetia," is admirably situated at the meeting-point of two torrents and of the two routes of the principal glaciers. I have seen many grander landscapes, but none more harmonious, better "composed," or more suitable for the artist, than that of the Roseg, the magnificent glacier which, from Pontresina, you see towering above the torrents.

Thanks to the excellent friends who inconvenienced them-selves in order to provide me with a more comfortable study, I had a very handsome and well-lighted spacious chamber, where I could read, write, and meditate at ease. One window looked eastward, another towards the south, and each furnished me with a picture. To the south, the Roseg, at an excellent distance for effect, and at the bottom of a winding valley, with woods on the right and left, and along the mountain-stream a green meadow, leading to Saint-Moritz. Eastward, the road which gently ascends to Upper Pontresina, the pic-turesque and tranquil village I have already spoken of, and then strikes onward to the glacier of Morterasch, which, from

this point, is invisible.   Of the village itself you can only see
the dominant feature, its cemetery-church, built prior to 1500.

All this, especially in the morning and towards noon, was
singularly attractive, and even blithesome.   It possessed a
touching cheerfulness, such as the rising sun lends in summer
to a country-side where one already anticipates the approach
of winter.   The meadow, somewhat sickly, with a fine short
grass ; the wood of sombre arollas ; the bridge of stone, with
its timber defences,—all gave serious warning of its advent.

I had resumed my ordinary habits.   I rested in the morning, reading, or at work.   The book I was then studying was
the learned " Géographie Botanique " of Alphonse de Candolle.

One day I came upon an expression which set me thinking, and which I may epitomize thus : *The commonplace will
prevail,* will invade and conquer the world.

" The plants common to different countries will become
more numerous.   The local flora will everywhere lose its
originality " (p. 803).

" Wayside flowers and cultivated plants will characterize
our epoch, and those of the forests and mountains grow more
and more restricted " (p. 806).

And he adds : " They belong to an ancient order of things,
and must give place to a new " (p. 807).

To this wild ancient order, which was in all things distinguished by original characteristics, strongly marked, will succeed the new order, much richer but less varied, and with
one object exactly like another.

Already, before De Candolle, Agassiz had laid down an
important fact, and an illustration which shows its range.
" Our European plants (about sixty in number, many of which
are noxious herbs) have invaded America, and swept away
the American plants, in the same manner and in the same

proportion as the white man has swept away the Indian"
(*Soc. de Neufchâtel, November* 1847).

A distinguished savant of the Engadine, M. Pallioppi,
having done me the honour to pay me a visit, I spoke to him
of the future of his country. He smiled sadly as he answered :
"Our language will disappear." But to adopt another language, to think in a strange tongue, is it not to change one's
soul, to grow dead to one's own genius ?

M. President Saratz told me another and very serious
fact : "Wood," said he, "will fail us."

This will be the end of all, will convert the country into a
desert.

His statement grieved me deeply, and I felt how warmly
I was interested in the Engadine.

I attempted to doubt its truth. Seeing many localities
still richly clothed with timber, you can hardly suppose that
such a calamity will ever take place. Nevertheless, life uses
it up ; the progress of human society, its increasing and
varied wants, wage a universal war against the trees. This is
everywhere discernible. Here the important difference is,
that they renew themselves with exceeding slowness.

What will become of the country when the frozen house
can only be warmed with wood brought from below, slowly,
at a great expense, and by a number of horses ! climbing the
steep ascents, and toiling up declivities so terrible as that of
the Maloya ?

But how shall the house be maintained, and how shall the
villages last, when, the woods which protect them wholly disappearing, the torrents and the avalanches obtain free way to
pour down upon them ? Will even such places as Pontresina,
situated at some distance from the mountain, be sufficiently
secure ? Who does not know that these sudden ruins, descending from a tremendous elevation, move forward with tremend-

ous leaps ? It is a matter of the utmost importance that a
forest still dominates over the town; and the day that it
perishes, Pontresina will no longer sleep in safety.

The whole life of the country has centred in two trees :
the heroic and vigorous arolla, which, if left to itself, would
endure almost for ever ; and the smiling larch, incessantly
renewed, and with its yearly verdure simulating eternal
youth.

Both are supported, in these severe regions, by a miracle
of nature which requires explanation. Heat and life are
cherished, guarded, and concentrated in them—are impenetrably shut in—by an internal defence, which is as good as a
house, and which, in the bitterest winter, preserves for them
the *home.* This defence is—the resin.

In general, the family of conifers or resinous trees, being
exposed to the extreme north, have only preserved life
through their prudent precautions. They breathe with much
care, never exposing their tracheas to the outer air. They
open only the narrowest loopholes (like the stomata of insects).
The air, entering slowly, and combining with their carbon, not
only nourishes them, but this nourishment gradually becoming thick and glutinous, turns into resin, and as such seals
them up against the breath of winter.

This resin resists the cold in three ways. First, it acts as
a solder. Then, owing to its density and thickness, it does
not freeze. Finally, as carbon, it is a non-conductor of heat,
and, far from permitting it to escape, preserves and concentrates it within.

Impervious to air, insoluble in water, and rebellious
against electricity, the resin repels these three great solvents,
which change everything in nature. It covers and defends
whatever has ceased to act, each cellule which has perished in
its turn. The great agent of preservation, it is also an instru-

THE DECAY OF THE MOUNTAIN FOREST.

ment of progress. It sustains the young cellule, and helps it
with its own fixity. And finally, in the spring (O wonder !)
it again grows pliable, resumes the softness of life, and once
more becomes a living thing.

The finest of all resins is that of the larch, which in commerce is known as Venetian turpentine,—a substance of
astonishing subtlety, and exceeding penetrability. An atom
introduced into any living organism penetrates it immediately,
and traverses the entire course of its circulation.

In all the arts these resins have proved of the greatest,
utility. Every painter has need of them. And even the
musician uses them for his stringed instruments, and by their
means makes his bow vibrate.

But is not the tree itself an instrument ? One is surprised to see, in the cold Engadine, the interior of the larch
exhibiting those warm hues which render the violin so pleasant in the eyes of colourists. Like the Alpine flowers, it
absorbs the living light, and thence derives that fine red tone
which one might suppose to be its youthful blood.

It inhales these colours through its numerous radiating
needle-like leaves, which may be compared to the polypus,
that all around it searches and seeks with its tiny arms. It
possesses no great exhausting branches, but a good strong
root, with which it plunges into its favourite soil, the mica-
schist, whose brilliant laminæ are like so many mirrors, excellent reflectors of heat and light.

With respect to its seeds it acts very wisely. Though
they are ripe in autumn, it retains and guards them, nor
ventures to let them forth until the spring. With this pledge
of the future shut up and concentrated within itself, abandoning to the wind its thenceforth useless leaves, it bends before
the hissing and raging gale, when stimulated into action by
the winter. Its bare branches, affording little hold to the

wind, come and go, and resist it all the more successfully that they do not offer any virtual resistance.

Far from exhausting itself by reproducing its leaves, it converts them into myriads of nourishing agents, which augment its sap and increase its vitality. And therefore it seems to be always young, a stranger to the country, the offspring of a happier clime. Its companion, the arolla, so grave and immovable, recognizes it no longer, and stares at it from the depths of its antiquity.

It is the hope and the joy of the mountain. It labours incessantly to re-create the forest. But the more it accomplishes, the more is demanded of it. It supplies the thousand wants of the country. Whence come those ceilings? From the larch. What builds up yonder noble and imposing grange? Again, the larch. Its beautiful, odorous wood, worthy of the highest artistic purposes, is wastefully expended upon the hearth.

Observe that nature everywhere treats it very harshly. Cheerful as it appears, and valiant against the winter, it is vulnerable in spring. The delicate sap which then rises in its veins dreads any sudden chill. And yet such a fate frequently befalls the adventurous larches, which climb up to the very glacier, in the teeth of a keen and subtle wind. You will see them looking very wretched, and frightfully attenuated, unable either to live or die.

It appears that the arolla accordingly said to the larch :—
" Child, what seek you here ? "

Only one being has the right to plant itself on the brink of the glacier. One alone can contemplate it face to face, through the long ten months of winter, and not perish. The winter cleaves the stone, but the tree laughs at its fury. The winter maddens and rages, but cannot subdue the tree's profound and vigorous vitality. The winds rush to the assault; the furious hurricanes heap up the mass of snows, and overwhelm everything, except the arolla. It has the royal privilege of never carrying a burthen. You see it speedily emerging from the snow, rising above it, and flinging it off its vigorous arms. It reappears with tranquil front, and raises heavenward its magnificent lustres; each of which is adorned with a lofty plume of leaves.

On the ascent to the glacier, the effect is impressive. All life gradually diminishes. The great trees are dwarfed, to live as humble and feeble coppices. The birch-tree of the far North—of Russia—that stout friend of the frost and rime, before the wild demon, the ferocity of the glacier, grows afraid, and lowers its crest. Yet, on the very edge you see the arolla, in its tallest stature, in its fulness of life, untouched and unchanged. On sheltered slopes it may be seen languishing, overloaded with lichens. But here, in the face of the terrible winds, and the midst of the mighty struggle, it flings off its garb of dree. Naked, like a skilled athlete, grasping the bare rock with its strong roots, it awaits the avalanche,— unconquerable and superb,—rearing aloft its conquering arms, and in these regions of death bearing witness to everlasting life.

Seeing it planted there so stoutly on the sterile rock, one asks how it contrives to nourish its strength. Some dust from the *débris* of the glacier may supply it with aliment, but it feeds especially upon the light.

Light! ethereal life! sublime nourishment! To this is due the noble character of our dwellers of the lofty Alps. Those who live in the plains, fed by the earth and the variable gifts of the cloud, remain in a condition of humble dependence. On lofty summits which the cloud never touches, the living, intense, and more equable light supplies the place of inferior food.

Hence results the strange splendour of this wholly solar flora. Hence the singular subtlety of the larch, and, at a still greater elevation, the sovereignty of the arolla, which reigns where nothing else lives; triumphs, where all is finished; and marks the supreme border-line of nature.

Do I say that it is therefore insensible ? Nay, its leaves, though apparently impenetrable, are really of a very delicate character, and feel most keenly the biting frost. This you may discern from their wan tints, which you would scarcely expect to find upon them. Our prince of the winter, in its warm soft lights, grows beautiful from its sufferings, and from the mighty calm with which it endures them.

Its internal magic—the tenacious resin—heals, protects, and endows it with a comparative eternity.

The ages being all its own, it is in no hurry. It does little, but does that little well. It slowly elaborates its admirable wood, and brings it to perfection. To accomplish its full growth it requires a thousand years.

One would fain form an idea of a life so slow and so strong. How curious it would be to divine what has succeeded to it in the obscure labour of the most persevering of vegetable souls ! Powerfully animated in its gloomy envelope, it must nevertheless preserve, through such a world of obstacles, the instinct of safety, the personal forethought, a prevision of the means by which life is saved or augmented.

An American imagines, with much probability, that between life and death exist numerous intermediate stages ; that these words are only relative. The dead life and the living death, the vague unconscious thought, the dream all powerless to act, and even to thoroughly comprehend or analyze itself,—are things that ought to be found in the prolonged existence of these trees, which one may describe as embalmed, like Egyptian mummies, but which live nevertheless under their voiceless mask.

To wound the arolla is a crime, for it is the only tree which one cannot renew.

Who will plant it, when, in the course of a hundred years, it does not acquire the thickness of a man's fist? In our hurried and utilitarian epoch, who will give any thought to future generations?

But, on the other hand, you may seek in vain to replace the arolla; in vain attempt it with the light (and soulless) birch, or the other meagre trees of the North. They are all powerless here. The glacier reduces them to the condition of dwarfs and abortions. But the sun is specially fatal and terrible to them; at certain times, it can annihilate them with a glance.

The arolla struggles and holds its ground successfully against both enemies, the sharp javelin of the frost, the overpowering sun. Since the Alps were Alps, it has defended the mountain against the two destroyers.

The misfortune of the arolla is that of all heroes. So brave against the blows of Fate—living so hard a life of trial and combat—it preserves, nevertheless, a tender heart. It is vulnerable from within. Its fragrant pleasant wood, of so fine and regular a texture, has the grave misfortune of being wholly free from defect, of being very easily wrought. It is cut without difficulty, and carved with the utmost ease. Hence a succession of sacrileges. An imbecile shepherd, with his rude knife, cuts out of this age-old timber ridiculous images of sheep and grotesque goats, which are sold at Vienna, at Nuremburg, and on the Rhine. To-morrow the foolish mother of this destructive child gives out the mighty heart which defended the Alps, to be used as a doll, dismembered, flung aside, and burned!

It is a sacred palladium. Living in it, the country maintains itself and maintains its own life. Dying, it also dies, perishes little by little, and when the last tree is cut, the last man will disappear.

My morning's labours concluded, I went out alone, and
crossing the torrent, ascended a little in front of it, to pay a
visit to the forest, salute my arollas, and converse with them.
These beautiful trees of the ancient forest suffered from the
visible wearing away of the mountain.   Many, with foot in
the peat-bog, and trunk encumbered with mosses, and arms
sadly draped with lichens which gradually overcome and suffo-
cate them, expressed but too plainly the idea which had
haunted me ever since my perusal of Candolle,—"The commonplace will prevail."

They were melancholy.   I said to them :—Dear trees,
you appear to me like men.   Your sickly groves remind me
of the human forest.   That from which you suffer is the
universal feature of the century—an ingenious and inventive
century, but with little liking for the grand.   None has
worked so hard to level all which might elevate it.   None
has so anxiously endeavoured to destroy the heroic races and
extirpate the heroes.

The plain is mistress of the age, and makes war against
the mountain.

The mountain of the Caucasus, where formerly shone the
most brilliant and the haughtiest of the white races ;

The mountain of Crete, the only country where Greece
(elsewhere mixed and polluted) has preserved the purity of
her blood ;

The Scandinavian mountain, the isles of the old kings of
the sea ;

All are razed, destroyed, or in a very short time will be so.

Where are the noble Indians of North America ?   Where
are the Welsh (whose daughter gave the world the illustrious
Shakespeare) ?   Where are the Highlanders ? torn from their
hills by England, and lying dead for her sake on the field of
Waterloo ?

The Low Dutch marches northward to ravage the country of Hamlet. The flat plain of Russia is reducing to its own level the land of Sobieski, and that of Charles XII.

There once existed in the world a city which one might have designated the Mountain of Mind ; and the jet of flame which issued from it has illuminated the earth. To-morrow its site will be occupied by a vulgar rendezvous of the rich, the rude, and the ignorant, who flock thither to enjoy their sensual pleasures, and to lavish contempt on intellectual delights.

XIII.

WILL OUR ERA SUCCEED IN REGENERATING ITSELF?

"REGRET is a sin," said the ancient Persian law.

By thinking our misfortunes incurable, we too frequently render them so.

By weeping over approaching death, we exhaust the life which remains.

Whatever reasonable causes of melancholy may be ours, I do not think a downward movement is our definitive law.

I have traversed too many ages—acquired too great an experience of the alternative phases through which human society passes—to suffer my spirits to sink, or my hope and faith to decline. I should have lost all the fruit of my two thousand years of history, if I forgot the all-powerful awakenings of man's soul, if I ignored the resources of that great centre of life—Europe. To ensure its abundant wealth and completeness it possesses, not only the ordinary vital organs, but, like the higher animals, supplementary organs with which to repair its losses, to supply its deficiencies,—energies hidden and unforeseen, which, in its days of despondency, spring from some unknown source.

If with a steady and tranquil gaze we contemplate the

world, we can without difficulty distinguish that our decay cannot be compared to the rottenness of some peoples of the past, such as the Chinese or the Byzantine, of whom sterility was the conspicuous and distinctive sign. Certain weaknesses of character have not prevented the mind from preserving its power and fertility. Our very weaknesses are, in truth, of extraneous origin, and due to the immense dispersion of those boundless works, and all those arts created long ago in the gigantic laboratory of our ancient continent.

The vigour of Anglo-Saxon America—that noble enthusiasm (*élan*) which now enraptures us, and fills us with hope and joy—does not prevent me from cherishing the belief that the sublime sensorium of earth still flourishes here, in the old mother Europe. Its four reverberating light-towers (France and England, Germany and Italy) feed it from their intercrossing rays with an infinitely vivid radiance, which enables it to know itself, to penetrate its inner soul, to distinguish its ills and their remedies. Europe is surpassingly lucid. Its singularly inventive genius, piercing to the very bottom of things, cannot fail to re-act upon itself, and analyze man. Among the numerous arts which it has created, another, and the loftiest, will yet arise—that which makes and re-makes the soul.

I know that, for this achievement to be effected, the supreme condition (and a difficult one) will be, to arrest for a moment the giddily-whirling wheel of external activity, which hurries us in all directions, and fixes our gaze on things out of and far apart from ourselves.

Would I could bestow on the spirits which are potent to renew our natures, some few of the choice delightful days I spent at Pontresina! A peculiar silence extinguished all the empty noises which mingle with our thoughts. There the senses seized upon every object with the utmost certainty.

The transparency of the air which clears away the mirages of
mist and fog, also diminishes distance, and enables us not only
to see things remote, but to see a multiplicity of things at one
and the same time.   What elsewhere we see in detail we
there survey as a whole.   And a glorious harmony which
embraces everything, is yet subject to a certain control, so as
to exclude the illusive, and protect the true.

This harmony enriches and extends our prospect, even
beyond the limits which we can actually discern.   Thus, in
the wonderfully harmonious landscape of the Roseg, I divined,

THE VALLEY OF ROSEG AND PONTRESINA.

by the aid of striking analogies, certain hidden beauties, and
with the mind's eye saw what I did not see.   This is the
secret of vision spoken of by the ancients, and not without
reason, but without their being able to afford a proper explanation.   Hence they were accustomed to say that the seer
could pierce through bodies with his glance.

It is, however, a task of extreme difficulty to penetrate
into oneself; it is the great effort of contemplation—the
object of the ancient sage in taking up his residence among

the mountains. It was only in their solitude that he could obtain a mastery over his own nature, could disengage his genius from the well-worn furrows of old routine, from the pressure and entanglement of the crowd, and from his internal self;—in a word, could by his own effort rise above himself.

The soul becomes sensible of an infinity, and augments its initiative faculty. Even humanity weighs little in the balance. Who does not remember that the world was on one side, Copernicus and Galileo on the other ?

In the presence of the Alps, all false greatness perishes. In the presence of the Alps, no worldly authority can preserve its lying prestige. The only sovereignty which there exists is that of reason, truth, and conscience.

I felt something of these truths when, in the neighbourhood of Mont Blanc, in August 1865, the first page of this book was written. I felt them still more powerfully in July 1867, during the hours of solitude which I enjoyed at Pontresina. While our travellers were overrunning the country and making their ascents, I too was accomplishing mine. For the second time this distinct and vivid idea of the mountain returned to my mind : " *It is an initiation.*"

It is interesting to observe how, shortly before the movement of '89, the great eighteenth century regained from Nature herself the heroic sentiment.

Voltaire, a child of the city and the drawing-room, whom one would have supposed all art had blinded to nature, in his poems written at the Lake of Geneva uttered the first sublime cry. Rousseau chose the framework of the Alps for his " Savoyard Vicar," and inbreathed their firm, bold tone into his " Letters from the Mountain."

Two great revolutionary spirits, Monsieur and Madame Roland, before they entered upon a life of action, attempered their stoicism in the mountain air.

BÜRGLEN, THE BIRTH-PLACE OF WILLIAM TELL.

The Swiss possess many beautiful chronicles in record of noble deeds, but have too much neglected to consecrate their memory by those monuments of stone which to generation upon generation read a silent lesson. A Frenchman, halting at the central point where the Lake of the Four Cantons crosses its heroic arms, was seized with a religious emotion, and trembled with a holy horror. He was neither king nor prince; he was only a philosopher. But it seemed intolerable to him that the three heroes of the Rutli who pledged their lives to the freedom of Switzerland should be without a monument. He remained on the spot, and erected in one of the islands of the lake a pyramid, which existed there until recently, when it was destroyed by lightning. The foes of liberty have effaced its remains. But they shall not efface this beautiful fact, and the mark it has made in literature. The Frenchman, a man of talent but of no genius, possessed an overflowing and inexhaustible heart ; a heart which, inspired by Switzerland, drew from it the idea of a book that for twenty years has been the bible of the world.

The book is fable, but the memorial sublime. It shows how fresh and genial hearts, even in an age which is reputed to be so corrupt still, found in these exalted regions the power of upward flight. This one, descending from their glaciers, brought back their spirit of austerity. That one, gazing upon their lofty peaks, felt an impulse of the heroic. All returned elevated and ennobled.

Such a recollection is in strong contrast with the sight we see to-day of worldly crowds, the noisy dregs of society, pouring every summer into Chamounix and Interlachen, taking the Oberland by storm, and vulgarizing each magnificent wilderness. Is it the love of Nature—a new sense—which has been suddenly developed among them ? Is it a manly impulse towards daring, dangerous, and difficult undertakings? We would wish to think so ; but a Tyndall, and two or three honoured names, cannot deceive us. As far as the mass is concerned, what we see is this : that those who in their own country still preserve some degree of moderation and show some respect for social decencies, in Switzerland believe themselves wholly unrestrained.

Let us cease to profane the Alps. Let us not carry into the mountains the grossness of the plains. Let us aim, at least, to render our pilgrimage a respite from vices, a moment of moral dignity.

We ought to reverence these places. The first consideration

which we owe them is, not to import the sickly and enervating
literature of our time.   Even eminent writers, whose genius
we admire, too strongly contrast by their subtle artifices and
excessive ingenuity with the spirit of the country, and are
unworthy of perusal here.   Elsewhere let them be read in
their turn.   But bring few books to this spot, I pray you.
A treatise or two on natural history, or some simple and
beautiful chronicles, will be enough.   All human works are
dwarfed into littleness before this grand, this living, this
imposing and wonderfully pure book.   Compared with *it*,
they do but excite our compassion.

Even religious and mystical books are here out of place.
Particular creeds speak with a feeble and, frequently, with a
deceptive voice in the presence of that sublime religion which
embraces and overawes them.   Ye worldly deities, be silent!
Let us hear *the* God.

The austere grandeur of the Alps, and the stainless poesy
of these sublime virgins, ought to keep at a reverential distance
our weaknesses and romances.   Man must be audacious
indeed if, in the presence of their eternity, he can take any
count of his miserable person ; can carry thither his little-
nesses, his sloth-engendered nervousness, and the maladies he
ought rather to seek to conceal.   What becomes of the weari-
ness of Obermann in these regions of active effort, in this ever
memorable cradle of European freedom, in this rude mountain-
life whose perilous and assiduous toil has furnished a great
example to the world!   Between the hardy pioneer of the
forests and the indefatigable workman of Geneva, what
signify fruitless dreams and the melancholies of emptiness ?

Love is upon a level with all,—is as divine as the Alps.   I
do not misunderstand the force and sincerity of Rousseau.
Yet who at Clarens can reperuse the "Eloise"?   No mere
rhetoric or talent can survive in such a place.   Nature is on
too grand a scale.   History too tragic in the war of these

CLARENS AND MONTREUX (LAKE OF GENEVA).

two shores, of which, happily, a witness still remains in the
prison of Chillon.

Some one has made an admirable remark on the striking
resemblance which exists between Meillerie and Clarens :—
" The feeling is of a still higher and more comprehensive order
than the mere sympathy with individual passion ; it is a sense
of the existence of love in its most extended and sublime
capacity, and of our own participation of its good and its
glory : it is the great principle of the universe."

A deep religious utterance ! Who would believe it was
Byron's ? * More than all his verses, it is truly worthy of the
Alps.

I wished while at Meyringen to read again his " Manfred,"
but could not succeed. Its desolate exaltation, its fictitious
mystery, its false tragedy, which belongs to no time or place,
jar on our minds in such a locality. It is a deplorable conception to have enthroned Nemesis, the vengeance and the
goddess of Ill, among these beneficent glaciers which pour out
in the flood of their mighty rivers the life, salubrity, and
fertility of Europe !

Switzerland is not perfect. But what I find particularly
admirable in her customs, and of superior excellence—in fact,
a true blessing—are the delightful liberties which childhood
there enjoys, its children's *fêtes,* so grateful to the heart, and
in all things so adorable. On one occasion, when entering
Vevay, I saw one of these entertainments, in which some
hundreds of children (about twelve years old, perhaps), girls
and boys pell-mell, with tiny flags, marched through the town
singing songs, with a prudence, and yet an amount of freedom, truly most affecting !

I frequently saw along the highroads little schools of
children bound on a journey. I met one at the Splügen—a

* [In his Notes to the third canto of "Childe Harold."]

THE REICHENBACH FALLS, AND GLACIER OF ROSENLAUI (FROM MEYRINGEN).

school which had come from a distance—from Neufchâtel, it appeared to me—and had traversed Switzerland. The children were very young, and yet, without suffering too much from fatigue, they went on foot, each carrying his small stock of baggage — undergoing already an apprenticeship to the traveller's life, and experiencing his little adventures;—happy in acting for the first time as men. They travelled along *with* — I will not say *under*—a master, who did but slightly interfere with their liberty of movement. He was a grave young man, who pleased me exceedingly. His wife was with him; young also, agreeable, attentive to all; not without some fatigue she followed her little flock, surrounding and enveloping them with her maternal grace (July 1867).

Nothing could be more charming or more touching. At a very early age, young Switzerland simply and soberly (whatever may be its fortune) traverses every canton of its free and beautiful country, learns as a child to love it, unites with it its existence, its habits, and its heart, and links to it its destinies.

Nevertheless, I am of opinion that, for the stranger, with whom the journey has no patriotic character, the Alps gain infinitely by being visited a little later in life ; that is, in youth. The child cannot properly feel their grandeur. He is much more impressed by a thousand prosaic details, which are sometimes insignificant, but especially accidental and not peculiar to the country ; are there only by chance, and give a false idea of it. The vivid memory of that age which ineffaceably preserves all that is impressed upon it, will throughout life retain these fantastic features. Of the sublimest locality, will it not preserve the recollection only of some chance passer-by, some *crétin*, or buffoon ?

"But if they should be revisited in later years, would not the Alps then produce their full effect ?" Do not believe it. They retain the character which originally arrested our attention.

Families are now tenderer in feeling than of old, separate themselves from their children less frequently than they were wont, and take them everywhere with them. From this excellent custom results an inconvenience which deserves to be recognized. The child grows weary of the world. All that in his childhood he saw from the narrow point of view of that young age, and looked upon as little, ever appears to him as little, and is regarded with indifference. It is only young men who have been led straight from the nursery to the sea or the mountain that cease in after life to feel an interest in such scenes. "The Alps! I was cradled among them.—The Ocean! I know it thoroughly."

There is an inconvenience in traversing a whole country in one tour, in embracing all at once its varieties and contrasts, its frequently antagonistic and discordant landscapes. To attempt in one season to examine the Alps or the Pyrenees is to undertake *ensembles* of overpowering extent. Our confused impressions efface or blend with one

22

another, and falsify themselves, if they are simultaneously formed.

It would be interesting to single out a particular mountain, and thoroughly to distinguish its grand scales of life. What could be more delightful than to mark down its every step, and to determine its relation to man as well as to nature itself? The progressive rarefaction of the air, the favourable manner in which the resinous forests absorb our electricity, the amphitheatre of plants which vary with each succeeding level, are a kind of education. Every mountain is a world, and may be in itself a living text-book of the sciences.

For a mature mind, a more changeable and exceedingly prolific study would be that of a single river—the Rhone, for instance, or the Rhine—following up all the chances and changes of its course, all the various products of its banks.

In no other way could one obtain so lofty or so healthy a conception of the reality of things. One would thus discern the true value of that which saddens and deceives in the incessant labour of the waters to ruin, demolish, and level the mountain. Cascade and brook incessantly say to us, "What is death? What is life? If we demolish the Alps, it is to dower and fertilize Germany with our alluvial deposits, to enrich Alsace, to raise the soil of Holland, and defend and maintain her against the invasion of the sea." This dissolution is, after all, nothing but a creation.

Rambert ingeniously notices the delight these elements seem to experience in quitting their solitary immovability to fraternize with the shore and the plain. You may hear them say: "Let us on! Let us become dead to our barren life, that we may enter on a life of work, and merge in the fertilizing course of nature."

It is a fatal tendency of our age to imagine that nature is a reverie, an idleness, a condition of languor. The Bernardin de Saint-Pierres and the Chateaubriands, and their imitators, have only too well succeeded in enervating us in this sense. Yet no view is more diametrically opposite to that of antiquity, whose wise Centaur,* in order to cultivate the energies of his youthful hero to the utmost, had him up in the mountain-caves, among the fresh and verdurous forests.

Far from believing that Nature, taken in its truth, produces any feebleness of heart, I would fain reserve its grand and salutary emotions for those critical periods of youth when the mind stands in need of special support.   Do not think that at such times mere preaching will suffice.   Keep your sermons, and let the Alps discourse !

The two grand communions of the Mountain and the Sea might be very usefully reserved for these perilous moments : the Sea, for the first awakening, the first impulse of life ; the Mountain, when the senses experience their crisis of intoxication.   It is then I would wish to carry man out of himself, avoiding all cold and empty words—drawing the lesson from Nature—and how ? —by leading him in the Alps to the very bosom of Nature.

I would not freeze up his heart.   On the contrary, I would warm it with the noblest and loftiest inspiration.

I would conduct him to the fields of Morat and of Sempach, to the memorable battles which secured the freedom of Switzerland, and prepared the liberty of the world.

I would show him, on the summits of Saint Gothard, the watershed of the rivers, the point where they say farewell to one another, before departing to fertilize their different nations. Their waters, sometimes salutary, sometimes wild and threatening, have confederated the valleys, and constrained the people of the lowlands to come to a mutual understanding and unite in powerful leagues, which prevailed against the torrents and

---

* [Alluding to the Centaur Cheiron, who, in the old mythology, is described as the instructor of Achilles.]

the floods—against the torrent of the Barbarians—against Frederick Barbarossa in the south, and Charles the Bold in the north. Thus did the Swiss brotherhood,—and the Lombard League,*—these great souls of the nation, issue forth, as it were, from the Alps; were awakened by their rivers and the mystery of their waters.

I content myself with these examples, and shall go no further.   In this book of "The Mountain" I have developed, from chapter to chapter, the heroic capabilities which we imbibe from Nature.   And now, just as in a journey we see behind the Alp a still loftier Alp arising, so beyond my present work I see another which begins from this point:— "The Regeneration of the Human Race."

But enough for the day, enough.   This little book, whatever it may be, has a claim on my gratitude.   I finish, and I thank it.   In the long struggle of life, and of art (for ever restless), in a season of sorrowful expectancy, it prevented me from sinking, and held my head above the waters.   By a happy alternation between History and Nature, I preserved my level.   If I had followed man alone, and his savage records, melancholy would have enfeebled me.   If I had wholly devoted myself to Nature, I should have fallen (as many have done) into an indifference to right.   But I frequently exchanged the two worlds.   When I found my breath

---

* [The great Lombard League was formed against Frederick Barbarossa in 1167. The principal cities united by it were Cremona, Verona, Milan, and Venice; and according to the terms of the compact it was to last for twenty years, and be maintained against any prince or power who should threaten their ancient liberties. Frederick found himself unable to contend against its energy and resources, and the great victory of Legnano in 1176, followed by the peace of Constance in 1183, ensured the independence of Lombardy.—*See Sismondi, "Histoire des Républiques Ital.," and Muratori, "Antiquitates Italiæ," Dissertation 48.*

Of the famous Swiss League against Charles the Bold, Duke of Burgundy, the story has recently been told with great eloquence and exhaustive fulness by Mr. Kirke. It is only necessary to state here that the Swiss cantons entered the field with 34,000 men against 60,000, but were nevertheless victorious—both at Granson, on the 5th of April, and at Morat, on the 22nd of June, 1476. They also contributed largely to the victory won by the Duke of Lorraine at Nancy, January 5, 1477, when their fierce but imprudent enemy was slain.]

failing me in my human studies, I touched Terra Mater, and recovered my vigour.*

This is the whole secret of my book. If it has again renovated *me*, if it has blotted twenty centuries from my memory, mayest thou, young traveller! who comest with strength unimpaired and all the day before thee, find herein a starting-point for thy career. May it be for thee one of those midway summits where we halt at dawn, to collect ourselves for awhile, to mark the goal with a sure eye, and then to ascend to a loftier elevation!

* [As Antaeus, the son of Poseidon and Gé, was invincible, so long as he could touch his mother Earth.]

AUTHOR'S NOTES.

PART THE FIRST.

COULD easily have invested my little books—"The Bird," "The Sea," "The Mountain"—with a scientific aspect, by multiplying my references and quotations. But in so narrow a framework these would have had the effect of obscuring the theme, and of arresting the reader's attention upon details which would have deprived of their due relief the principal subjects.

Let it not be forgotten that when a work of genius appears on any topic it is immediately followed by numerous meritorious and useful books of theory or travel, observation or verification, until the mother work is apt to be pushed aside. On glaciers, the subject of our earlier chapters, the standard authority is that of Agassiz (*Etudes*, 1840). Preceded by Hugi, Venetz, and Charpentier, he systematized and enlarged their results, and first poured a strong flood of light on the great secret. He has been followed with much honour by Desor, Martins, Tyndall, Schlagentweit.* How it is that Europe did not retain in her most eminent professorial chairs so illustrious a man of science? How is it that so great a master teaches beyond the seas?

It was Agassiz who first asserted (*Etudes*, p. 304) that there had existed as an age of the world's history, *the Glacial Period*. This was not a simple hypothesis. He demonstrated irrefragably that if such a theory were not accepted, all the facts on which it was founded became inexplicable. Has he been answered? No. All later observation, and our increasing acquaintance with the earth, support his assertion, and the Glacial Period has gradually received the adhesion of the scientific world. Many writers refer to it in their books as a thing admitted and agreed upon, but without doing justice to him who first opened up the way.

* [See also Professor Forbes, on the Glaciers of Norway and Savoy.]

It was Agassiz again who first (after Hugi) perceived that mere passing ascents of the mountain would not suffice; that what science required was a *lengthened residence* among the glaciers,—to dwell there,—to live upon their mass and grow thoroughly acquainted with them,—to spend months and seasons in their companionship. Hugi, Agassiz, and Desor established themselves in these dreary regions, persevered in enduring their rigorous climates, and gave the world a bright example of courage, patience, and devotion.

The alternate advance and recoil of the glaciers,—a phenomenon of immense importance, which, as I have said, is a kind of physical (and may I not add, moral?) thermometer of the condition of Europe,—has been observed for the last fifty years. In 1811, owing to the drought, they receded. Three cold damp years—1815, 1816, 1817—made them move forward considerably (Venetz). In 1840, says Agassiz, they took a great stride in advance. They recoiled in the warm and potent year 1857, which prepared for us a cycle of fine seasons. In fact, Mr. Charles Martins,* in his ascent of 1865, detected an enormous recession. But, without doubt, they will have advanced again during the wet years of 1866 and 1867.

The illustrious Lyell † attempts to explain the transport of Erratic Blocks, not by the movement of the glaciers, but by rafts of ice similar to those which now descend from the North, and, in their progress, scarify the rocks. But here a difficulty arises which Agassiz has pointed out (*Etudes*, p. 283)— namely, that such rafts sink to an enormous depth beneath the surface of the sea; their upper part is, in magnitude, nothing compared with their lower. To carry such burthens as the Erratic Blocks, they must therefore have floated in waters of extreme depth, like those of ocean.

As a description and animated picture of mountain-life, Tschudi's work—so rich, moreover, in curious facts and personal researches—has never been excelled.‡ It is a small bible of the Alps, which every traveller should carry with him. He should also be accompanied by the following charming books : the "Essais" of Rambert ; the "Grimpeurs" (Climbers) and "Ascensions" of Margollé and Zürcher, the "Lake Leman" of Rey, and "Les Chamois" of A. Michiels.§

It is a matter of great interest to compare three standard books, three men, and three nations : the sagacity of M. de Saussure, courageous, judicious,

* [See his "Voyage du Spitzberg au Sahara."]

† [See his "Principles of Geology," 2 vols., 10th edition.]

‡ [An English abridgment exists, under the title of "Nature among the Alps."]

§ [The list might be easily extended, for equal, if not superior to the above, are Professor Tyndall's "Glaciers of the Alps," Wills's "Eagle's Nest," "A Lady's Tour of Monte Rosa," "Vacation Tourists," the publications of the Alpine Club, &c.]

harmonious, and well-balanced; the fine German genius of Tschudi, in such perfect communion with nature, and reflecting it so vividly, like a pure and beautiful Alpine lake; and, finally, the rough and feverish Ramond, the Frenchman of the South, thrilled with the spirit of the year '93. Putting aside his declamations, we must acknowledge that passion sometimes gifts him with a "second sight" to discover and divine the '93's of earth. One cannot but feel strongly interested in his prolonged exploration of Mont Perdu, in his hazardous career, and in his feelings, when, seated on the ruined rocks, he gives utterance to the lament: "How many are the irreparable and deplorable losses in the bosom of Nature!"

Is it easy to separate man from nature, human society from the great community whence it springs? We are amused and interested by the old travellers because, in their pages, we always catch glimpses of our kind through the landscapes. Most modern travellers, devoting themselves to special objects, —as one to plants, and another to shells,—furnish us only with matter-of-fact; they are instructive, but unreadable.

In CHAPTER X., p. 113—*The Upward Progress of Earth*—I have dwelt upon a circumstance which is too frequently neglected—namely, that our men of science, while believing that they pursue it apart from all social influences, are really affected by them unwittingly, and carry them into their very systems. It must be thoroughly understood, however, that I by no means assert that men so eminent as the Lyells, on the one side, the Buchs and Elie de Beaumonts, on the other, have been solely dominated by them.

What I have said of the boldness of Elie de Beaumont, and the grandeur of his *tentative*, will not astonish those who (like myself, at this very moment) have under their eyes his article *Systèmes de Montagnes*, an article which is in itself a colossal work (see d'Orbigny's "Dictionnaire," 1849, vol. xii., pp. 187–311). In its opening paragraph he gives expression to the idea that "a rigorous analysis will demonstrate the existence upon earth of a general order of which the heavens present no trace." Never before has Geology, that new-born science, thus dared to speak of its elder sister, which looks down upon us from such a height—Astronomy.

A word or two in reference to Chapter X., on the earth in general, and the creation of our globe :—

The sciences of observation did not really begin their existence until inaugurated by Galileo in 1600. The sciences of creation were commenced shortly before 1800 by Lavoisier.

The latter are the great and characteristic feature of our century, which has first created machines and forces; has created plants (not simple varieties, but permanent varieties); has created for these plants different soils, and cycles of cultivation which remake and renew them; has created races of animals, of useful and admirable monsters.

A strange and daring progress! It has outstripped Nature. No natural colour can vie with our *anilines*, introduced within the last ten years. The sun grows pale before the lightning invented by man—before his Electric Light. But note his greatest triumph: from the inert mineral we extract that which seems the most impalpable; all kinds of perfumes, spirits, and essences. Stone is alcoholized. And (must we finish? the Middle Ages would have recoiled in horror) stone is also *animalized*. We have drawn from pebbles the milk of the breast, the sweet milk of woman.

In the processes of fermentation and electricity we have discovered the stages by which the inert mounts to the organic state. The eternal barrier which was supposed to exist between them sinks and disappears. We put all things in a condition to live. What we believed to be matter dead everlastingly, will be life to-morrow. All *is* life, present or future. Everything incessantly glides from one living form to another.

What have become of the three kingdoms, the beautiful divisions of ancient science? Between the mineral and the vegetable—the highest vegetable energy (the blood of the vine, the essence)—there is no barrier of separation. Still less is there a barrier between the vegetable and the animal. Morren has discovered some semi-aquatic plants which, in the warm light, become animals for four hours daily, and then, when the day declines, resume a vegetable existence. But the equality of the two lives, the vegetable and the animal, is most plainly seen,—is, in fact, complete,—at the divine moment of love. Some flowers rise to the level of the highest animals, and even equal the mammalia. (See L. Lortet, on the *Preissia*, published in 1867.)

In a word, through fermentation, the stone creates itself mind. Through love, the plant makes itself man.

"Creation!" It was the enigma, the scarecrow of the Middle Ages. But for us it is the common life, it is what we see and do every day. It needs no miracle. The miracle would be if, in a world of such fertility, all things did not incessantly create.

How can a continent, a new quarter of the world, create itself? We enjoy to-day the pleasure of witnessing the process. Earth, by its polype-life, its little animals, is secreting a new field for human activity—who knows? perhaps an Europe? It prepares in the Southern Ocean a new continent for our use, if we should exhaust our own, or if it should be destroyed by some catastrophe.

It commences with a great number of islands, with hundreds and thousands of little circular mountains rising above the level of the wave. This form is excellent. It affords the fewest points of attack to their great enemy, the huge Austral wave, which, sweeping downward from the Pole without encountering a single obstacle, propelling and accumulating its confused billows, bears against them with a terrible weight, but being turned aside on either hand, loses a portion of its force. Each of these isles—of these graceful little worlds (very dangerous, notwithstanding, to the navigator)—with its white coral reefs, soon gathers in its bosom a little water suitable for the nourishment of vegetables, and frequently a fine cocoa-nut tree, which is able to endure the brine. And thus, behold, arises a miniature of the earth, an abridgment of the globe!

The island is seldom alone. A sister isle, and yet other islands, spring up by its side. Each forms a ring. And the group, too, is a ring, which, how-ever, by permitting the ingress of the seas, breaks their violence, and defends itself the more successfully. These annular groups, seventeen in number, present as a whole a great elongated circle, and, as it were, a colossal ring of nearly three hundred leagues in length. This promises well. The work advances. And it is continued by a prolongation of coral reefs, which, within the last few years, have arrested navigation.

The obstacle to these good workers is the avidity of the fish, which under the waters pasture upon the tender polypes, and assimilate the lime. They digest it, and restore it in the shape of chalk, which in its turn will produce the infusoria that form the food of the polypes, and will thus return to them again. In this manner the lime of the polypes, destroyed and digested, becomes the nourishment of their descendants ;—a curious circle, which vividly illustrates the very simple process of Nature's exchanges.

This truth was divined by Lamarck, who says : "Limestone is an animal substance ; it is produced by animals. That enormous portion of the world, which counts for so much in the terrestrial crust, and enters into so many soils and mountains, into these beds and quarries out of which we hew our towns, is a secretion. In an eternal revolution, the lime, alternately dissolved and restored to life, digested by plants and animals (and itself an animal), will go on, rolling and changing, inert in certain ages, and in others organic."

When was it all made? The process, probably, has been continuous. In the oldest strata deposited by the boiling sea we find the diatomaceæ ; those tiny creatures of silex, which exactly resemble organisms of the present epoch. The warm lakes of the Upper Andes have their fishes, and, accordingly, they also possess the infusoria on which these fishes feed. Why, even in the ages of fire, should there not have existed animals capable of living under such con-ditions? Do you say they have left no traces in the porphyries and basalts?

That proves nothing. They may have entered and re-entered into chemical combinations contrary to their own elements,—have been lost and annihilated in them.

Earth will create its creators. The natural upward movement of liquids—their *endosmose* in the bosom of the mineral very nearly resembles the vegetable *absorption*, which, if the plant be athirst, becomes *aspiration*—I was going to say, *suction*. Ought this last word to be restricted solely to animals, since, like them, the plant also aspires and sucks? The first-created animals, differing but slightly from plants, were all tiny suckers.

The *plant-animal*, or polype—half life and half rock—that freak of Nature mimicking Earth—imitated its immobility. Tiny organisms afterwards succeeded in the image of mobile Earth—erratic creatures and dwarf-plants springing from the bosom of the great mother, and permitted to move about their rock. Following the example of the Earth, which carries with it its terrestrial crust, these too travelled along with *their* crust, their shell, their protecting dwelling-place and asylum. Some composed of lime, others of silex, they have silently constructed, with their bodies and their small *débris*, the lofty mountains of the world, storing up for the earth the elements of superior beings.

The smaller existences, in order to reproduce themselves, are gifted with an obscure instinct, like an attraction, an interior gravitation, which is *Love*. First comes the love of self for self (to use Geoffroy Saint-Hilaire's expression). They love themselves, and seek their own good. And this is the origin of the development of every being, its taste, its choice, its "preference" (*Darwin*), for all that it has of good for itself, for all that ought to save and augment it, —make its little fortune, perhaps transform it, and raise it to a higher condition.

Such is the ordinary procedure of life, which we are ready enough to admit to-day so far as relates to the world of the little, the minor existences of animals. But why should it be otherwise with the grander life of the Earth? Why should not this transpire on the same principles as the little Earth (the animal-rock-plant) which we call *polype?* But working with very different agents, and means of every kind, it has not preserved the extreme regularity of the polype or bee. With an enchanting charm of variety it has built up the superb and delightful polypid which we inhabit.

I have a horror of the two hypotheses of creation without love.

First, The hypothesis of chance. Can any one suppose "that the attraction of a wandering star, passing near the earth, to the north of the Equator, can have diminished the general pressure, stirred up a tide in the interior fluids of our globe, and by this movement have elevated those mountains which we call the Old and New Continents!" (Poulett Scrope).

Here, indeed, is a fine stroke of chance ! But common sense rejects it. Who can believe that a simple shock has created so admirable and so felicitously combined a system of the universe ?

Second, The hypothesis of an all-powerful mechanician, who, elaborating and equipping the inert machine, by a stroke of address and force, a plain, indisputable miracle, has suddenly urged into life this world, without any mutuality of feeling or communion of love,—has mounted it on wheels,—has set it going without effort, and said to it, "Onward !" This is not worthy of God.

The Divine idea implies the two processes of life—the tender incubation and the maternal infoldment—above all, the patient succession and the infinity of time.

Violent shocks, thunder and lightning, the barbarous apparatus which barbarians supposed to have produced the world, are invariably (as everybody may observe) the cause of abortive births.

It is through the inspiration of that Power which preserves in the egg the delicate life of the tiniest bird—of that Soul of goodness which we feel in Nature—that the worlds create themselves—the worlds, the suns, and the Milky Ways.

Each star, endowed and sustained by its share of the Universal Soul, in its attraction towards its neighbouring sun, loves itself in loving the universe, unites, and harmonizes, and fashions itself in accordance with the whole.

A pacific mildness characterizes all the gods of the remotest antiquity. The Agni (*ignis*, the Fire-Spirit of the Rig-Veda), which vivifies the world, is, at the same time, the kindly companion of our roof-tree, the friend between *him* and *her*—between the husband and the wife—the cherished mediator of love. It is in later and more troublous times that humanity dreams of the fierce creative powers, the lightnings and the thunder of Indra.

CHAPTER XI., p. 129.—*On the Decadence of India.*—This decadence, and the neglect and brutality of Europeans, appear only too conspicuously in our books of travel, and especially in the interesting work of Warren, an authority beyond suspicion, since he served in the English army, admires the English, and in the English gentleman recognizes the ideal of man. The works of Hugh Cleghorn (1861), and of Brandis (1863-1865), point out the decay of the forests, and the tardy efforts made to remedy it.* Animals have decayed, as well as trees. The elephant, whose sagacity was still proverbial in the last century (see, particularly, Foucher d'Obsonville), is now embruted, and has sunk into a mere beast of burden, if I may believe the evidence of the East

* [To the importance of these subjects the Indian Government is now fully awake.]

India Company's Director of Commissariat.   See his important article on the
Elephant in D'Orbigny's " Dictionary."

CHAPTER XIII.—*On Java, &c.*—I have consulted the important and highly
instructive works of Sir Stamford Raffles and Mr. Crawford (1824); Blume,
Flora Javæ (1828); and Hogendorp (1830).   Walcknaer's excellent compila-
tion is also useful for reference.   It is interesting to compare Borneo with
Java.   See Mr. Spenser St. John's volumes, particularly respecting the
marvel of the *Nepenthes Edwardsiana.*

PART THE SECOND.

THE FIRST CHAPTERS OF PART II.—We cannot separate from the mountain
the forest, which is not only its clothing, but under many relations its revelation, its explanation—I would venture to say, its word and voice.   We have
eagerly read all we have been able to get hold of in reference to the German
foresters, who have most completely preserved their ancient traditions.   The
magnificent book of Schact's, " L'Arbre," commands and overshadows the whole
of this grand subject.   We read it for the first time in the beautiful summer of
1857, under the oaks of Fontainebleau ; and since, we have carried it with us
everywhere,—to the *pinadas* of Bayonne, the firs and arollas of the Alps, and
the cork-oaks of Provence.

Those agreeable and handy books, " La Plante " of Schleiden, " Le Monde
Végétal " of Karl Muller, and numerous erudite articles in Borie-Saint-Vincent
and D'Orbigny's " Dictionary," we have found very useful.   Karl Muller has
an excellent chapter on the " Social Relations " of Plants.

Our remarks on Coniferous Trees are based upon the *mémoires* of Richard,
M. Carrière, and the illustrious Hooker, and also, largely, on our own observations.

Modern botanists too much neglect and despise the myths relative to trees;
they are legends which enshrine many truths among their errors.   Nothing is
more important, even for the naturalist, than the " Histoire du Culte du
Cyprès," by Lajard.   It includes a number of facts of great value in reference
to the general history of the tree, and the points of view from which it was
anciently considered.

CHAPTER IX.—*The Engadine.*—I have quoted in the text M. Binet-
Hentsch's excellent work (Geneva, 1859).   It is the only one which I

know of in French. The valuable books of Papon (1857), Lechener (1858), and Theobald, are in German. I have before me a graceful little English work, by Mrs. Freshfield (1862), interesting, but somewhat too minute, with a long enumeration of dinners, breakfasts, and the like. But more useful than any books I found the instructive and judicious conversation of the men of the country. Will they permit me here to express my acknowledgments, and especially to Monsieur the President Saratz?

CHAPTER XIII.— *The Alpine Climbers.*—On this subject the reader should consult those who know the most,—the guides, who haul the climbers to the summit—who, for a little money, afford them the pleasure of the boast—who, up to the very glaciers, carry their viands, dishes, and liqueurs. They relate with what peril they guide the great drunken and terrified *marmots* in their descent, hewing out for them flights of steps, planting their feet in each secure position, and frequently only able to extricate them from their danger by literally carrying them in their arms.

The Swiss, either through habit, or the annoying affectation of an airy superiority, appear to me very frequently to speak in a scarcely suitable tone of their glorious country. It is this false wit which renders so fatiguing the books of Tœpfer, despite their spirit, amusement, and facility of pencil. He constantly dwells upon accidental traits, and the chances of caricature. This laughter and these antics sadden us. I resemble little children; grimacing, far from amusing me, makes me weep. In the presence of scenery so grave and serious, the contrast is oppressive.

In a work to which I am very partial, a work full of wit and ability, I saw the other day a few lines which one would willingly efface—those wherein it describes the sensation, quite peculiar to the Swiss, which they experience on the glaciers :—"They run, they leap, they gambol; they wander to the right and the left. They fasten themselves to one another for the safer passage of an obstacle. They hurry past the most beautiful objects, and only pause just as butterflies rest themselves." And again : " In those lively pastimes, there comes a moment when one begins to recognize a distant kinship between man and the bird, and one surprises oneself chirping......What merriment in these wild descents, when one goes dashing through a bed of pebbles, which rattle and rush along with one !"

Very different ideas may be gathered from the men who not only traverse the glaciers, but dwell among them, and make long sojourns in their solitudes ; such men as Hugi, Agassiz, and Desor. They do not find them a theatre for the display of levity. They are not places where man feels himself free. The difficulty of the ascents, the painful respiration, the necessity you are under of fastening yourself to your companions,—in all this there is nothing of gaiety !

CHAPTER XIII. p. 286.—*Regeneration of the Species.*—A change of medium may undoubtedly produce a great effect, but not the vain and giddy mobility resulting from the introduction of railways. We see nowadays none but people hurrying along, and travelling at high pressure. Whither? They can scarcely tell themselves. What is required is, a prolonged residence in the best localities. I wish some special books might be written on this subject ; first, a good general work in which one might compare the different *maritime resorts* (all useful for different physical conditions), and, second, a book on the different *mountain stations.* M. Lombard's little treatise (Geneva, 1858) is very good and very valuable, but dwells too much on the circumstances and local maladies of the Swiss, too little on those of the stranger.

ANALYTICAL TABLE OF CONTENTS.

Part the First.

Part the Second.

INDEX.

———◆———